A Research Agenda for Strategic Human Resource Management

Elgar Research Agendas outline the future of research in a given area. Leading scholars are given the space to explore their subject in provocative ways, and map out the potential directions of travel. They are relevant but also visionary.

Forward-looking and innovative, Elgar Research Agendas are an essential resource for PhD students, scholars and anybody who wants to be at the forefront of research.

Titles in the series include:

A Research Agenda for COVID-19 and Society
Edited by Steve Matthewman

A Research Agenda for Civil Society
Edited by Kees Biekart and Alan Fowler

A Research Agenda for Tax Law
Edited by Leopoldo Parada

A Research Agenda for Animal Geographies
Edited by Alice Hovorka, Sandra McCubbin and Lauren Van Patter

A Research Agenda for Food Systems
Edited by Colin L. Sage

A Research Agenda for International Political Economy
New Directions and Promising Paths
Edited by David A. Deese

A Research Agenda for Social Networks and Social Resilience
Edited by Emmanuel Lazega, Tom A.B. Snijders and Rafael P.M. Wittek

A Research Agenda for the Gig Economy and Society
Edited by Valerio De Stefano, Ilda Durri, Charalampos Stylogiannis and Mathias Wouters

A Research Agenda for Strategic Human Resource Management
Bringing Variety in Forms, Theory, Methodology and Outcomes
Edited by Peter D. Sherer

A Research Agenda for Strategic Human Resource Management

Bringing Variety in Forms, Theory, Methodology and Outcomes

Edited by

PETER D. SHERER

Professor of Organizational Behaviour and Human Resource, Haskayne School of Business, University of Calgary, Canada

Elgar Research Agendas

Cheltenham, UK • Northampton, MA, USA

Published by
Edward Elgar Publishing Limited
The Lypiatts
15 Lansdown Road
Cheltenham
Glos GL50 2JA
UK

Edward Elgar Publishing, Inc.
William Pratt House
9 Dewey Court
Northampton
Massachusetts 01060
USA

A catalogue record for this book
is available from the British Library

Library of Congress Control Number: 2022944611

This book is available electronically in the **Elgar**online
Business subject collection
http://dx.doi.org/10.4337/9781800883802

ISBN 978 1 80088 379 6 (cased)
ISBN 978 1 80088 380 2 (eBook)

Printed and bound in Great Britain by TJ Books Limited, Padstow, Cornwall

Contents

Figures

Tables

Contributors

Minseo Baek is a PhD candidate in Management at the Wharton School, University of Pennsylvania. Her research examines how young professionals from diverse backgrounds make career choices and navigate increasingly fluid and open contemporary work settings, with a special focus on its implications for social stratification. She is particularly interested in how individuals' distinct perceptions on career options or strategies for navigating the workplace shape their career choices and outcomes, with potential variations according to their social backgrounds. In another research stream, she studies the unique challenges of fluid and open work settings in career management, such as frequent changes of bosses or multiple bosses' demands in project-based work settings. Before coming to Wharton, she was a founder of a Korea's leading travel tech company.

M. Diane Burton is a Professor in the ILR School at Cornell University where she chairs the Human Resource Studies department, directs the Institute for Compensation Studies, and serves on the advisory board for the Center for Advanced Human Resource Studies. Professor Burton studies employment relations and organizational change in entrepreneurial companies. Her research has been published in leading scholarly journals including the *Academy of Management Journal, American Sociological Review*, the *American Journal of Sociology*, and *Organization Science*. In addition to her scholarly publications, she is the author of several best-selling HBS cases. She earned her Ph.D. in organizational sociology at Stanford University.

Peter Cappelli is the George W. Taylor Professor of Management at The Wharton School and Director of Wharton's Center for Human Resources. He is also a Research Associate at the National Bureau of Economic Research in Cambridge, MA, served as Senior Advisor to the Kingdom of Bahrain for Employment Policy from 2003–2005, was a Distinguished Scholar of the Ministry of Manpower for Singapore, and was Co-Director of the US Department of Education's National Center on the Educational Quality of the

Workforce from 1990–1998. He was recently named by HR Magazine as one of the top 5 most influential management thinkers, by NPR as one of the 50 influencers in the field of aging and was elected a fellow of the National Academy of Human Resources. He received the 2009 PRO award from the International Association of Corporate and Professional Recruiters for contributions to human resources and an honorary Doctorate degree from the University of Liege in Belgium. He is a regular contributor to *The Wall Street Journal* and writes a monthly column for *HR Executive* magazine. His work on performance management, agile systems, and hiring practices, and other workplace topics appears in the *Harvard Business Review*. His latest book is *The Future of the Office: Work from Home, Remote Work, and the Hard Choices We Face.*

Clint Chadwick is a Professor of Strategy and Human Resource Management at the University of Kansas. Clint received his PhD in Management from the Wharton School and has previously served on the faculty of the University of Illinois and the University of Alabama in Huntsville. Clint's research interests include the impact of human resource systems and human capital on firm competitiveness, the strategic roles of HRM departments, and downsizing and strategic renewal in organizations. His work has appeared in such outlets as *Academy of Management Review, Academy of Management Perspectives, Organization Science, Strategic Management Journal, Journal of Management, Industrial Relations, Industrial and Labor Relations Review, Human Resource Management, Human Resource Management Review,* and *Personnel Psychology.* Clint has been an active participant in the Academy of Management Human Resource Division and in the Strategic Human Capital interest group in the Strategic Management Society. Clint currently serves as the Management and Entrepreneurship Area Director in the University of Kansas' School of Business.

Christopher J. Collins is an Associate Professor of Human Resource Studies in the ILR School at Cornell University. He received his PhD in organizational behavior and human resources from the Robert H. Smith School of Business at the University of Maryland. His research interests include strategic human resource management, firm innovation and knowledge creation, social capital, employee recruitment, and employer brand equity.

David Cross is a Lecturer in Organisational Behaviour and Human Resource Management at Southampton Business School. His research interests include workplace commitment, self-employment, and professions in an increasingly changing world of work. Recently he has investigated project networks from an intellectual capital perspective, and he recently secured funding from the CIPD to examine the relationship between the HR profession and self-employment. His work has been published in journals such as *Human Resource Management Journal, Organization Studies, British Journal of Management,* and *Human Resource Management Review.*

David received his PhD from the University of Bath where he also gained an MSc, and he received his BA from the University of Warwick.

Anne Keegan is Full Professor of Human Resource Management (HRM) at University College Dublin, College of Business. Her primary research interests are HRM in online labor platforms, gig work and project-based organizations and her recent work draws on paradox theory and institutional theory. Her work is published in peer-reviewed journals including *Human Resource Management Journal, Human Resource Management, International Journal of Human Resource Management, Journal of Management Studies, Organization Studies, Journal of Applied Psychology, Journal of Managerial Psychology and International Journal of Project Management* where she is former Associate Editor for HRM and OB and currently sits on the Strategic Advisory Board. She has contributed to scholarly handbooks including *Oxford Handbook of Organizational Paradox, Cambridge Handbook of Organizational Project Management,* and the *Elgar Introduction to Theories of Human Resources and Employment Relations.*

Joonyoung Kim is a PhD student in the ILR School at Cornell University. He earned his Bachelor of Business Administration degree from Korea University and Master of Industrial and Labor Relations degree from Cornell University. After working as an HR consultant for ten years, he entered the PhD program at the ILR School. Joonyoung's research focuses on how organizations achieve competitive advantage through adopting a set of systematic HR practices. As the overarching research stream, he studies strategic human resource management and investigates how and when organizations elicit intended firm-level outcomes through the design and implementation of HR systems. He is particularly interested in the intersection between HR and entrepreneurship research. For example, he examines how and when HR systems may benefit or hinder the performance of new firms.

Nicholas Kinnie is Emeritus Professor in the School of Management, University of Bath, UK. His principal research interests lie in exploring the links between HR practices and business performance both within and between organizations. This has involved extensive empirical research in private and public sector organizations as well as various networks of organizations. This research has been published in a variety of academic and practitioner publications including *Human Resource Management, Human Resource Management Journal* and the *International Journal of Human Resource Management.*

Mengwei Li is a doctoral candidate in the Management and Entrepreneurship Area in the University of Kansas' School of Business. Her research interests include strategic human resource management, human capital resources, and topics that connect and/or extend these two streams of research.

Jeroen Meijerink, PhD is Associate Professor of Human Resource Management (HRM) at the University of Twente (The Netherlands). His research activities focus on the value(s) of HRM in platform-based organizations, including online labor platforms (e.g., Uber and Deliveroo), social media platforms (e.g., YouTube and Instagram), talent and crowdsourcing platforms (e.g., Open Opportunities) and shared service organizations. He has a special interest in the use of algorithms and artificial intelligence in human resource management.

His research is multidisciplinary in nature, draws on the service-dominant logic and institutional theories, and has been published in peer-reviewed international outlets such as *Human Resource Management Review, Human Resource Management, International Journal of Human Resource Management, Journal of Business Research, Journal of Managerial Psychology*, and the *Research in Personnel and Human Resource Management series.*

Jeroen Meijerink is the co-editor of the edited volume *"Platform Economy Puzzles: A Multidisciplinary Perspective on Gig Work"* (Edward Elgar Publishing, 2021) and serves as associate editor at the *International Journal of Human Resource Management.*

Ilhwan "Ian" Na is a doctoral candidate in the Management and Entrepreneurship Area in the University of Kansas' School of Business. He examines phenomena discussed in the Strategic Human Capital and Organizational Learning literature, such as human capital acquisition, specific human capital, employee mobility, and knowledge transfer.

Karin Sanders is a professor of Human Resource Management and Organizational Psychology at the School of Management and Governance, University of New South Wales (UNSW) Business School, Sydney, Australia. Her research focuses on the human resource (HR) process approach, in particular the impact of employees' understanding and attributions of HR on their attitudes and behaviours. Karin published on these and other topics in journals such as Human Resource Management (Wiley), Human Resource Management Journal, Journal of Vocational Behavior, Organization Studies, Organization Science, and International Journal of HRM. Karin is Editor for the special issues of International Journal of HRM, and Associate Editor for Human Resource Management (Wiley), and Frontiers of Business Research in China. She is in the editorial board of several HRM and Organizational Psychology journals.

Peter D. Sherer is a professor of Organizational Behaviour and Human Resources and Director of the PhD program at the Haskayne School of Business of the University of Calgary. His interest lies in understanding the role of competitive, behavioural, and institutional processes in looking at what goes on inside of organizations and how these processes generate variety in forms of work arrangements. He (with KyungMook Lee) was awarded the *Academy of Management Journal* best paper award for 2002. He has been published in a diverse range of major journals and has contributed to several research volumes. He is a long-standing member of the editorial board for the *Academy of Management Journal*. He received his PhD from the University of Wisconsin-Madison.

Scott Snell is the Frank Sands, Sr. Chair in Business Administration and former Senior Associate Dean for Executive Education at the University of Virginia's Darden Graduate School of Business. He teaches courses in strategic management and works internationally with senior executives to help their companies align strategy, organizational capability, and investments in talent. His research has been published in a number of top journals, and he is an author of several books, notably *Strategic Execution: Driving Breakthrough Performance in Business* (Stanford Press, 2019), *Management: Leading and Collaborating in a Competitive World* (McGraw-Hill, 2016), and *Managing Human Resources* (Cengage, 2018). He currently serves on the board of directors for SHRM and has served on the boards of the Strategic Management Society's Human Capital Group, HRPS, the SHRM Foundation, the Academy of Management's HR Division, the *Academy of Management Journal* and the *Academy of Management Review*.

Prior to joining the Darden faculty, Scott was Professor and Director of Executive Education at Cornell University's Center for Advanced Human Resource Studies and a Professor of Management in the Smeal College of Business at Pennsylvania State University. He received his BA from Miami University, as well as his MBA and PhD in business from Michigan State University.

Juani Swart is a Professor in Human Capital Management and she seeks to understand the nature of contemporary work contexts. In particular, she is interested in cross-boundary working (which includes gig-working and artificial intelligence), its impact on commitment and knowledge sharing. Her research is focused on human capital as a strategic resource, innovation, ambidexterity and employee attitudes and behaviours. She has published widely in journals such as *Human Resource Management, Human Resource Management Journal, Organisation Studies and the Journal of Management Studies.*

Pamela S. Tolbert is the Lois S. Gray Professor of ILR and Social Sciences in the ILR School at Cornell. She joined the faculty of the ILR School after receiving her Ph.D in sociology from UCLA, and is currently chair of the Department of Organizational Behavior. She is broadly interested in processes of organizational and institutional change, culture and entrepreneurship, and organizational practices and social inequality.

Her research has been published in a variety of journals, including *Administrative Science Quarterly, Organization Studies, Organization Science, Work and Occupations,* and *ILR Review,* among others. She has served on the editorial boards of *American Sociological Review, Administrative Science Quarterly* and *Journal of Professions and Occupations,* as a senior editor for *Management Science, Academy of Management Review, Organization Science* and *Administrative Science Quarterly,* as well as a guest editor for a special issue of *Organization Studies* on careers, and an issue of the *ILR Review* on diversity management practices. Her work has been funded by grants for the National Science Foundation, the Institute for Social Sciences at Cornell, and the Center for Advanced Human Resources Studies in ILR.

Preface

My late colleague, Huseyin Leblebici (of the University of Illinois at Urbana-Champaign), and I wrote a chapter in 2001 for *Research in Personnel and Human Resources Management* in which we argued Strategic HRM had taken a best practices perspective, focusing on the positive effect on firm performance of the high commitment HRM system, at the expense of identifying and assessing other possible forms of HRM systems. The idea there was one best way, and that the underlying theoretical argument was driven solely by competitive forces, drew our attention for several reasons given our backgrounds.

Huseyin was an organizational theorist who had written important work to understand the variety in organizational forms (e.g., Salancik & Leblebici, 1988). He had an interest in institutional theories dating back to John R. Commons (Leblebici, 1985) as well as the more recent work of neo-institutionalists like Meyer and Rowan (1977) and DiMaggio and Powell (1983, 1991) as reflected in his work on institutional change in business models in radio broadcasting (Leblebici, Salancik, Copay, & King, 1991). I shared many of the same interests and perspectives with Huseyin and had a front row seat during the early development of Strategic HRM. I had also published work in which I had examined non-traditional contexts for research in Strategic HRM, especially in law firm partnerships (e.g., Sherer, 1995, 1996), which were distinct from managerial or industrial settings and relied on partners to make key decisions on such matters as granting partnership and promotion to full partner.

Our backgrounds sensitized us to be wary of arguments on the universality of a management practice, organizational structure, and the like. There were invariably environmental contingencies (e.g., turbulence, uncertainty) and possibly equifinality (i.e., different practices could lead to the same outcome) that raised suspicions there was one best way. Sherer & Leblebici (2001) pointed out that if there was only one best way, how was it possible to study change – as there would be nothing to change to, unless firms sought out something less beneficial, which was not something we saw firms doing purposefully. Moreover, we argued the sources of organizational forms like HRM systems were driven in varying degrees by both competitive and institutional pressures, which could lead to different forms of HRM systems.

Sherer & Leblebici (2001) proposed a framework that joined competitive based arguments which were the staple of Strategic HRM with institutional-based arguments to understand when we might see more or less variety in forms of HRM systems within an organizational population. We looked to theoretical arguments from population ecology (Hannan & Freeman, 1977, 1984), neo-institutionalism (DiMaggio and Powell, 1983) and Stinchombe's (1965) notion of founders' imprinting effects. The framework provided insights into when there would be "… random and idiosyncratic variety and change, variety through imprinting effects, organizational adaptation, and also uniformity and stability through legitimacy and competitive selection" (Sherer & Leblebici, 2001: 201). The framework called for studying how at the level of firms and organizational populations we could identify and understand the variety in forms of HRM systems and the changes in those forms that would be expected. Our framework placed emphasis on understanding the processes by which we would observe the occurrence and incidence of forms and the dynamics by which we would see changes in forms in organizational populations.

We were something of an island of thought in Strategic HRM given our organizational theory perspective. And, given the success Strategic HRM was having, there was no reason to reflect back on the field, rethink it at a fundamental level, and complicate things by bringing in institutional based arguments, which suggested that firms' behavior was not entirely based on competitive processes, and instead that coercive, normative and mimetic processes (DiMaggio and Powell, 1983, 1991) needed to be considered. The compelling competitive-based argument, captured in the resource-based view of the firm (RBV), was providing important insights, and generating quite a lot of excitement.

The state of the field is different now. As time has passed, Strategic HRM has lost some of the excitement and momentum it once had, and the more recent field of Strategic human capital (HC) has garnered interest. The world of work has changed too, with new forms of work such as we see in the gig economy, providing new contexts and novel HRM forms to study. With these developments, the time is right to address the variety in forms of HRM practices and arrangements, deepen our theoretical understanding of processes, and bring in insights from Strategic HC and other fields and from theories that have not been the focus of Strategic HRM researchers but that can provide further insight.

A few words of appreciation. First, to the authors of the chapters in this book, I thank all of you for your efforts and the exceptionally high-quality chapters you have written. Second, I want to thank my former PhD student, Scott Rankin (Thompsons River University), whose deep knowledge and strong interest in Strategic HRM has kept me up-to date on the field over the years through our many conversations and work together. Third, to the editors at Edward Elgar, I thank them for their patience and support. Finally, to my late colleague and close friend, Huseyin Leblebici, I want to thank him for encouraging and developing my interest in seeing not just what is being studied, but what should be studied, and with that the understanding that goes with going down a different path than the one most taken. The idea and inspiration for this book is the culmination of my many conversations with Huseyin over the years.

REFERENCES

DiMaggio, P.J. & Powell, W. W. 1991. Introduction. In W.W Powell & P.J. DiMaggio (Eds.), *The New Institutionalism in Organizational Analysis*. Chicago: University of Chicago press.

DiMaggio, P. J., & Powell, W. W. 1983. The Iron Cage Revisited: Institutional isomorphism and collective rationality in organizational fields. *American Sociological Review*, 48: 147–160.

Hannan, M. T., & Freeman, J. 1984. Structural inertia and organizational change. *American Sociological Review*, 49: 149-64.

Hannan, M. T., & Freeman, J. H. 1977. The population ecology of organizations. *American Journal of Sociology,* 82: 929–64.

Leblebici, H. Salancik, G., Copay, A & King, T. 1991. Institutional change and the transformation of interorganizational fields: An organizational history of the US radio broadcasting industry. *Administrative Science Quarterly*, 36: 333-63.

Leblebici, H. 1985. Transactions and organizational forms: A reanalysis. *Organization Studies*, 6: 97–116.

Meyer, J. W., & Rowan, B. 1977. Institutionalized organizations: Formal structure as myth and ceremony. *American Journal of Sociology*, 83: 340-63.

Salancik, G. R., & Leblebici, H. 1988. Variety and form in organizing transactions: A generative grammar of Organization. *Research in the Sociology of Organizations*, 1–32. Greenwich, CT: JAI Press.

Sherer, P. D & Leblebici, H. 2001. Bringing variety and change into the study of strategic human resource management. *Research in Personnel/Human Resources Management,* Oxford, GB: Elsevier Science LTD, 19, 199–230.

Sherer, P. D. 1996. Toward an understanding of the variety in work arrangements: The organization and labor relationships framework. In C. L. Cooper & D. M. Rousseau (Eds.), *Trends in Organizational Behavior*, New York: John Wiley, 99-122. Also appears *in Journal of Organizational Behavior*, 3: 99–122.

Sherer, P. D. 1995. Leveraging human assets in law firms: Human capital structures and organizational capabilities. *Industrial and Labor Relations Review*, 48, 671–691.

Stinchombe, A. L. 1965. Social structure and organizations. In J. G. March (Ed.), *Handbook of Organizations*, 142–93. Chicago: Rand McNally.

1 Introduction to *A Research Agenda for Strategic Human Resource Management*

Peter D. Sherer

Strategic human resource management (HRM) came into its own in the mid 1990s by demonstrating empirically that the management of human resources mattered to strategy and firm performance. Several ground-breaking empirical studies (Arthur, 1992, 1994; Huselid, 1995; MacDuffie, 1995) drew attention to interrelated HRM practices that served as best practice, referred to by such names as the high commitment HRM system, the high involvement work system, or the high-performance work system, and were evidenced in positive effects on firm performance. The finding of a best practice was a windfall for Strategic HRM as an academic field and set it down a path from which it did not stray far. Empirical studies followed by meta-analyses (e.g., Combs et al., 2006) confirmed the best practice's positive effect on firm performance, while limited support was found for a contingency theoretic view that called for a best-fit perspective (e.g., Becker & Gerhart, 1996). By these accounts, Strategic HRM was a success in generating a widely accepted academic field.

The very success of Strategic HRM had the unintended effect of narrowing and reducing the field largely to the following question: what is the effect of the best practice HRM system on firm performance (Sherer & Leblebici, 2001)? Underlying this question was the view that, even though there were other forms of HRM systems, the best practice was the only option that led to competitive advantage (e.g., Lepak & Snell, 1999). Research focused on estimating the effects of the best practice on how organizations or subunits fared on firm performance. What was used as a comparison to the best practice HRM system was with few exceptions (e.g., Delery & Doty, 1996) its null, its absence, not alternative forms of HRM systems that put it to a competitive test (Sherer & Leblebici, 2001). What was concerning, though, was that the effect found in studies was not grounded theoretically. Why the effect occurred was conjectured in one way or another, which was particularly striking because the distance from the HRM system to firm performance was so distal. There was the proverbial black box.

Given the path Strategic HRM went down, numerous questions have not been fully answered or have gone unaddressed. Why didn't all or at least most organizations use the best practice if it was in fact superior to alternative HRM forms? What were the micro foundations and behavioral processes that underlay HRM systems as they related to employees and managers? What were the processes involved for more proximal effects? What role did human and social capital play in understanding the linkage between HRM systems and firm performance? Were other HRM forms being ignored or emerging but were not studied, and did they lead to equal to or higher performance than the best practice HRM system? Could different HRM forms engender equifinality in valued attitudes and behaviors? What processes and dynamics occurred in entrepreneurial and start-up firms that differed from what was observed in larger, more established organizations? Was critical "HR" performed by leadership in firms outside of the HR function being sufficiently addressed? And were there outcomes, such as job creation and economic well-being of employees, that were important to study but receiving limited attention – because they did not fit neatly into the outcome of firm performance?

These and other such questions were always there. Despite their importance in building our understanding, they got pushed to the side and out of the way, or they got less attention than they deserved. Moreover, the answers to some of them were not found in the cross-sectional data and standard regression methods that were typically applied in Strategic HRM studies as they require longitudinal data analysis or in-depth qualitative studies.

Several of the questions have, however, gained traction over the years. The authors in this volume are leading thinkers on these and other related questions. Other of these questions are still very much in need of attention. The authors in this volume offer key insights to move theory and research ahead on these critical yet less attended-to questions.

A brief history of the field: how did we get here?

Strategic HRM did not come out of nowhere. It had its origins in a number of academic fields, with diverse intellectual traditions, including institutional labor economics and internal labor market theory (Doeringer & Piore, 1971; Kerr, 1958), behavioral theory (Simon, 1951), transaction cost economics

(Williamson, Wachter & Harris, 1975; Williamson, 1980, 1985), structural contingency theory (Drazin & Van de Ven, 1985; Lawrence & Lorsch, 1967; Thompson, 1967), international and comparative labor studies (Cole, 1979; Dore, 1973), business strategy and managerialist arguments (Beer et al., 1984; Porter, 1980), and the quality of work life movement (e.g., Walton, 1973, 1985). These fields provided a variety of theoretical bases regarding competitive, institutional and behavioral forces, as the sources of individual and organizational actions. While elements of the fields were integrated early in the development of Strategic HRM (Wright & McMahan, 1992), over time the field was winnowed down to something less of a synthesis to a limited set of questions.

Origins of the field

Dating back to the 1950s, institutional labor economists noticed the rise in markets inside firms that had institutionalized rules that did not exist in the neoclassical economists' conception of the labor market. Clark Kerr (1958), a leading figure in observing this divergence, wrote colorfully of the "balkanization of labor markets." Firms operated under institutional rules that differed from the rules of supply and demand that guided the external market. These rules were institutionalized in that they did not change readily in response to market conditions. Accordingly, these rules insulated and buffered employees from the vicissitudes of the external labor market and economy. Identifying the rules required looking into the personnel policies of organizations and conducting detailed case analyses. Institutional labor economists suggested the rules were the result of the interplay of institutional forces (e.g., unions) and market forces. And they saw these forces as often opposing each other. They did not see the rules as necessarily profit maximizing in their aim, but instead the result of various actors (e.g., unions, employers, and personnel departments) contestations over the "rules of the game" and ultimately on what parties could agree to given market factors acting as constraints.

Doeringer and Piore (1971) took these early institutional labor economists' arguments to the next step by identifying the critical role of human capital (Becker, 1964) in explaining the development of institutional rules inside firms, which they referred to as internal labor markets (ILMs). They showed how Becker's notion of firm-specific human capital provided a key to explaining the rules operating in industrial settings. They argued that firms with industrial ILMs sought to develop, nurture, and protect the firm-specific human capital of employees through ILMs. Accordingly, firms offered employees promotions, seniority-based pay, and various benefits as incentives to stay and develop their internal human capital. Equally important, the rules ensured workers cooperated and shared their firm-specific knowledge with one another.

Simon (1951) provided a behavioral approach to the employment relationship. He argued that employment was an authority relationship that required an employee to perform a set of activities (X) within a zone of acceptance, of which specific activities could vary day by day, in exchange for a wage. Having employees with an agreed upon set of activities from which the employer could select gave employers an internal liquidity to have employees perform work activities as needed (Sherer, Rogovsky, & Wright, 1998), a type of internal flexibility, and in return it gave employees a guaranteed wage and job security.

Williamson, Wachter and Harris (1975) examined both Simon's authority relationship model of employment and the ILM argument using transaction cost theory. Williamson et al. specified how ILMs minimized transaction costs related to firm-specific human assets, creating a protective shield, which the authority relationship alone could not do. Doeringer and Piore, Williamson et al., and Williamson's later work (1985) would presage the field of Strategic Human Capital (HC), with its starting point of Gary Becker's (1964) theory of human capital.

Managerialist views on the importance of HRM practices bridged the study of HRM practices with that of strategy and leadership in organizations. Foulkes (1980) foreshadowed later works that looked to high commitment work systems, arguing that various large non-union firms built commitment in their employees through such HR practices as promotion from within and employment security. Beer et al. (1984) took a general manager's view of HR, looking to key decisions by senior managers outside of the HR function that directly or indirectly had effects on employees, and which required taking a systems perspective to HRM practices. Fombrum, Tichy and Devanna (1984) addressed the need for organizations to build HRM into formulating and implementing strategy.

Walton (1985) argued for a commitment-based approach to supplant the control-based approach that was common in the US and other countries in their manufacturing sector. His work tied back to the Quality of Work Life movement in the US, with its emphasis on the well-being of workers (Walton, 1973). Having a work environment for employees that contributed to their well being was a "win-win." Those organizations that adopted the commitment-based approach would be better off and so would their employees.

Empirical work by Jackson, Schuler and Rivero (1989) followed. They integrated various theoretical perspectives to examine the relationship between HRM practices, firm strategy (Porter, 1980), and organizational and environmental characteristics (e.g., Lawrence & Lorsch, 1967; Thompson, 1967). Jackson et al. showed empirically how HRM practices fit with internal and external characteristics of organizations.

Strategic HRM: A field in search of a theory

A key point in several of the above perspectives was that HRM systems had important implications for firm strategy and performance, but it took several ground-breaking empirical papers to set the foundation more firmly for Strategic HRM. The evidence came when researchers, particularly Arthur (1994), Huselid (1995) and MacDuffie (1995), demonstrated the positive effects of HRM systems on firm performance. With these studies, Strategic HRM focused on competitive forces that affected firm performance. What was missing was a theoretical explanation for why the effect occurred.

Strategic HRM addressed the theoretical gap by going in two distinct directions. One was to examine micro processes that mediate the effects of HRM systems on firm performance. Micro-organizational work by Bowen and Ostroff (2004) built on Kelley's covariation model in attribution theory (Kelley, 1967, 1973) to argue that the strength of an HRM system regarding the signals HRM systems sent to employees affected their attitudes and behaviors. Another avenue for micro-oriented research was the Ability Motivation Opportunity (AMO) framework of Applebaum et al. (2000). They argued that HRM systems affected employees' ability levels, their motivation, and their opportunities, which in turn affected firm performance. These advances laid a foundation for understanding the micro dynamics by which employees and managers' perceptions, motivations and attitudes, actions, and skills play a key mediating role in the effectiveness of HRM systems (Guest et al., 2020; Ostroff & Bowen, 2016).

The other direction to filling the theoretical gap was to tie Strategic HRM to business strategy through the resource-based view (RBV) of the firm, given its focus on identifying the resources and capabilities that are the basis of firm competitive advantage (e.g., Barney & Wright, 1998; Wright, McMahan, & McWilliams, 1994). The RBV provided critical insights into (Barney & Wright, 1998; Wright, Dunford, & Snell, 2001; Wright, McMahan, & McWilliams, 1994) competitive processes that shaped firm behavior and influenced firm performance. However, this important integration downplayed or ignored other theoretical arguments. Among those arguments not considered were institutional forces that influence organizational actions for which earlier institutional labor economists drew attention, and which had seen advances in neo-institutional theory, beginning with several seminal pieces (DiMaggio & Powell, 1983; Meyer & Rowan, 1977). As Baron, Dobbin, and Jennings (1986) and Tolbert and Zucker (1983) showed, organizations mimic the HRM practices of larger more visible organizations in their field to gain legitimacy. While there was important work combining institutional and resource-based arguments (e.g., Oliver, 1997), very little of that thinking showed up in the Strategic HRM literature.

Strategic HRM loses out

Given the success but increasingly narrowing focus of Strategic HRM, the field lost momentum over time. As such, it has been argued that the field is not progressing (Delery & Roumpi, 2017; Rankin & Sherer, 2019). Taking the place of Strategic HRM is Strategic human capital (HC), which examines how individual human capital is aggregated into higher level units that have value and influence firm performance (Wright, Coff, & Moliterno, 2014).

Important insights have come out of this line of research. Coff (1997) and Chadwick (2017) examine the significance of human capital rents through the notions of value creation and value capture. Ployhart and his colleagues (Ployhart & Moliterno, 2011; Ployhart et al., 2014) address the emergent properties that allow individual human capital to become team, unit, and larger aggregations. Campbell, Coff, and Kryscynski (2012) challenge the notion of general human capital as Becker (1964) proposed it. Sirmon et al. (2011) and subsequently Chadwick, Super, and Kwon (2015) argue for the critical role of resource orchestration in firms' decisions on configuring resources and capabilities.

Social capital also gained traction in Strategic HRM. Work in this area builds on the view in Kogut and Zander (1992) and Nahapiet and Ghoshal (1998) of organizations as communities in which social capital is critical to building employee trust and cooperation. Collins and Clark's (2003) foundational paper in this area looked at the role of social capital and Strategic HRM while Collins and Smith (2006) examined how high commitment HRM systems build trust and sharing among employees which then allows for organizational innovation. Recent advances in work on social capital and Strategic HRM bring in creativity and the notion of psychological safety (Liu et al., 2017; Agarwal & Farndale, 2017).

Mining the variety out there

Various authors established that there was greater variety in forms of HRM systems than the best practice system. Katz and Darbishire (2001) found increasing divergence within countries in forms of HRM systems, and that variety was mirrored across countries, suggesting a convergence across countries. The Stanford Project on Emerging Companies (Baron, Hannan, & Burton, 2001; Baron, Burton & Hannan, 1996: Hannan, Baron, & Burton, 1996; Baron & Hannan, 2002) identified five HRM systems in high tech start-ups and entrepreneurial firms and many other admixtures of these forms. Considerable work was also done on how firms managed employee mobility (Cappelli, 1999; Saxenian, 1994) and how market-based employment posed a competitive test to the high commitment HRM system given its value to firms (Delery & Doty, 1996; Rao & Drazen, 2002).

A great deal more variety has been only partially addressed. Gig work has paved the way for seeing how work that might have been done previously through employment can be done by workers contracted in (Sherer, 1996; Sherer, Rogovsky & Wright, 1998) as independent contractors, given the enabling effects of information technology. Important work has been done (e.g., Meijerink & Keegan, 2019) on online labor platform work. However, more theory and research needs to be done looking at the variety in platform work. For example, high skilled platform work where workers have significant bargaining power differs in kind not in magnitude from low skilled platform work where workers are in great supply relative to demand. Furthermore, strategic HRM research has been primarily done in large and mature companies, not the entrepreneurial firms that are the source of considerable job creation, and where novel HRM practices and alternative HRM systems have arisen. Finally, while various authors over the years talked about models with networks and quasi-like firms in which multiple entities act together (Eccles, 1981; Williamson, 1980), little was said about these sorts of arrangements, with some notable exceptions (Swart & Kinnie, 2014).

Concluding remarks

As this brief review of the field suggests, the advances in Strategic HRM over the years have been many. Nonetheless, the field has lost momentum and excitement in recent years. There is an even greater need for theoretical development in identifying the processes by which HRM systems affect employees, how that relates to value creation and value capture, and what the outcomes are associated with employees and organizations (but not limited to firm performance). Novel HRM practices and emerging forms of HRM systems renew interest in the field by expanding the context and calling for us to broaden and enrich our theoretical lens. This volume aims to restore vitality to what made Strategic HRM an area of study that was both exciting and critically important.

The research agenda: the chapters

This research volume develops a research agenda for Strategic HRM by advancing theory and further identifying the variety in forms of HRM systems. Four chapters speak to a wider theoretical lens by providing an institutionalist perspective, advancing the role of attribution theories, offering a greater role for social capital theory, and linking Strategic human capital (HC) with Strategic HRM. Taken together, these four chapters provide theoretical lenses at the micro, meso, macro, population, and organizational field levels, and are important in filling the black box. Four chapters then address the variety in existing or emerging HRM forms by addressing the liquid workforce, online labour platform work, network based HRM models, and HRM entrepreneurial models. Taken together, these four chapters highlight the very real diversity in HRM systems, and the experimentation with new models which may lead to enduring new forms.

Expanding the theoretical base of Strategic HRM

Pamela Tolbert retraces the history of Strategic HRM through a neo-intuitionalist lens. Her in-depth review of ground-breaking studies in the 1990s' key articles reveals there were different arguments being made about what constitutes high performance work systems (HPWS) and different operationalizations, rather than mere differences in wording. She looks to the literature on institutional logics (Friedland & Alford, 1991; Thornton & Ocasio, 1999), the notion that there are logics or models with constituent elements that speak to broader meanings, to suggest what underlies these differences. Tolbert identifies a managerial engineering logic, with its focus on how to engineer work to generate high individual performance from workers (through ability, motivation, and opportunity) versus an employee control logic which focuses on practices that provide decision rights to employees. She argues that not only is there a lack of consensus in the theorization of what constitutes HPWS, but there is also a strikingly low adoption rate of HPWS across countries. In so doing, her work has important implications for theory building. It asks the fundamental question why the adoption of HPWS did not approach what would be considered institutionalization. Moreover, Tolbert's in-depth analysis of the early empirical work in Strategic HRM cautions us on the importance of construct clarity regarding HPWS (Suddaby, 2010). Different logics will presumably involve different micro dynamics.

Karin Sanders provides an in-depth examination of developments in Strategic HRM regarding its link to the two main approaches in attribution theory (Heider, 1944; Kelley, 1967, 1973; Weiner, 1985). As she points out, the approach referred to as HR attributions provides answers on how employees perceive HRM practices as signals about management's intentions (Nishii, Lepak, & Schneider, 2008). The "decoding" of signals by employees of HRM practices is critical for how they perceive their organizations view them and how they will be managed (Guest et al., 2020). Sanders points out that tests of the HR attribution approach have been limited largely to single practices (Hewett et al., 2018). Thus, as she argues, more work is needed is in examining HRM arrangements that are comprised of multiple and interrelated practices. Second, as she points out, the approach labeled HR strength, originating with Bowen and Ostroff (2004), examines how strong the message is that organizations send with HRM systems. Such messaging creates an organizational climate and collective sense of what is expected of employees, which in turns affects employee behavior and attitudes. As Sanders argues, these two approaches help to lay a groundwork for the micro foundations of strategic HRM, connecting micro dynamics to macro level HRM practices and systems. Moreover, as Sanders discusses, these approaches look to differing yet interrelated arguments on attributions, and she points to promising efforts to integrate them further.

Clint Chadwick, Mengwei Li and Ilhwan Na make the case for integrating Strategic HRM with Strategic HC. They first distinguish between the two fields, noting their key similarities but also their critical differences. They then make a compelling argument for cross-fertilization. They argue that integration of the fields can come about by looking at how economic rents follow from the interplay of value creation and value capture. As they point out, value creation has to do with maximizing the use value of an organization's strategic resources, and value capture has to do with minimizing the associated costs associated with those resources. Chadwick et al. argue that much of strategic HRM research has focused on the value creation that arises through HRM practices and systems, but there is the need to look more at value capture. They argue that, while an HPWS could be beneficial in providing value creation, its net benefit must be weighed against its costs in wages and benefits, its administration, and other potential costs. Chadwick et al. also point to research that links HR practices to HC by treating the latter as a mediating variable, and here too they argue that looking at the interplay of value creation and value capture advances thinking. Finally, they argue for building on the notions of complementarities in Strategic HC to bolster arguments in Strategic HRM, particularly in looking at not only beneficial or redundant complementarities but also dysfunctional bundling, which has been rarely done in the strategic HRM literature. Their arguments hold forth the promise that Strategic HRM can renew its importance by better integrating with Strategic HC.

Chris Collins takes us beyond the HRM Practices-Firm Performance relationship. He specifies social capital as a critical mediating variable. He argues that the notion of external fit, which has been tested in studies as the link from business strategy to HRM practices, needs to incorporate a critical role for social capital. He also points to critical contingencies that have not gotten sufficient attention, focusing on leadership behavior (e.g., transformational leadership), alternative HRM forms to HPWS, and organizational structure. He argues for looking at resource orchestration as a key moderator that affects a firm's ability to use social capital to gain competitive advantage. He argues that managerial capability, ability to generate and manage slack, and organizational design are potentially critical factors in determining whether social capital does in fact lead to competitive advantage. Collins' work points to the importance of social capital, returning to macro variables that have not been sufficiently addressed, and to bringing leadership behavior and managerial capability further into the discussion.

Populating the variety in forms

Alternative forms of HRM systems are not new. Nonetheless, we are going through a period where the diversity has grown and is continuing to grow even more. The four chapters that speak to the variety in forms of HRM systems offer novel perspectives in this regard.

Peter Cappelli and Minseo Baek address the liquid workforce, which they define as non-employees embedded in organizations though employed by other firms. They point out that almost a third of workers in organizations operate as employees in this way, indicating that the liquid workforce is a dominant HRM arrangement and outweighs the gig workforce, which they specify is only around 6% of the workforce. While liquid workers are still employees, they operate in a different model from traditional employment relationships, given they are physically externalized from their employer and take some level of direction from an organization that does not employ them. Cappelli and Baek identify managed service providers (MSPs) as important players in the liquid workforce who operate on premises for clients. They ask the crucial question: Why do organizations tap into the liquid workforce so heavily? Cappelli and Baek argue that employers believe they gain flexibility and reduce labor costs by using liquid workers since they do not not have to carry inventories of their own employees. However, they challenge the claim of flexibility and are not convinced that employers reduce labor costs with liquid workers given the myriad of transaction costs, hidden costs, turnover, losses in productivity, and stifling of innovation in organizations with liquid workers and traditional employees. Even so, they argue that there may be no turning back now. Their work raises the issue of what types of HRM practices and systems organizations use with leased employees and in their combinations with actual employees of organizations, and what ends these arrangements serve for organizations.

Juani Swart, David Cross, Nicholas Kinnie, and Scott Snell address the growing use of networked forms of organizations. They address the more conventional networks we see in which individuals are contracted in to work alongside employees. These teams include Cappelli and Baek's liquid workers working alongside employees. They also address inter-organizational relationships involving organizations collaborating on a major project, particularly Integrated Project Teams (IPTs) and alliances, which we see in such industries as aerospace and pharmaceuticals. Finally, they identify loosely coupled networks, Project Network Organizations (PNOs), which include individuals and firms that operate to produce network level outcomes. They argue that these network forms require greater collaboration, a focus on sustained access to human capital, and speed to complete projects, all of which critically depend on social capital. As they point out, concerns with Strategic HRM practices do not go away, but the nature of the practices change. Critical to their argument, social capital takes on increasing importance with HRM practices. Recruiting changes into resourcing, formal training gives way to informal learning. Moreover, a commitment to the network, as opposed to the organization, becomes a crucial element of what ties stakeholders together. Human capital too becomes a property of not just individuals, firms, or industries, but of networks. With work being disaggregated more than ever before, their work raises questions whether these arrangements counter or compete with the seemingly more impersonal models that we see in many online labour platforms, or if they are simply orthogonal to one another.

Anne Keegan and Jeroen Meijerink provide an integrative framework that provides insights into online labour platforms. Keegan and Meijerink view online labour platform work through the lens of an ecosystem, which they treat as a "a group of interacting, yet semi-autonomous entities that depend on each other's activities..." (2022: 168). They note the hierarchy in these relations, which is evident in that platform workers, and even customers are notably secondary to the tech companies, and the investors in these companies. As they argue, online labour platforms bring the parties together through a mobile app or crowd work platform, which acts as a labor market intermediary matching labor demand by customers with labor supply. They point to the various contradictions found in the literature that online labour platform workers are in most instances independent contractors and have autonomy and work hour flexibility that employees do not have, but at the same time they are under very significant control by the platform. Keegan and Meijerink look to the notions of value creation and value capture to begin to answer, "who is gig work good or bad for?" As they argue, online platforms succeed at value creation in ways that were harder if not impossible to do in the past, generating a pool of workers and creating opportunities for them, providing revenues for platform providers, and services for customers. Whether online labor platform workers are significant beneficiaries of the value creation, as they point out, is subject to debate. They go on to discuss HRM practices that allow for value creation and value capture. Online labour platform companies have made use of algorithmic management to both collect and analyze data as well as to direct and incentivize workers through dynamic pricing and the use of customers to rate and rank gig workers, substituting for the performance management practices of an employer. While online labour platform companies have had the upper hand in capturing value, Keegan and Meijerink argue that there is contestation by workers to extract more of the value creation through unionization activities, regulatory pushes, and social mobilization efforts. We will see in the years to come whether more of the value creation goes to online labour platform workers, but their discussion provides guidance on what we should be looking for regarding value creation and capture.

Joonyoung Kim and Diane Burton address HRM in entrepreneurial firms, which they treat as "new and independently created organizations" (2022: 200). They rightly caution us to view these firms as not simply immature organizations but instead as organizations with their own distinctive qualities. Kim and Burton point to the important insights gained by studies (e.g., Baron, Burton, & Hannan, 1996) in the Stanford Project on Emerging Organizations (SPEC) that identified significant variety in HRM systems, highlighted the important role of initial founders' choices and imprinting effects (Stinchombe, 1965), and demonstrated the disruptive effects of change in models on organizations. Notwithstanding that ground-breaking project, they argue that entrepreneurial organizations have largely been ignored by HR scholars. They point out that a key to this gap is that HR researchers focus on the HR function rather than the questions that follow from the study of people management, such as what the leadership of the firm wants to convey more broadly to employees in terms of their people management practices. As they point out, entrepreneurial organizations' experimentation and adaptation with novel HRM practices, such as at Valve, Netflix, Zappos, and Gravity Payments, are important to study because their practices potentially get diffused, modified, refined, or serve as failed experiments, all of which are equally instructive. And they further instruct us to look broadly, not just at hi-tech firms, because we will miss out on firms such as Amazon, which started off as a mail order book seller. They present a research agenda wherein studying entrepreneurial firms can benefit the study of Strategic HRM more generally. These include addressing more proximal outcomes and mechanisms, locating novel HR practices, taking a broader view of HR beyond the HR function to that of people management, and taking stock of the role of HR in job creation. They close by making the case for more balance in research methods to the quantitative bias found in HRM research on entrepreneurship. They argue for more qualitative research, mixed methods, and longitudinal research designs. Their chapter offers many opportunities for HRM scholars in a context which is both dynamic in its variability, replete with experimentation, and rich for investigation.

Conclusion

This research volume speaks to a renewed Strategic HRM. Authors in this volume address critical processes at the micro, meso, macro, population and organizational field levels, identify the greater variety in HRM forms, look beyond the HR function to those actors who lead organizations and are responsible for key elements of the people management of organizations, and expand the outcomes of interest beyond that of financial performance to include societal level questions of economic and social well-being of individuals. These authors' works renew excitement and bring novelty to Strategic HRM.

References

Agarwal, P., & Farndale, E. 2017. High-performance work systems and creativity implementation: The role of psychological capital and psychological safety. Human Resource Management Journal, 27: 440–458.

Applebaum, E., Bailey, T., Berg, P., & Kallerberg, A. (2000). *Manufacturing Advantage: Why High-Performance Work Systems Pay Off*. Ithaca, NY: Cornell University Press.

Arthur, J.B. 1994. Effects of human-resource systems on manufacturing performance and turnover. Academy of Management Journal, 37: 670–687.

Arthur, J.B. 1992. The link between business strategy and industrial relations systems in American mini mills. Industrial and Labor Relations Review, 45: 488–506.

Barney, J.B. & Wright, P.M. 1998. On becoming a strategic partner: The role of human resources in gaining competitive advantage. Human Resource Management, 37: 31–46.

Baron, J.N. & Hannan, M.T. 2002. Organizational blueprints for success in high-tech start-ups: Lessons from the Stanford project on emerging companies. California Management Review, 44: 8–36.

Baron, J.N., Burton, M.D., & Hannan, M.T. 1996. The road taken: Origins and evolution of employment systems in emerging companies. Industrial and Corporate Change, 5: 239–275.

Baron, J.N., Dobbin, F.R., & Jennings, P.D. 1986. War and Peace: The evolution of modern personnel administration in U.S. industry. American Journal of Sociology, 92: 350–383.

Baron, J.N., Hannan, M.T., & Burton, M.D. 2001. Labor pains: Change in organizational models and employee turnover in young, high-tech firms. American Journal of Sociology, 106: 960–1012.

Becker, B. & Gerhart, B. 1996. The impact of human resource management on organizational performance: Progress and prospects. Academy of Management Journal, 39: 779–801.

Becker, G.S. 1964. *Human Capital*. New York: National Bureau of Economic Research.

Beer, M., Spector, B., Lawrence, P.R., Mills, D.Q., & Walton, R.E. 1984. *Managing Human Assets*. New York: The Free Press.

Bowen, D.E. & Ostroff, C. 2004. Understanding HRM-firm performance linkages: The role of the "strength" of the HRM system. Academy of Management Review, 29: 203–222.

Campbell, B.A., Coff, R., & Kryscynski, D. 2012. Rethinking sustained competitive advantage from human capital. Academy of Management Review, 37: 376–395.

Cappelli, P. 1999. *The New Deal at Work: Managing the Market Driven Workforce*. Boston: MA: Harvard Business School Press.

Chadwick, C. 2017. Toward a more comprehensive model of firms' human capital rents.
Academy of Management Review, 42: 499–519.

Chadwick, C., Super, J.F., & Kwon, K. 2015. Resource orchestration in practice: CEO emphasis on SHRM, commitment-based HR systems, and firm performance. Strategic Management Journal, 36: 360–376.

Coff, R.W. 1997. Human assets and management dilemmas: Coping with hazards on the road to resource-based theory. Academy of Management Review, 22: 374–402.

Cole, R.E., 1979. *Japanese Blue Collar: The Changing Tradition* (Vol. 86). University of California Press.

Collins, C.J. & Clark, K.D. 2003. Strategic human resource practices, top management team social networks, and firm performance: The role of human resource practices in creating organizational competitive advantage. Academy of Management Journal, 46: 740–751.

Collins, C.J. & Smith, K.G. 2006. Knowledge exchange and combination: The role of human resource practices in the performance of high-technology firms. Academy of Management Journal, 49: 544–560.

Combs, J., Liu, Y.M., Hall, A., & Ketchen, D. 2006. How much do high-performance work practices matter? A meta-analysis of their effects on organizational performance. Personnel Psychology, 59: 501–528.

Delery, J.E., & Doty, D.H. 1996. Modes of theorizing in strategic human resource management: Tests of universalistic, contingency, and configurational performance predictions. Academy of Management Journal, 39: 802–835.

Delery, J.E. & Roumpi, D. 2017. Strategic human resource management, human capital and competitive advantage: Is the field going in circles? Human Resource Management Journal, 27: 1–21.

DiMaggio, P.J. & Powell, W.W. 1991. Introduction. In W.W. Powell & P.J. DiMaggio (Eds.), *The New Institutionalism in Organizational Analysis*: 1–38. Chicago: University of Chicago Press.

DiMaggio, P.J. & Powell, W.W. 1983. The Iron Cage revisited: Institutional isomorphism and collective rationality in organizational fields. American Sociological Review, 48: 147–160.

Doeringer, P. & Piore, M.J. 1971. *Internal Labor Markets and Manpower Adjustment*. New York: DC Heath and Company.

Dore, R. 1973. *British Factory-Japanese Factory: The Origins of Diversity in Industrial Relations*. London: Allen & Unwin.

Drazin, R. & Van de Ven, A.H. 1985. Alternative forms of fit in contingency theory. Administrative Science Quarterly, 30: 514–539.

Eccles, R.G. 1981. The quasi-firm in the construction industry. Journal of Economic Behavior & Organization, 2(4): 335–357.

Fombrun, C., Tichy, N.M., & Devanna, M.A. 1984. *Strategic Human Resource Management*. New York: John Wiley & Sons.

Foulkes, F. 1980. *Personnel Policies in Large Nonunion Companies*. Englewood Cliffs, New Jersey: Prentice Hall

Friedland, R. & Alford, R.R. 1991. Bringing society back in: Symbols, practices, and institutional contradictions. In W.W. Powell and P.J. DiMaggio (Eds.), *The New Institutionalism in Organizational Analysis*: 232–263. Chicago: University of Chicago Press.

Guest D.E., Sanders K., Rodrigues R., & Oliveira T. 2020. Signalling theory as a framework for analysing human resource management processes and integrating human resource attribution theories: A conceptual analysis and empirical exploration', Human Resource Management Journal. http://dx.doi.org/10.1111/1748-8583.12326.

Hannan, M.T., Baron, J.N., & Burton, M.D. 1996. Inertia and change in the early years: Employment relations in young, high technology firms. Industrial and Corporate Change, 5: 503–536.

Heider, F. 1944. Social perceptions and phenomenal causality. Psychological Review, 51: 358–374.

Hewett, R., Shantz, A., Mundy, J., & Alfes, K., 2018. Attribution theories in human resource management research: A review and research agenda. The International Journal of Human Resource Management, 29: 87–126.

Huselid, M.A.. 1995. The impact of human resource management practices on turnover, productivity, and corporate financial performance. Academy of Management Journal, 38: 635–672.

Jackson, S.E., Schuler, R.S., & Rivero, J.C. 1989. Organizational characteristics as predictors of personnel practices. Personnel Psychology, 42: 727–786.

Katz, H.C. & Darbishire, O.R. 2001. *Converging Divergences: Worldwide Changes in Employment Systems*. Ithaca, New York: ILR Press.

Kelley, H.H. 1973. The processes of causal attribution. American Psychologist, 28: 107–128.

Kelley, H.H. 1967. Attribution theory in social psychology. In D. Levine (Ed.), *Nebraska Symposium on Motivation*. Lincoln, NE: University of Nebraska Press.

Kerr, C. 1958. The balkanization of labor markets. In E.W. Bakke (Ed.), *Labor Mobility and Economic Opportunity*: 92–110. Cambridge, MA: Technology Press of MIT.

Kogut, B. & Zander, U. 1992. Knowledge of the firm, combinative capabilities, and the replication of technology. Organization Science, 3: 383–397.

Lawrence, P.R. & Lorsch, J.W. 1967. *Organization and Environment: Managing Differentiation and Integration*. Boston: Harvard Business School Press.

Lepak, D.P. & Snell, S.A. 1999. The human resource architecture: Toward a theory of human capital allocation and development. Academy of Management Review, 24: 31–48.

Leung, A., Foo, M.D., & Chaturvedi, S. 2013. Imprinting effects of founding core teams on HR values in new ventures. Entrepreneurship Theory and Practice, 37: 87–106.

Liu, D., Gong, Y., Zhou, J., & Huang, J.C. 2017. Human resource systems, employee creativity, and firm innovation: The moderating role of firm ownership. Academy of Management Journal, 60: 1164–1188.

MacDuffie, J.P. 1995. Human resource bundles and manufacturing performance: Organizational logic and flexible production systems in the world auto industry. Industrial and Labor Relations Review, 48: 197–221.

Meijerink, J. & Keegan, A. 2019. Conceptualizing human resource management in the gig economy: Toward a platform ecosystem perspective. Journal of Managerial Psychology, 34: 214–232.

Meyer, J.W. & Rowan, B. 1977. Institutional organizations: Formal structure as myth and ceremony. American Journal of Sociology, 83: 340–363

Nadler, D.A. & Tushman, M.L. 2003. *Competing by Design: The Power of Organizational Architecture*. New York: Oxford University Press.

Nahapiet, J. & Ghoshal, S. 1998. Social capital, intellectual capital, and the organizational advantage. Academy of Management Review, 23: 242–266.

Nishii, L.H., Lepak, D.P., & Schneider, B. 2008. Employee attributions of the "why" of HR practices: Their effects on employee attributions and behaviors, and customer satisfaction. Personnel Psychology, 61: 503–545.

Oliver, C. 1997. Sustainable competitive advantage: combining institutional and resource-based views. Strategic Management Journal, 18: 697–713.

Ostroff, C. & Bowen, D.E. 2016. Reflections on the 2014-decade award: Is there strength in the construct of HR system strength? Academy of Management Review, 41: 196–214.

Ployhart R.E., & Moliterno, T.P. 2011. Emergence of the human capital resource: A multilevel model. Academy of Management Review, 36: 127–150.

Ployhart, R.E. Nyberg, A.J., Reilly, G., & Maltarich, M.A., 2014. Human capital is dead; long live human capital resources! Journal of Management, 40: 371–398.

Porter, M.E. 1980. *Competitive Strategy: Techniques for Analyzing Industries and Competitors*: New York: Simon and Schuster.

Rankin, S. & Sherer, P.D. 2019. Is Strategic HRM losing its way – and possibly its identity? A social network perspective. Academy of Management Proceedings, 151–157.

Roa, H.R. & Drazin, R. 2002. Overcoming resource constraints on product innovation by recruiting talent from rivals: A study of the mutual fund industry, 1986–94. Academy of Management Journal, 45: 491–507.

Saxenian, A. 1994. *Regional Advantage: Culture and Competition in Silicon Valley*. Cambridge, MA: Harvard University Press.

Sherer, P.D. 1996. Toward an understanding of the variety in work arrangements: The organization and labor relationships Framework. Appears in Journal of Organizational Behavior and in C.L. Cooper and D.M. Rousseau (Eds.), *Trends in Organizational Behavior*: 99–122. New York: John Wiley.

Sherer, P.D & Leblebici, H. 2001. Bringing variety and change into the study of strategic human resource management. In J. Ferris (Ed.), *Research in Personnel/Human Resources Management*: 199–230. Oxford, England: Elsevier Science Ltd.

Sherer, P.D., Rogovsky, N., & Wright, N. 1998. What drives employment relationships in taxicab organizations? Linking agency to firm capabilities and strategic opportunities. Organization Science, 9: 34–48.

Simon, H.A. 1951. A formal theory of the employment relationship. Econometrica, 19: 293–305.

Sirmon, D.G., Hitt, M.A., Ireland, R.D., & Gilbert, B.A. 2011. Resource orchestration to create competitive advantage: Breadth, depth, and life cycle effects. Journal of Management, 37(5): 1390–1412.

Stinchombe, A.L. 1965. Social structure and organizations. In J.G. March (Ed.), *Handbook of Organizations*: 142–193. Chicago: Rand McNally.

Suddaby, R. 2010. Editor's Comments: Construct clarity in theories of management and organization. Academy of Management Review, 35: 346–357.

Swart, J. & Kinnie, N. 2014. Reconsidering boundaries: Human resource management in a networked world. Human Resource Management, 53: 291–310.

Thompson, J.D. 1967. *Organizations in Action*. New York: McGraw Hill.

Thornton, P. H., & Ocasio, W. 1999. Institutional logics and the historical contingency of power in organizations: Executive succession in the higher education publishing industry, 1958 to 1990. American Journal of Sociology, 105: 801–843.

Tolbert, P.S. & Zucker, L.G. 1983. Institutional sources of change in the formal structure of organizations: The diffusion of civil service reform, 1880–1935. Administrative Science Quarterly, 28: 22–39.

Walton, R.E. 1985. From Control to Commitment in the Workplace. Harvard Business Review, 63: 77–84.

Walton, R.E. 1973. Quality of working life: what is it? Sloan Management Review, 15: 11–21.

Wang Y., Kim S., Rafferty A., & Sanders, K. 2020. Employee perceptions of HR practices: A critical review and future directions. International Journal of Human Resource Management, 31: 128–173.

Weiner, B. 1985. "Spontaneous" causal thinking. Psychological Bulletin, 97: 74–84

Williamson, O.E. 1985. *The Economic Institutions of Capitalism*. New York: Free Press.

Williamson, O.E. 1980. The organization of work: A comparative institutional assessment. Journal of Economic Behavior and Organization, 1: 5–38.

Williamson, O.E., Wachter, M.L., & Harris, J.E. 1975. Understanding the employment relation: The analysis of idiosyncratic exchange. Bell Journal of Economics, 6: 250–278.

Wright, P.M. & McMahan, G.C. 1992. Theoretical perspectives for strategic human-resource management. Journal of Management, 18: 295–320.

Wright, P.M., Coff, R.W., & Moliterno, T.P. 2014. Strategic human capital: Crossing the great divide. Journal of Management, 40: 353–370.

Wright, P.M., Dunford, B.B, & Snell, S.A. 2001. Human resources and the resource-based view of the firm. Journal of Management, 27: 701–721.

Wright, P.M., McMahan, G.C., & McWilliams, A. 1994. Human resources and sustained competitive advantage: a resource-based perspective. International Journal of Human Resource Management, 5: 301–326.

PART I

Variety in theoretical perspectives and processes

2 Failure to institutionalize? The case of high-performance work systems

Pamela S. Tolbert

Over two decades ago, the field of strategic human resource management 'converged on a "best practice" or universalistic paradigm that presumed the superiority of a single HR system – namely, the "high performance work system" (HPWS) – in supporting competitive advantage across all organizations' (Kehoe, 2021: 175). Despite this early convergence and human resource scholars' ongoing advocacy of HPWS, a common, recurring plaint in the literature is that very few organizations have adopted many of the HR practices that constitute HPWS (Pfeffer, 1998; Blasi and Kruse, 2006; Posthuma et al., 2013). In this chapter, I draw on institutional theory to explain this outcome, treating HPWS as an example of a failure to institutionalize.

Frequently used as a framework in analyses of the diffusion of various human resource management practices across organizations, institutional theory draws attention to two core social processes that shape the environment of organizational decision-making. One is the promotion of some set of formal structures – that is, specific organizational policies, positions and/or practices – by a set of advocates as good solutions to common organizational problems. The second process is tied to this. As a growing number of organizations adopt the structures (presumably partly in response to advocacy efforts), the structures increasingly become expected components of 'well-run' organizations, and the emergence of this social definition increases pressure on non-adopters to follow suit, fostering self-perpetuating diffusion. These processes are referred to as institutionalization (Meyer and Rowan, 1977; Zucker, 1977; DiMaggio and Powell, 1983; Tolbert and Zucker, 1983).[1]

---

[1] 'Institutionalization' is also used to refer to the outcome of these processes – i.e., to the general acceptance and persistence of the structures over time (Zucker, 1977).

Institutionalization has been identified as the source of diffusion for a variety of administrative innovations – new kinds of organizational subunits, job titles, and specific policies and practices (e.g., Rowan, 1982; Baron, Dobbin and Jennings, 1986; Still and Strang, 2003; Fiss, Kennedy and Davis, 2012). Empirical work in this tradition has almost always focused on arrangements that have become relatively widespread, that is, cases of what could be deemed successful institutionalization.[2] But not all such innovations achieve this status; some fail to spread to more than a few firms, despite the backing and promotion of experts. Unfortunately, from the standpoint of empirical study, these are readily forgotten and evidence of their existence is ephemeral – much like social movements that fail to catch fire (Snow and Soule, 2010). Hence, it is not surprising that institutional theorists have given little or no attention to this phenomenon.

In this context, HPWS provides a useful case for considering the question of why failures of institutionalization occur. Broadly, the chapter has two key aims. The first involves clarifying a central construct in strategic human resource management studies, denoted by the label HPWS, and in doing so, identifying needed areas of further theorization and research in the field. The second entails contributing to our understanding of institutionalization as a process by examining a case where the process failed to launch.

Below, a brief sketch of the core arguments constituting institutional theory, along with key elaborations offered by later theorists, provide a point of departure for the analysis. Following this, I turn to a review of the historical background and development of HPWS, noting its lineal relation to other similar constructs, in particular, 'high commitment organizations' and 'high involvement organizations,' popularized in the mid-1980s. Although seemingly similar, I note some differences in work using each construct, differences reflected and amplified in empirical studies published in the mid-1990s that commonly are taken as evidence for the impact of HPWS by advocates. Based on the review of its history, I make the case that the construct of HPWS has come to be associated with two distinct institutional logics, or different views of how it is linked to intended outcomes. These unacknowledged disagree-

---

[2]   Some may quibble over whether a distinction should be made between 'institution' and 'fad' or 'fashion,' but these terms are similarly used by organizational researchers to refer to structures that have been nominally adopted by a relatively large number of members of a population. A distinction might be made based on the length of time different structures persist, but research in this tradition has not explicitly addressed how to make this distinction (Tolbert and Zucker, 1996), and thus, the terms are treated here as interchangeable.

ments that developed over time among advocates resulted in ambiguity about the key practices tied to HPWS, and such implicit disagreements and ambiguities, I argue, have played a key role in its failure to become institutionalized in contemporary work organizations.

Institutional theory overview

Institutional theory (or sometimes, neo-institutional theory) comprises a large, diverse body of work in contemporary organizational studies connected by an emphasis on the importance of shared, normative expectations as influences on the choices of organizational decision-makers. Its roots can be traced to the writings of Max Weber (1978) on legitimacy and authority in organizations, and to observations of Parsons (1956) and Selznick (1957) about organizations' need to demonstrate consistency with general societal values to ensure social support (David, Tolbert and Boghossian, 2019).

But its rise as a dominant theoretical paradigm in contemporary organizational studies began in the late 1970s with the publication of a now-classic article by Meyer and Rowan (1977) suggesting a very different approach to explaining formal structures in organizations than that taken in much of the prior sociological work. The latter, by and large, rested on two critical (albeit typically implicit) assumptions about how and why organizations adopt formal structures, viz., that choices to adopt structures are made independently by atomistic decision-makers, and that organizational decision-makers are driven exclusively by concern with maximizing efficiency in operations. In contrast, Meyer and Rowan underscored the symbolic properties of formal structures, arguing that structures could become identified with certain values (e.g., commitment to shareholders, social responsibility and/or employee welfare), and their adoption could thus provide information to potential transaction partners and other audiences about a focal organization, signaling its commitment to 'good management.'

So how do formal structures acquire such signaling value? Early work by Tolbert and Zucker (1983), sometimes characterized as a 'two stage model,' suggested a process in which first, a set of organizations seeking to address certain operating problems create new structures as solutions. Other organizations, attempting to solve similar problems, observe and create similar structures (or engage in simultaneous invention). Second, as a growing number of organizations create such structures, they become increasingly accepted as parts of well-managed organizations or viewed as 'best practices' (Sherer and Lee, 2002; Still and Strang, 2009). The emergence of this social definition propels the structure's diffusion, either because decision-makers take others' adoption as evidence of the value of the structure (informational conformity) or because they are concerned with the legitimacy costs the organization could incur by failing to adopt the structure (normative conformity) (Tolbert and Darabi, 2019).

Following Meyer and Rowan's arguments, a second classic work in this tradition by DiMaggio and Powell (1983) expanded on different ways in which signal/structure links develop. The approach proposed by Tolbert and Zucker (1983) corresponds to which they label 'mimetic processes' (driven simply by imitation) but they note that social definitions of formal structure as desirable can also be explicitly promulgated by groups with recognized expertise or other forms of credibility ('normative processes') as well as by powerful organizations with the resources to enforce adoption through resource-tied network relations ('coercive processes').

The role of intentional efforts by groups advocating for the adoption of particular structures was elaborated by Strang and Meyer (1993), who added an additional, middle-stage process, 'theorization,' to the two-stage model. Per their account, theorization involves 'the self-conscious development and specification of abstract categories and the formulation of patterned relationship such as chains of cause and effect.' Thus, it entails the purposeful dissemination of information about formal structures, including arguments concerning how they work, purported consequences, and who is a relevant adopter (see Hardy and Maguire, 2008; Boghossian and David, 2021 for examples). Key disseminators are 'culturally legitimated theorists' – academics, policy makers, professionals and popular analysts – also denoted as 'institutional entrepreneurs' in other work (DiMaggio, 1988; Hardy and MacGuire, 2008). By providing a coherent cultural template, theorists play a central role in the diffusion of many organizational structures and practices, facilitating their spread across sets of actors who have no direct contact with or even observation of the originators or previous adopters.

A somewhat ironic example of this process is provided in Still and Strang's (2009) discussion of the rise of systematic benchmarking, involving regular surveys of competitors' practices as a planning technique. As they note, this practice was heavily promoted in the 1980s by both the American Productivity and Quality Center (APQC) and the National Institute of Standards and Technology (NIST). The latter organization included it as a key criterion for the award of its Malcolm Baldrige National Quality Award, a much-touted prize given to firms that exemplified 'world-class' performance. Both APQC and NIST embody the culturally legitimated theorists described by Strang and Meyer, and their voluminous publications and promotion of benchmarking as an important management practice were critical to its widespread adoption in the late 1980s.

Although not made explicit in Strang and Meyer's discussion of theorization, this concept is closely linked to another often invoked by institutional theorists: institutional logics. At its simplest, this concept refers to core social values that are implicated in justification or support for the utility of some practice (Friedland and Alford, 1991; Thornton and Ocasio, 1999).[3] Different logics are typically associated with different sets of institutionalized practices and formal structures. For example, Thornton and Ocasio (1999) noted that, from the 1970s onward, academic publishers found themselves facing two competing logics: market and editorial. According to a market logic (based on the valorization of market efficiency), publishing firms were expected to maximize market position, to be run as an impersonal corporate entity, and to have staffing and governance decisions tied to firms' stock market performance. On the other hand, per an editorial logic (valorizing academic professionalism), firms were expected to maximize their prestige and status in scholarly communities, to be run in a more personalistic, adaptive fashion, and to have executive succession reflect owners' personal planning. The idea that particular logics are apt to be more readily associated with some practices than others is also compatible with Strang and Meyer's observation (1993: 497) that a belief in effective information processing as key to success is compatible with the promotion of strategic planning arrangements and adoption of various information technologies, while an emphasis on the virtues of cooperation and sharing are consistent with job rotation and group-based rewards.

Of course, different logics and associated practices can overlap to some extent, but it seems likely that effective theorization (in terms of stronger institutionalization outcomes) will entail a focus on a particular logic, and on a limited set of practices tied to it. As Strang and Meyer observed in their discussion of theorization (1993: 497): 'Theoretical accounts of practices simplify and abstract their properties and specify and explain the outcomes they produce. Such accounts make it easier to perceive and communicate about the practice.' A few sentences later, they add that theorizing typically 'emphasizes certain

---

[3]   Although some definitions of 'logics' include practices and behaviors as well as the underlying values that guide behaviors (e.g., Thorton and Ocasio, 1999), here the term is applied only to subjective factors (beliefs, values) and distinguished from behavioral outcomes (practices, formal structure).

features as central and relevant, while treating others as variable, or unnecessary or derivative.'

Examples of the use of an institutional theoretic framework in studies of the spread of HR practices abound. In an early application, Tolbert and Zucker (1983) adopted it in explaining the diffusion of civil service examinations at the turn of the twentieth century as a means of selecting municipal employees. Baron, Dobbin and Jennings (1986) examined the institutionalization of job evaluation systems and dedicated departments of employment relations among US businesses, emphasizing the advocacy role played by members of the emergent profession of personnel management. Likewise, a number of studies of the spread of diversity management specialists and related policies have taken an institutional lens, treating their adoption as efforts to signal organizational compliance with anti-discrimination laws (Dobbin et al., 1988; Edelman, 1992; Dobbin, 2009). Fiss, Kennedy and Davis (2012), describing the spread of a controversial compensation arrangement for CEOs (informally known as 'golden parachutes'), made note of the theorization efforts by proponents, who suggested that these arrangements actually benefitted shareholders by reducing CEOs' propensity to resist stock-price-enhancing acquisition offers. As they argue, CEO interests undoubtedly provided an important spur to adoption of this practice, but both the theorization and its increasing prevalence among large corporations are likely to have contributed to its spread as well. Other examples of analyses using institutional theory to explain the spread of HR practices include those by Sherer and Lee of senior and staff attorney positions in law firms (2002), Still and Strang's study of family-friendly arrangements in firms (2003) and the analysis of the spread of CFO positions among public corporations in the 1980s by Zorn (2004).

Hence, institutional theory seems likely to offer a useful lens for studying HPWS as well. As described below, one issue illuminated by this application is the existence of potentially competing logics and theorization associated with this construct, differences that have been largely unacknowledged and undeveloped. Tracing the history of writings that are associated with the construct provides insights into how this came to be.

Origins and evolution of HPWS

Meeting the Japanese challenge in the 1980s

While explicit references to HPWS emerged only in the early to mid-1990s, most work using these labels recognizes their connection to a line of work that began a decade earlier. This includes two well-cited publications by Walton (1985) and Lawler (1986), both reflecting a context in which US firms faced intense competitive pressure created by the economic ascendance of Japanese firms in a number of industries. Hence, interest in determining the sources of that ascendance ran high (Cappelli and Neumark, 2001). One result was the publication of a number of studies of Japanese organizations (e.g., Cole, 1979; Ouchi, 1981; Womack, Jones and Roos, 1990). These studies highlighted strong employee loyalty, delegated decision-making responsibility and team production as defining features, and fueled other work that drew on these findings to offer prescriptions for improving US firms' ability to compete (e.g., Katz, 1985; Katz, Kochan and Weber, 1985; Osterman, 1994).[4]

In line with this literature, Walton (1985) proposed a form of organization that he called 'high commitment.' Given the general *zeitgeist*, his arguments had a great deal of resonance, and the array of touted benefits of such systems – higher production quality, better utilization of equipment and space, reduction of turnover and absenteeism, and greater flexibility – seemed plausible. Contrasting high commitment organizations with what he deemed 'control' organizations, he described a number of defining characteristics of the former (1985: 81), including: use of teams as the locus of accountability; broad, overlapping assignment of work responsibilities to individuals; high levels of autonomy for production workers; sharing of business information with employees to assist them in their decision-making; group-based rewards/ gain-sharing/profit-sharing; and employment security (or conversely, 'equality of sacrifice').

Lawler's conception of high involvement management, laid out in several volumes (Lawler, 1986; Lawler 1998), was similar, albeit summarized more compactly in a catalog of four core enablers of employee performance: power; information; knowledge; and rewards. In Lawler's conception, power entails rights to make or at least influence decisions about how to carry out tasks; information involves the sharing of data with employees about current organ-

---

[4]   Some (e.g., Jewell, Jewell and Kaufman, 2022) suggest that the core ideas and recommendations of this work can be traced back even further, to post-WWII notions of organizations as socio-technical systems (Emery, 1959).

izational functioning (quality of outputs, costs, revenues, profitability, etc.); knowledge refers to access to training in new skills and theoretical understandings that allow employees both to be more efficient and to adapt to changes more easily; and rewards encompass compensation for discretionary efforts and performance, thereby incentivizing or motivating continuing efforts.

Although similar in their focus on the benefits of delegating substantial decision-making to line employees (and thus to reducing layers of lower-level management), Lawler's schema gave less attention than Walton's to reconfiguring work specifically through the use of teams. It was even more muted on the importance of group-based performance as part of reward systems, and of 'employment assurance' – employer commitment to employees in the form of job security. Though subtle, the different emphases on particular practices arguably reflect underlying differences in core values underpinning the two authors' analyses. Walton's explicit discussion of potential concerns for his advocated approach (and managerial ambivalence about), such as role ambiguities, threats to managers, and financial commitments associated with a high commitment form of organization (1985: 80–83) is consistent with a logic of genuine employee control. While Lawler's analysis certainly has points of affinity with this, his focus on effective use of employee knowledge is more consistent with a management-dominant logic, in which management's role as 'an enabler, a culture setter, and a supporter' of employee productivity (Lawler 1998: 5) holds a prominent place.

However, these differences were typically downplayed in research and theory that followed this line of work, and the labels have often been used interchangeably, both with one another, and with HPWS. As Pfeffer notes (1998: 64), '(A) plethora of terms have been used to describe management practices: high commitment, high performance, high involvement, and so forth. Throughout this book I will use these terms interchangeably, as they all tap similar ideas about how to obtain profits through people.' Despite this synonymous usage, the subtle differences, and attendant ambiguities about what constitutes HPWS, are evidenced in the range of operationalizations of these constructs in empirical research.

Foundational empirical studies

In the mid-1990s, a trio of empirical studies appeared, aimed at demonstrating links between performance outcomes and human resource arrangements, and these soon became staple citations (often as a set) in studies advocating for the use of HPWS (e.g., Huselid and Becker, 1995; Pfeffer, 1998; Jiang et al., 2012). The first, by Arthur (1994; see also Arthur, 1992), explicitly drew on both

Walton and Lawler, and was based on data collected from steel mini-mills, a relatively young and growing industry at that time. The data were obtained from surveys sent in 1988–1989 to all existing firms in the US, asking relevant informants for information on both the firms' industrial relations practices and performance outcomes. He obtained usable survey responses from a little more than half of the plants (30 of 54).

A second study, by MacDuffie (1995), focused on automotive manufacturing firms and used a combination of survey and interview data collected between 1985 and 1990, part of an international research project of the industry. While 70 plants responded to the initial request for participation (approximately 75 percent), he confined his analysis to 62 volume-based producers. The data included information on whether an organization was characterized by the use of lean production (aimed at minimizing inventory of both parts and finished output), the types of work practices used, and a number of performance measures. Like Arthur, MacDuffie referred to 'high commitment' organizations (though he cited only Lawler).

A third study, conducted by Huselid (1995), used survey data from a large set of US firms, ones that were publicly held, had more than 100 employees, and represented a variety of industries. Sampling criteria produced a set of approximately 3,500 firms, and a questionnaire was sent to the firm-level human resources department of each. Useable responses were received from 968 firms (28 percent). These survey data were supplemented by financial performance data for each firm, using an existing data base, Compact Disclosures, containing information from firms' 10-K reports. Of these three studies, only Huselid referred to 'systems of high performance work practices,' and the theoretical connection of his study to the work of Walton and Lawler is less clear, though he does cite MacDuffie.[5]

Although these studies are often treated as reflecting a fundamental similarity in their general conclusions, as suggested in the quote above from Pfeffer, differences in theoretical sources and terminology suggest potentially more substantial divergences in underlying conceptualizations, perhaps part of the reason for notable variations in the empirical measures used in each study. Table 2.1 shows a side-by-side comparison of the latter.

---

[5]   A monograph published in 1993 under the imprimatur of the U.S. Department of Labor (no individual authors were identified) provided a catalogue of 'high performance work practices,' similar to that used by Huselid (1995).

Table 2.1   Comparison of measures in studies linking high performance characteristics to organizational performance outcomes

Arthur 1994	MacDuffie 1995	Huselid 1995
1) *Decentralized decision-making scale* (high employee participation in decisions about: a) investment in equipment b) work flow c) developing new products d) firm performance data	1) *Work systems scale* a) percent employees in formal work teams b) percent employees in employee involvement groups c) number of work suggestions made per employee d) percent of employee suggestions implemented e) extent of job rotation f) degree of production employee responsibility for monitoring quality data	1) *Employee skills and organizational structure scale* a) percent employees getting information on the organization (e.g., newsletters) b) percent employees regularly receiving attitude surveys c) percent employees participation in QWL, QC or labor/management teams* d) percent employees whose jobs are subject to job analysis e) percent employees receiving group incentives (e.g., gain-sharing plans) f) percent jobs filled from within g) percent employees with grievance or complaint resolution system h) percent employees given a test as part of hiring
2) *Employee participation scale* (percent of employees who): a) meet regularly in group to discuss production issues b) Get training in group problem-solving c) Are involved in employee/management committees	2) *HRM policies scale* a) Selection focus (using openness to learning and interpersonal skills as criteria) b) Compensation based on performance (lower scores for individual performance only, higher for plant performance and individual skills acquired) c) Elimination of status barriers (use of uniforms, common cafeteria, etc.) d) Level of training (separate questions about new and continuing EEs)	2) *Employee motivation scale* a) percent employees receiving formal performance appraisals b) percent employees whose compensation reflects performance appraisal c) Greater reliance on merit and performance than seniority for compensation d) Average number of applicants for a given job
3) *General training scale* (whether a large part of training activities involve): a) seminars or classes away from work area b) 'people skills' training		
4) *Skill level*: ratio of craft employees to total employees		
5) *Supervision*:Supervisor/ production employee ratio		
6) *Due process*: what percent of employee complaints handled through formal grievance procedures		

Arthur 1994	MacDuffie 1995	Huselid 1995
7) *Social relations*: number of social events for employees organized annually by managers		
8) *Wage level*: employment cost per production and maintenance employees		
9) *Benefits*: benefits costs divided by total employment costs		
Outcomes: productivity (labor hours/ton of process steel); scrap rate; turnover	Outcomes: productivity (number of hours to produce one vehicle); quality (number of defects/100 vehicles, as reported by consumers)	Outcomes: turnover; sales per employee; gross rate of return on capital; market value of a firm/replacement cost of assets

Note: QWL and QC refer to Quality of Working Life and Quality Circles, respectively. These terms were popular in the 1980s, and like the work of Walton (1985) and Lawler (1986), were tied to efforts to make US firms more competitive by engaging workers more fully in the production process.

Arthur's analysis used a combination of 10 total measures to capture human resource practices associated with what he labeled commitment-maximizing organizations. These included three scale measures: *decentralized decision-making* (with items tapping employee contributions to firm-level decisions on investments, work design and product development); *employee participation* (containing items on the use of teams to address production concerns); and *general training*. He also included a number of single-item measures indicating average employee skill level, the intensity of supervision, use of formal processes to handle employee grievances, company-organized social events, general wage levels, level of employee benefits, and additional bonus or incentive compensation.

MacDuffie's analysis used two main scales of human resource arrangements, denoted as *work systems* and *HRM policies*. The first, *work systems*, contains items primarily tapping employee participation in work design, along the lines suggested in Lawler's work (e.g., employee involvement groups and input via suggestions, along with feedback to employees on output quality). A few items in the scale also indicate the use of production teams and job rotation. The second scale, *human resource policies*, seems more eclectic (despite a respectable reported Cronbach's alpha coefficient of .70). It contains items that tap criteria used to select employees (particularly, the importance given to the ability to learn and to work well with others) and to compensate them (group-level performance and individual acquisition of new skills). It also includes items measuring the provision of training and minimization of status differences within the company.

Huselid also used two main scales in his analysis. The first, referred to as *employee skills and organizational structure*, includes measures of a wide range of practices – sending information to (e.g., via newsletters) and receiving information from employees, the use of employee/management groups, the use of job analysis, the presence of internal labor markets, using tests to screen job applicants, and having formal grievance procedures. The second scale, labeled *employee motivation*, primarily taps performance appraisal and compensation practices, though it also includes an item measuring recruitment practices, indicated by the average number of applicants per job opening.

There are certainly overlaps in the predictors used in these studies. For example, Arthur's scale measure of *participation* contains items similar to ones on teams and employee involvement groups in MacDuffie's *work systems* scale, and to an item on percent employees involved in labor/management teams in Huselid's *employee skills* scale. MacDuffie's scale of *HRM policies* includes two items on employee training that are somewhat analogous to Arthur's *general training* scale. And there are other points of intersection, but the differences are equally, if not more striking. While each study has a measure of compensation, Arthur's reflects a concern with relatively high pay levels, MacDuffie's measures involve overall group and organizational performance as a basis, while Huselid's emphasis is on individual performance and merit as critical criteria. Moreover, the relative number of items tapping particular features, and their aggregation into different scale measures also suggests different conceptualizations of the underlying core factors.

There are also variations in the types of performance outcomes each considers. The measures of rate of production and quality used by Arthur and MacDuffie are most similar, probably because both studies were set in manufacturing firms, where outputs are more tangible. Arthur also included turnover, which is treated as an outcome that mediates the effects of human resource management practices on quality and production rates. Although Huselid also examined a measure of turnover as a mediating variable, by and large his performance measures were notably different from both Arthur's and MacDuffie's, partly due to the fact that his sample spanned industries, and included firms in the service sector as well as those in manufacturing. This breadth makes creating general measures of rates of productivity and quality of output inherently challenging, if not impossible. Instead, Huselid examined outcomes more commonly studied in the economics-oriented strategy literature, including sales, rates of return on investment, and stock performance.

Thus, although the results of each study provide some general support for broad claims of positive influences of human resource practices on organizational performance outcomes, because they examine different bundles of practices and different outcomes, whether they should be treated as providing replicating evidence for the value of HPWS is debatable (see also Becker and Gerhart, 1996: 785). All emphasize the importance of using various practices as part of an integrated human resource system, but which practices are truly central to such systems and how or why they produce positive effects is obscured by the differing logics they implicitly or explicitly embody.

Arthur's theoretical discussion and measures most clearly reflect a logic of greater employee control as articulated in Walton's work. This logic also seems to underlie MacDuffie's analysis, although perhaps less clearly. On the other hand, both Huselid's discussion and his measures, from the example of company newsletters as a communication indicator to the use of job analysis, hiring tests and formal performance appraisals, reflect more of a concern with rationalized human resource management, or what could be called the logic of managerial engineering.

Failure to institutionalize?

Given ambiguities about what practices are key to HPWS and the underlying logic that ties these together, gauging the adoption of HPWS by firms is a challenging task. Nonetheless, there is a common perception (and plaint) among advocates of HPWS that despite evidence of positive effects, a very limited number of companies have complied with their prescriptions. A few empirical studies do provide some support for these concerns.

For example, Blasi and Kruse (2006) used data from the 1994 and 1997 National Employer Survey to assess the proportion of firms using eight practices they identify with high performance. Conducted by the US Census Bureau, the survey was sent to a representative sample of over 4,000 private establishments employing at least 20 workers, and approximately 75 percent responded in each year. The eight practices included: self-managed work teams; work-related meetings with non-managerial employees; employee training; use of benchmarking; job rotation; shorter administrative hierarchy; higher expenditures for recruiting; higher levels of compensation and benefits; and the provision of pension plans and health insurance. This list appears closest to that offered by MacDuffie (1995), but, once again, represents a unique combination (with benchmarking and offering pension and healthcare as novel additions). Coding firms that reported having five or more of these as 'strong,' those with three or four as 'medium,' and those with two or fewer as 'weak,' their analysis indicated that only about 1 percent of the respondents met the criteria for 'strong,' and the vast majority, about 85 percent, fell into the 'weak' category.

Another study often cited in this context is one conducted by Osterman (1994) which drew on data from a 1992 survey of a national, representative sample of US firms. His findings indicated that only about a quarter of surveyed establishments reported using *any* of three practices he identified with flexible specialization (equated with 'high performance work organization'): teams, job rotation and employee problem-solving groups, such as quality circles. Less than 4 percent used all three.[6]

It is worth noting that the measures used in both of these studies are more reflective of the logic of employee control characteristic of older work. Whether a contemporary study that included measures more closely identified with a managerial engineering logic (e.g., employee attitude surveys, regular formal performance appraisals, merit-based compensation) would produce different results is an open question. However, in this context, it is worth noting that a casual search of textual content in several current practitioner journals published within the last five years (including *Forbes*, *Fortune*, *Harvard Business Review*, and even the Society for Human Resource Management's *People and Strategy*) turned up no references to 'high performance work systems' or 'high performance work practices.' This suggests that if organizations do use practices better identified with the logic of managerial engineering, they probably do not consciously adopt them as a coherent system or use the HPWS rubric.

As Zucker (1983) argued, only when beliefs and values are reflected in action can they be deemed to be institutionalized. Thus, the argument that HPWS has failed to become institutionalized among organizations appears to have validity. Pfeffer (1998: 132) has catalogued some of the possible reasons for firms' resistance to adopting HPWS, including stock market and individual career pressures to reduce short-run costs (with labor expenses being a common suspect in the search for 'unnecessary fat'), leading to oblivion to the potential long-run revenues that HPWS could produce (see also Johns, 1993). These reasons may provide part of an explanation, but ambiguities about the core component practices and how and why they should produce effects are apt

---

[6]   Osterman also queried respondents about the use of total quality management (TQM), but since TQM often encompasses the use of teams and employee problem-solving groups, this seems a redundant survey item.

to be equally, and possibly a more important part (see also Jewell, Jewell and Kaufman, 2022).

Summing up

A review of the history of academic studies commonly linked to HPWS helps clarify why and how ambiguities surrounding this construct developed. Per the preceding review, earlier work viewed as foundational typically reflected the logic of employee control, based on the presumption that greater delegation of decision-making and sharing of returns to point-of-production workers would lead these employees to engage in thinking about ways to improve organizational functioning, and to work hard. This logic is linked to practices involving shared responsibilities and shared outcomes – the use of teams, employee involvement in making key decisions about jobs and the organization, and group-based compensation (e.g., Arthur, 1992, 1994; Osterman, 1994, 2000; MacDuffie, 1995; Cappelli and Neumark, 2001).

Progressively, however, research has come to reflect more of a managerial engineering logic, suggesting that the right design (i.e., use of a system of 'best practices') will produce the required set of skills among employees, appropriate levels of motivation, and avoidance of the pitfalls of a rigid bureaucracy; these arguments are often encapsulated in the popular acronym, AMO (for abilities, motivation, opportunities). Practices such as employee attitude surveys, testing as part of hiring, use of job analysis, performance appraisals and career planning (see, for example, Huselid, 1995; Combs et al., 2006; Posthuma et al., 2013) – all of which firmly insert human resource managers in the driver's seat – are compatible with this logic.

The evolution from a logic of employee control to one of managerial engineering in the literature on HPWS did not entail a sharp break. Instead, the former was overlaid gradually by the latter. A key result is the proliferation of number of practices that are identified with HPWS. This is notably reflected in a review conducted by Posthuma et al. (2013) of peer-reviewed academic publications from 1992 to 2011 that they identify as part of the HPWS tradition. Their analysis came up with an astounding total of 61 separate practices suggested across the various studies.

Moving forward: implications for strategic human resource management

The observation that the referent of the label, HPWS, is unclear is not a novel one. Ambiguities in the literature on HPWS have been called out in a number of previous studies (see Gerhart (2012) for a particularly trenchant, critical review) yet there seems to have been a curious reluctance to resolve these concerns. For example, in a meta-analysis of prior studies of the link between HPWS and firm performance, Combs et al. (2006) admit that some practices commonly promoted as part of the systemic whole may be redundant (e.g., training and formal selection procedures, if the latter results in employees already possessing the skills targeted by training), or even contradictory (e.g., the use of teams and individual performance-based compensation) (see also Becker et al., 1997). But their analysis includes these components as part of HPWS without further qualification.

Likewise, Becker and Gerhart (1996: 784) observe, 'Studies of so-called high performance work systems vary significantly as to the practices included…and sometimes even as to whether a practice is likely to be positively or negatively related to high performance.' Yet, later in the same article, reviewing research by Huselid and Becker (1995) which links practices to firms' market value, they posit that the highest performing firms 'arguably have all the appropriate best practices' (p. 788).

Approaches to resolving the problems

Given the purported centrality of the notion of HPWS to the field of strategic HRM (the quote from Kehoe at the outset of this chapter echoes similar views found in other work), if the field is to influence decisions of organizational leaders (Rynes, Bartunek and Daft, 2001; Rynes, Giluk and Brown, 2007), the ambiguities surrounding this core construct need to be tackled head on. Some recent work has begun to move towards this end, but different scholars suggest very different resolutions.

One approach is to associate HPWS more firmly with a logic of employee control, in line with the originating studies in the 1980s. This is reflected in a recent description offered by two consultants of how they present HPWS to client organizations:

> As HPWS organizational architects, we try to provide a clear and detailed blueprint of the end-product and also its price tag. The blueprint typically features a flattened, delayered management hierarchy, a reorganized work system built around broad-

ened jobs with employees grouped in production or project teams (where interdependencies warrant), an opened-up and facility-wide in-training and development, new gain-sharing forms of pay, a substantial measure of employment security, greater sharing of information and a more egalitarian culture. (Jewell, Jewell and Kaufman, 2022: 7)[7]

The authors go on to note that these recommendations rest 'on a foundation of core beliefs and values – broadly humanistic, democratic, entrepreneurial, and open-systems.' They are also clear that this system is not suited for every organization, thus implicitly endorsing a contingency rather than a best practices framework. Critical contingencies they note include ones long-recognized in traditional organizational studies (e.g., Scott, 1975), such as the size of the organization and its dominant technology.

This approach is compatible with Strang and Meyer's (1993) discussion of effective theorization – i.e., providing a simplified, easily communicated model of a few core elements and a causal linkage of these to outcomes. (See also Abrahamson, Berkowitz and Dume (2016) and Piazza and Abrahamson (2020) on forces that affect diffusion processes.) However, given the evolution in the use of the HPWS label over time, the prospects for trying to forge a consensus among academics, consultants and other practitioners on de-limiting the application of the construct in this way seem dim.

An alternative solution, suggested in recent work by Jiang, Takeuchi and Jia (2021), would be to abandon the HPWS label altogether. This might entail work among strategic human resource scholars to develop alternative, consistently-defined bundles of practices tied to a distinct logic. Jiang, Takeuchi and Jia propose one, termed High Investment Human Resource System (HIHRS), which includes 13 practices that involve various aspects of firms' expenditures on its members (e.g., career development, bonuses, health and pension plans, improvements to health and safety, etc.). The implicit logic valorizes commitment to employees by firms for its own sake. In their words (p. 1340), 'A high level of HIHRS indicates that the company places a high value on its employees regardless of whether the investment in employees can lead to performance gains.'

Given problems of trying to gain consensus on a redefinition of an existing, commonly-used and long-standing label like HPWS, this approach has some appeal. However, whether a logic that was not tied to the ultimate goal of

---

[7]   The third author on the paper helped co-write the article, but the quoted description is based on the consulting experiences of the first two authors.

enhancing financial performance could find much of an audience among practitioners is doubtful. But even if investments in employees could be theoretically (and/or empirically) linked to economic outcomes, new constructs like HIHRS need a logic that also provides criteria for de-limiting those practices that are truly core if they are to become attractive from a practitioners point of view. As noted above, theoretical work from institutional theory as well as the case of HPWS suggests the importance of this.

'Best practice' systems

Whatever approach is taken to resolving the ambiguities inherent in the construct of HPWS, another issue that needs more attention by strategic human resource scholars is identification of factors that affect the boundaries of application of any system. In part, this involves giving more explicit attention to identifying key contingencies that affect whether and when a given practice or bundle of practices is relatively more or less effective. Research on HPWS has found differences in its impact by sector and occupational groupings (e.g., Combs et al., 2006; Liao et al., 2009), but researchers have been slow to theorize or empirically explore these differential effects in more depth. Research undertaken nearly 70 years ago convincingly undermined the value of the quest for 'one best way' (Woodward, 1958; Burns and Stalker, 1961), yet the concept of best practices returned, zombie-like, in the 1980s and still lives today. Happily, current work in HR is increasingly abandoning the notion of a single best system (Shuler and Jackson, 1987; Jackson, Shuler and Jiang, 2014; Kehoe, 2021), but much work remains to be done.

Moving forward: implications for institutional theory

Treated as a case of failure to institutionalize, HPWS offers useful insights into why some advocated organizational changes are unlikely to diffuse, a problem given scant attention in work going under the banner of institutional theory. The historical analysis of this case draws attention to the development of competing logics over time, and attendant ambiguities in the practices that signify its adoption.

At a most basic level, management innovations are labels that connote particular policies, positions, and/or practices and that reflect means-and-ends arguments about the attainment of some valued objective. Previous work on specific innovations, including TQM, golden parachutes and academic tenure systems, indicates that it is probably more common than not for a given label to be identified with a variety of practices, ones that often expand over time, and that are not uniformly implemented by organizations purporting to have adopted the innovation (Kennedy and Fiss, 2009; Fiss, Kennedy and Davis, 2012; Park, Sine and Tolbert, 2011; see also Ansari, Fiss and Zajac, 2010).

However, at least to begin the process of institutionalization, the case of HPWS suggests the importance of the label being associated with a few core, distinctive practices that exemplify a single general institutional logic. Per the historical account offered here, the construct, HPWS, was identified with two different logics at the outset – a melding of older work reflecting the valorization of employee control and new work emphasizing advantages of more systematic HR practices. This combination encouraged its widespread use by scholars with very different interpretations of the basic cause-and-effect relations embodied by HPWS. One could hypothesize that this inherent ambiguity limited its promotion by consultants and highly visible manager champions who are often key to the transmission of ideas from academia to managerial practice (Abrahamson, Berkowitz and Dumez, 2016). This beginning also made it virtually impossible to distinguish 'certain features as central and relevant, while treating others as variable, or unnecessary or derivative' (Strang and Meyer, 1993: 497).

From the standpoint of institutional theory, then, the case of HPWS suggests the need for greater attention to the content as well as the process of theorization associated with management innovations. Doing so will allow for greater understanding of the factors that may influence both the extent of adoption of a management innovation, as well as its endurance – two key dimensions of institutionalization.

References

Abrahamson, Eric and Micki Eisenman. 2008. 'Employee-management techniques: Transient fads or trending fashions?' *Administrative Science Quarterly* 53 (4): 719–44.
Abrahamson, Eric, Heloise Berkowitz and Herve Dumez. 2016. 'A more relevant approach to relevance in management studies: An essay on performativity.' *Academy of Management Review* 41 (2): 367–381.
Ansari, Shahzad M., Peer Fiss and Edward Zajac. 2010. 'How practices vary as they diffuse: A framework for analysis.' *Academy of Management Review* 35 (1): 67–92.
Arthur, Jeffrey B. 1992. 'The link between business strategy and industrial relations systems in American steel minimills.' *Industrial and Labor Relations Review* 45 (3): 488–506.

Arthur, Jeffrey B. 1994. 'Effects of human resource systems on manufacturing performance and turnover.' *Academy of Management Journal* 37 (3): 670–87.

Baron, James N., Frank Dobbin and P. Devereaux Jennings. 1986. 'War and peace: The evolution of modern personnel administration in U.S. industry.' *American Journal of Sociology* 92: 350–83.

Becker, Brian and Barry Gerhart. 1996. 'The impact of human resource management on organizational performance: Progress and prospects.' *Academy of Management Journal* 39 (4): 779–801.

Becker, Brian E., Mark A. Huselid, Peter S. Pickus and Michael F. Spratt. 1997. 'HR as a source of shareholder value: Research and recommendations.' *Human Resource Management* 36: 39–47.

Blasi, Joseph R. and Douglas L. Kruse. 2006. 'U.S. high-performance work practices at century's end.' *Industrial Relations* 45 (4): 547–578.

Boghossian, Johnny and Robert J. David. 2021. 'Under the umbrella: Goal-derived category construction and product category nesting.' *Administrative Science Quarterly* 66 (4): 1084–1129.

Burns, Tom and George M. Stalker. 1961. *The Management of Innovation*. London: Tavistock.

Cappelli, Peter and David Neumark. 2001. 'Do "high-performance" work practices improve establishment-level outcomes?' *Industrial and Labor Relations Review* 54 (4): 737–75.

Cole, Robert E. 1979. *Work, Mobility and Participation: A Comparative Study of American and Japanese Industry*. Berkeley CA: University of California Press

Combs, James, Yongmei Liu, Angela Hall and David Ketchen. 2006. 'How much do high-performance work practices matter? A meta-analysis of their effects on organizational performance.' *Personnel Psychology* 59: 501–28.

David, R.J., Tolbert, P.S. and Boghossian, J. 2019. 'Institutional theory in organization studies.' *Oxford Research Encyclopedia, Business and Management*. doi: 10.1093/ acrefore/ 9780190224851.013.158.

DiMaggio, Paul J. 1988. 'Interest and agency in institutional theory.' 3–21 in L.G. Zucker (ed.), *Institutional Patterns and Organizations: Culture and Environment*. Cambridge MA: Ballinger.

DiMaggio, Paul J. and Walter W. Powell. 1983. 'The iron cage revisited: Institutional isomorphism and collective rationality in organizational fields.' *American Sociological Review* 48 (2): 147–60

Dobbin, Frank. 2009. *Inventing Equal Opportunity*. Princeton NJ: Princeton University Press.

Dobbin, Frank, Lauren B. Edelman, John W. Meyer, Richard Scott and Ann Swidler. 1988. 'The expansion of due process in organizations.' 71–98 in L.G. Zucker (ed.), *Institutional Patterns in Organizations: Culture and Environment*. Cambridge MA: Ballinger.

Edelman, Lauren B. 1992. 'Legal ambiguity and symbolic structures: Organizational mediation of civil rights law.' *American Journal of Sociology* 93 (6): 1531–76.

Emery, Fredrick E. 1959. *Characteristics of Socio-Technical Systems*. London: Tavistock Institute Document 527.

Fiss, Peer, Mark T. Kennedy and Gerald F. Davis. 2012. 'How golden parachutes unfolded: Diffusion and variation of a controversial practice.' *Organization Science* 23(4): 1077–99.

Friedland, Richard and David Alford. 1991. 'Bringing society back in: Symbols, practices and institutional contradiction. 232–263 in W.W. Powell and P.M. DiMaggio (eds.), *The New Institutionalism in Organizational Analysis*. Chicago: University of Chicago Press.

Gerhart, Barry. 2012. 'Construct validity, causality and policy recommendations: The case of high performance work practices systems.' *Human Resource Management Review* 22 (2): 157–160.

Hardy, Cynthia and Steve Maguire. 2008. 'Institutional entrepreneurship.' 198–217 in R. Greenwood, C. Oliver, K. Sahlin and R. Suddaby (eds.), *The SAGE Handbook of Organizational Institutionalism*. Los Angeles CA: SAGE Publishing.

Huselid, Mark. 1995. 'The impact of human resource management practices on turnover, productivity and corporate financial performance.' *Academy of Management Journal* 38 (3): 635–672.

Huselid, Mark and Brian Becker. 1995. 'The strategic impact of high performance work systems.' Paper presented at the Academy of Management meetings, Vancouver CA.

Jackson, Susan E., Randall S. Schuler and Kaifeng Jiang. 2014. 'An aspirational framework for strategic human resource management.' *Academy of Management Annals* 8: 1–56.

Jewell, Donald O., Sandra F. Jewell and Bruce E. Kaufman. 2022. 'Designing and implementing high-performance work systems: Insights from consulting practice for academic researchers.' *Human Resource Management Review* 32: 1–16.

Jiang, Kaifeng, David Lepak, Jia Hu and Judith Baer. 2012. 'How does human resource management influence organizational outcomes? A meta-analytic investigation of mediating mechanisms.' *Academy of Management Journal* 55 (6): 1264–1294.

Jiang, Kaifeng, Rikki Takeuchi and Yingya Jia. 2021. 'Taking peers into account: Adoption and effects of high-investment human resource systems.' *Journal of Applied Psychology* 106 (10): 1539–1556.

Johns, Gary. 1993. 'Constraints on the adoption of psychology-based personnel practices: Lessons from organizational innovation.' *Personnel Psychology* 46 (3): 569–592.

Katz, Harry C. 1985. *Shifting Gears: Changing Labor Relations in the U.S. Auto Industry*. Cambridge MA: MIT Press.

Katz, Harry, Thomas A Kochan and M.R. Weber. 1985. 'Assessing the effects of industrial relations systems and efforts to improve the quality of working life on organizational effectiveness.' *Academy of Management Journal* 28: 509–526.

Kehoe, Rebecca R. 2021. 'Revisiting the concepts of vertical and horizontal fit in HRM: What we know, what we don't know, and where we might go.' *Academy of Management Perspectives* 35 (2): 175–180.

Kennedy, Mark and Peer Fiss. 2009. 'Institutionalization, framing and diffusion: The logic of TQM adoption and implementation decisions among U.S. hospitals.' *Academy of Management Journal* 52 (5): 897–918.

Lawler, Edward E. 1986. *High-Involvement Management: Participative Strategies for Improving Organizational Performance*. San Francisco, CA: Jossey-Bass Inc.

Lawler, Edward E. 1998. *The Ultimate Advantage*. San Francisco, CA: Jossey-Bass Inc.

Liao, Hui, Keiko Toya, David P. Lepak and Ying Hong. 2009. 'Do they see eye to eye? Management and employee perspectives of high-performance work systems and influence processes on service quality.' *Journal of Applied Psychology* 94 (2): 371–391.

MacDuffie, John Paul. 1995. 'Human resource bundles and manufacturing performance: Organizational logic and flexible production systems in the world auto industry.' *Industrial and Labor Relations Review* 48 (2): 197–221.

Meyer, John W. and Brian Rowan. 1977. 'Institutional organizations: formal structure as myth and ceremony.' *American Journal of Sociology* 83 (2): 340–363.

Osterman, Paul. 1994. 'How common is workplace transformation and who adopts it?' *Industrial and Labor Relations Review* 47 (2): 173–188.

Osterman, Paul. 1987. 'Turnover, employment security and the performance of the firm.' 275–317 in M.M. Kleiner, R.N. Block, M Roomkin and S.W. Salsburg (eds.), *Human Resources and the Performance of the Firm*. Washington DC: BNA Press.

Ouchi, William G. (1981). *Theory Z*. New York: Avon Books.

Park, Sangchan, Wesley D. Sine and Pamela S. Tolbert. 2011. 'Professions, organizations and institutions: Tenure systems in colleges and universities.' *Work and Occupations* 38 (3): 340–371.

Parsons, Talcott. 1956. 'Suggestions for a sociological approach to the theory of organizations.' *Administrative Science Quarterly* 1: 63–85.

Pfeffer, Jeffrey. 1998. *The Human Equation*. Boston MA: Harvard Business School Press.

Piazza, Alessandro and Eric Abrahamson. 2020. 'Fads and fashions in management practices: Taking stock and looking forward.' *International Journal of Management Reviews* 22: 264–286.

Posthuma, Richard A., Michael C. Comapion, Malika Masimova and Micahel A. Camion. 2013. 'A high performance work practices taxonomy: Integrating the literature and directing future research.' *Journal of Management* 39 (5): 1184–1220.

Rowan, Brian. 1982. 'Organizational structure and the institutional environment: The case of public schools.' *Administrative Science Quarterly* 27 (2): 259–279.

Rynes, Sara L., Jean M. Bartunek and Richard L. Daft. 2001. 'Across the great divide: Knowledge creation and transfer between practitioners and academics.' *Academy of Management Journal* 44 (2): 340–355.

Rynes, Sara, Tamara L. Giluk and Kenneth G. Brown. 2007. 'The very separate worlds of academic and practitioner periodicals in human resource management: Implications for evidence-based management.' *Academy of Management Journal* 50 (5): 989–1008.

Schuler, Randall S. and Susan E. Jackson. 1987. 'Linking competitive strategies with human resources management practices.' *Academy of Management Executive* 1 (3): 207–219.

Scott, W. Richard. 1975. 'Organizational structure.' *Annual Review of Sociology* 1: 1–25.

Selznick, Philip. 1957. *Leadership in Administration*. New York: Harper and Row.

Sherer, Peter D. and Kyungmook Lee. 2002. 'Institutional change in large law firms: A resource dependency and institutional perspective.' *Academy of Management Journal* 45 (1): 102–119.

Snow, David and Sarah Soule. 2010. *A Primer on Social Movements*. New York: W.W. Norton.

Still, Mary and David Strang. 2003. 'Institutionalizing family-friendly policies.' 327–45 in P. Moen (ed.), *It's About Time: Couples and Careers*. Ithaca NY: Cornell University Press.

Still, Mary and David Strang. 2009. 'Who does an elite organization emulate?' *Administrative Science Quarterly* 54 (1): 54–8.

Strang, David and John W. Meyer (1993). 'Institutional conditions for diffusion.' *Theory and Society* 22: 487–511.

Thornton, Patricia and William Ocasio. 1999. 'Institutional logics and the historical contingency of power in organizations: Executive succession in the higher education publishing industry, 1968–1990.' *American Journal Sociology* 105: 801–839.

Tolbert, Pamela S. and Tiffany Darabi. 2019. 'Bases of conformity and institutional theory: Understanding organizational decision-making.' *Research in the Sociology of Organizations* 55: 587–611.

Tolbert, Pamela S. and Lynne G. Zucker. 1983. 'Institutional sources of change in the formal structure of organizations: The diffusion of civil service reform, 1880–1935.' *Administrative Science Quarterly* 28 (1): 22–39.

Tolbert, Pamela S. and Lynne G. Zucker. 1996. 'The institutionalization of institutional theory.' 175–190 in Stewart Clegg, Cynthia Hardy and Walter Nord (Eds.), *Handbook of Organization Studies*. London: Sage.

Trist, Eric L. 1950. 'The Relations of Social and Technical Systems in Coal-Mining.' Paper presented to the British Psychological Society, Industrial Section.

Walton, Richard. E. 1985. 'From control to commitment in the workplace.' *Harvard Business Review* (March–April): 77–84.

Weber, Max. 1921/1978. *Economy and Society: An Outline of Interpretive Sociology*. Berkeley: University of California Press.

Womack, James P., Daniel T. Jones and Daniel Roos. 1990. *The Machine that Changed the World: The Story of Lean Production*. New York: Rawson Associates.

Woodward, Joan. 1958. *Management and Technology*. London: HMSO

Zorn, Dirk. 2004. 'Here a chief, there a chief: The rise of the CFO in the American firm.' *American Sociological Review* 69 (3): 345–364.

Zucker, Lynne G. 1977. 'The role of institutionalization in cultural persistence.' *American Sociological Review* 42 (5): 726–743.

Zucker, Lynne G. 1983. 'Institutional theories of organization.' *Annual Review of Sociology* 13: 443–464.

3 The human resource management–outcomes relationship: an attributional HR process perspective

Karin Sanders

1. Introduction

There is a long-standing research tradition in human resource management (HRM) research to examine the relationship between HR practices and organizational performance. To understand the nature of this relationship, also referred to as the 'black box', scholars have focused on the effect of (bundles of) HR practices – such as recruitment and selection, training and development, performance appraisal and rewards on different outcomes, such as profit and revenue of the organization. Although for many decades HRM scholars have focused on the understanding of this relationship, we still do not know the exact mechanism by which these bundles of HR practices contribute to organizational performance (Boon, Den Hartog and Lepak, 2019; Bowen and Ostroff, 2004).

As a response to this mainly macro-level research, scholars have turned their attention to the role of employees and focus on the *HR process* to explain the 'black box' (see Bowen and Ostroff, 2004; Sanders, Shipton and Gomes, 2014; Ostroff and Bowen, 2016; Hewett et al., 2018; Wang et al., 2020; Sanders, Bednall and Yang, 2021). This HR process research, in which two main research streams can be identified, can be considered as the micro-foundations of the HRM–outcomes link research. In the first research stream scholars have focused on the influence of employees' beliefs about intentions of organization to design and implement HR practices (i.e., *HR attributions*; Nishii, Lepak and Schneider, 2008). When an organization implements a new practice, for instance a new pay for performance or recruitment practice, employees will ask the question *why* this new policy is implemented by the organization. The answers on these questions, for instance 'this practice is implemented because the organization wants to cut costs' or 'this practice is implemented because the organization takes care of their employees', are called HR attributions. Research shows that these HR attributions influence employees' attitude and behaviours.

The second research stream is initiated by Bowen and Ostroff (2004)'s theoretical framework on *HR (system) strength* and focuses on the process of *how* employees can make sense of the HR practices within an organization. This approach proposes that when information on HR practices is perceived by employees as distinctive (the information is standing out), consistent (across the different HR practices, and across time) and consensual (different policy makers within an organization are sending out the same message), employees can make sense of this information, and can understand what is expected from them and what is rewarded within this organization. Research shows that perceptions of HR strength also have an influence on employees' attitudes and behaviours.

Both research streams have their foundations in an influential theoretical framework within the social psychology: namely the *attribution(al) framework*. Under the umbrella of this attribution(al) framework, a family of attribution theories can be identified. All these attribution theories (Heider, 1944; 1958; Kelley, 1967; 1973; Weiner, 1985) have in common that they assume that individuals act as naïve psychologists who seek to explain events and behaviours, including their own behaviour and the behaviour of people around them. Therefore, individuals make inferences (attributions) about the causes of these events and behaviours. In this way attributions can be seen as naïve, common-sense explanations for events and behaviours around them. For instance, employees try to understand the behaviour of organizations in managing their employees.

In addition to the HR attribution model based on the work of Nishii and colleagues (2008) and HR (system) strength model based on the work of Bowen and Ostroff (2004), the implementation of HR practices by line managers, also known as the transfer of HR tasks from HR to line managers, is sometimes seen as part of the HR process research (see Patel, Yang and Sanders, 2021). However, in this chapter I focus on the HR attributions and HR strength research as these two research streams are both based on theories of the attribution(al) framework and are in comparison to the implementation of HR by line-managers more focused on sending out signals to employees and on the sense-making of HR by employees. For a recent overview of the research on the implementation of HR practices by line managers, I refer to work of Guest (2021) and Bos-Nehles, Trullen and Valverde (2021).

The impact of the HR process research has been accumulated in the last two decades and acknowledged in several recent review papers and chapters (Ostroff and Bowen, 2016; Hewett et al., 2018; Wang et al., 2020; Hewett, 2021; Sanders et al., 2021). Also, a recent meta-analysis on perceived HR strength (Bednall et al., 2021) has been accepted in an influential journal and an edited book on the HR process has recently been published by Edward Elgar (Sanders, Yang and Patel, 2021). Yet, a lot of questions remain unanswered (see also Patel et al., 2021). I will elaborate more in this chapter on one of the remaining questions, namely 'how do HR strength and HR attributions can work together?' in addition to a presentation of the two research streams.

In this chapter, the background, as well as areas for improvement and avenues for future research of the two research streams are presented (HR attributions research in Section 2 and HR strength research in Section 3). In Section 4, I discuss how these two research streams can work together.

2.   HR attributions research

In this section I provide an overview of the foundations of the research on HR attribution, starting with the causal model of the attribution theory (Weiner, 1985; Heider, 1958). For this overview I refer to earlier reviews (Hewett et al., 2018; Wang et al., 2020) and chapters of Hewett (2021) and Sanders and Rafferty (2021) in the HR process book (Sanders et al., 2021).

Causal attributions are the explanations that individuals form for their own behaviour (e.g., 'Why did I not get this promotion?') and of behaviours of others (e.g., 'Why did my colleague receive a bonus, while I did not?'). People make attributions to enhance their ability to understand, predict, and control their environment (Wong and Weiner, 1981). One of the key dimensions of Heider's (1944; 1958) attribution theory is the *locus of causality*, which concerns whether an individual considers the cause of a behaviour to be internal (i.e., generated by the person) or external (i.e., generated by the situation). Dependent on success or failure people attribute the event or behaviour to internal or external causes (as 'naïve, common-sense explanations'). In general, people attribute own success (e.g., receiving a bonus, or promotion) to internal factors as 'own abilities', 'hard working' and 'talents', while failures (e.g., not receiving a bonus or promotion) are attributed in general to external factors, such as 'bad luck', 'the supervisor does not like me', or 'the HR department is only promoting females lately'. However, in explaining success and failures of other people, we attribute their success in general to external factors, as 'luck' or 'the supervisor likes him more' and failure to internal factors such as 'a lack of capabilities and talents'. The explanations (attributions) of one own and other's behaviour influence individuals' responses in terms of their attitudes and behaviours (Weiner, 1985).

Scholars in the HR field have considered whether the locus of causality influences employees' responses to the implementation and design of (new) HR practices. For instance, in the early 1990s, Koys (1988; 1991) argued that employees make an internal attribution if HR activities appear to be freely chosen by the organization rather than forced by external pressures. Koys also suggested that HR activities that are done 'out of a spirit of justice' or 'to attract and retain employees' represent internal attributions. On the other hand, HR activities that were done to 'encourage individual or organizational performance' or 'to comply with government relations' are examples of external explanations. Empirical results show that while internal explanations are positively related to commitment, external explanations are unrelated to commitment (Koys, 1988; 1991).

In their personnel psychology paper, Nishii et al. (2008) build on the work of Koys (1988; 1991) to study HR attributions in a more systematic way. They define HR attributions as the beliefs that employees form about the intentions of management to design and implement HR practices. Nishii et al. defined internal attributions as the beliefs that actions are due to factors over which management has control. For example, if an employee feels that an HR practice is designed to comply with trade unions, employees attribute the implementation of this HR practice to external factors. In contrast, external attributions are defined as the beliefs of external, environmental forces that require management to adopt certain practices.

In addition to one external attribution ('trade union attribution'), Nishii et al. argue that internal attributions are more complex and they organize these internal attributions along two dimensions: (1) the extent to which the (internal) attributions represent business goals versus employee-oriented philosophies underlying HR practices (e.g., Lepak et al., 2002; Osterman, 1994), and (2) whether the practice is designed to engender commitment or enforce control (Arthur, 1992; 1994). By crossing over these two dimensions, Nishii et al. identify four types of internal HR attributions: service quality, employee wellbeing, cost reduction and employee exploitation ('how are we getting the most out of employees?'). The five HR attributions as formulated by Nishii et al. are presented in Table 3.1.

Table 3.1   Typology of HR attributions

	Internal attributions		
	Business/strategic goal underlying HRM	Employee-oriented philosophy	External attribution
Commitment-focused	Service quality	Employee wellbeing	Union compliance
Control-focused	Cost reduction	Exploiting employees	

Using data from 4,500 employees and 1,100 department managers from a service firm, Nishii et al. show that employees make varying attributions for the same HR practice. In addition, their results show that these HR attributions are differentially associated with employee commitment and satisfaction. More specific, attributions that HR practices are motivated by the organization's concern for enhancing service quality and employee well-being (commitment attributions) were positively related to employee commitment and satisfaction. However attributions focused on reducing costs and exploiting employees (control attributions) were negatively associated with these attitudes. The external attribution involving union compliance was not associated with these attitudes. These employee attitudes – satisfaction and commitment – were related to different dimensions of employee Organization Citizenship Behaviours (OCBs) which were in turn related to customer satisfaction.

Hewett (2021) has reviewed the work on HR attributions and has found 14 empirical papers that examined aspects of the HR attribution framework. The majority of these papers tested the effects of the HR attributions within the relationship between HR practices and attitudinal and behavioural outcomes. These studies showed that commitment-focused (service quality and employee well-being) attributions are positively related to affective commitment (Fontinha et al., 2012; Khan and Tang, 2016; Nishii et al., 2008; Van De Voorde and Beijer, 2015), job satisfaction (Valizade et al., 2016), performance-related outcomes (Chen and Wang, 2014; Yang and Arthur, 2019) and negatively to intention to quit (Lee et al., 2019), supporting the findings of Nishii et al. In addition, control-focused (cost reduction and employee exploitation) attributions are found to be related to stress-related outcomes such as work overload, emotional exhaustion, and burnout (Shantz et al., 2016; Van de Voorde and Beijer, 2015; see Hewett et al., 2018 and Wang et al., 2020 for reviews).

Instead of examining the outcomes of HR attributions, only a few articles have focused on high-performance work practices (HPWP) as an antecedent of HR attributions (Van de Voorde and Beijer, 2015; Sanders, Yang and Li, 2019).

For example, Van de Voorde and Beijer found that the presence of HPWP, as rated by unit managers, was positively related to the commitment attributions. In a vignette study and cross-sectional survey, Sanders et al. found that the employee perception of HPWP was positively related to service-quality attributions and negatively to cost-saving attributions.

In addition, a few papers have focused on interactions between antecedents to explain the HR attributions. For example, Sanders and colleagues (2019) examined the effect of power distance orientation, referring to the extent to which people accept unequally distributed power in a society or an organization (Hofstede, 1984) and found that the relationships between HPWP and HR attributions (service-quality and cost-saving attributions) are stronger for low-power, distance-oriented employees, indicating that individuals who rely less on hierarchically senior managers to shape their interpretations are more likely to perceive HPWP as it was intended. Montag-Smit and Smit (2020) examined the effect of three dimensions of pay secrecy policies (i.e., distributive nondisclosure, communication restriction, procedural nondisclosure) on employee trust in management, and found that attributions generally mediated the relationships between pay secrecy and trust in management. Employee preferences for sharing pay information moderated some of these relationships; those who were unwilling to share personal pay information did not make negative attributions of secretive distributive pay policies. However, employees with a preference for disclosure thought that pay secrecy had more malevolent intentions. Finally, Hewett and colleagues (2019) found an interaction of organizational cynicism and perceptions of distributive fairness predicting HR attributions, such that perceptions of distributive fairness buffered the effects of cynicism; fairness was negatively related to cost-saving attributions when employees are cynical.

In the same year as Hewett finished her review chapter a special issue of *Human Resource Management Journal* (Sanders, Guest and Rodrigues, 2021) was published, containing five articles on HR attribution, including the article by Montag-Smit and Smit (2020). One of topics in their call for papers (Sanders, Guest and Rodrigues, 2017) was the integration of HR attribution and HR strength research. Two articles in this special issue addressed this call (Katou et al., 2021; Guest et al., 2021; see section 4 of this chapter). These two articles also addressed the call for more research on the role of communication in this field. Alfes, Veld and Furstenberg (2021) addressed the call for research (Sanders et al., 2017) on the combination of HR attributions. They found that a combination of well-being and exploitation attributions, which they called performance attribution, mediates the relationship between HPWP and employee engagement. The article by Fan, Huang and Timming addressed the call for more multi-level research and explored the effect of team-level HR attributions; they found that transformational leadership moderates the relationship between team-level commitment HR attributions and team performance. The chapter by Zhang, Wei, and Wang (2021), entitled 'Team Leaders' HR Attribution: The Teams-Level and Employees-Level Consequences' in the book on HR process approach (Sanders et al., 2021) is an example of a team-level study on HR attributions.

Despite the very valuable work done on the antecedents and consequences of HR attributions according to both Hewett (2021) and Sanders et al. (2021), there are still important topics that are largely neglected, and which still need to be effectively addressed in future research on HR attributions. One of them concerns the wider context in which the HR attributions are formed and are effective (see Sanders et al.). Until now, research on HR attribution assumes a universalistic approach mainly since the research in this field lacks the influence of institutional factors or cultural values on HR attributions. In addition, sscholars have argued that people make attributions, especially following a threatening or dramatic event, such as an organizational change or the Covid-19 crisis (Wong and Weiner, 1981). Research about the forming of HR attributions in different times should be encouraged.

Hewett (2021) also discussed some challenges with the HR attribution frame-work. One of them is the HR attributions dimensions of Nishii et al. In addition to locus of causality (whether the attribution is internal or external), Weiner (1985; 1986) also distinguished a dimension of controllability (the extent to which the focal actor can influence the outcome), and a dimension of stability (whether this is a typical behaviour or an exception) of a behaviour or event. Until now, scholars seem to avoid incorporating these two dimensions, while Weiner (2018) explained that these dimensions are necessary to distinguish a scientific theory of causal attributions from the theory of causal explanations (see also section 4 of this chapter). Related to the lack of acknowledging the other dimensions, the inconsistency in the use and terminology in the current research of service-quality, employee exploitation and performance attribu-tions can be mentioned. While Nisii et al. (2008) use employee exploitation, Beijer and van der Voorde call this attribution a performance attribution. The use of different terms for the same HR attribution is not helpful in the cumula-tion of knowledge in this field. With a few exemptions (Guest, Rodrigues and Oliviera, 2019; Hewett et al., 2019; Montag-Smit and Smit, 2020), external HR attributions have been largely ignored in empirical research work. Although external attributions are seen as less predictive of behavioural outcomes (Jones and Davis, 1965), it would be valuable for future research to explore these external attributions more (Hewett, 2021). It may for instance be the case that

that external attributions are important for specific HR practices, but not for all.

Based on their findings, Hewett et al. (2019) suggested an alternative dimensional structure which focuses on two dimensions. First, they suggested a continuum ranging from more organization-centric (exploitation attributions) to more employee-centric (commitment attributions; employee well-being and service quality), while cost-saving attributions are more ambiguous. Second, they proposed that this continuum applies to both internal and external attributions. Although this revised framework is yet to be fully tested, it highlights the need to re-evaluate the Nishii et al. typology considering the empirical research so far. Finally, the dynamic nature of HR attributions (see Hewett, 2021) is underexplored in the current research. Sanders et al. (2021) also encourage longitudinal research in this field to understand the causality between HR attributions and outcomes.

In the next section I discuss the other research stream within the HR process research, namely research on the HR strength research.

3.   HR strength research

In this section I review the research on HR (system) strength and provide an overview of the foundations of this research stream, namely the co-variation model of the attribution theory (Kelley, 1967; 1973). This section is based on earlier reviews (Hewett et al., 2018; Wang et al., 2020) and chapters of Sanders, Bednall and Yang (2021) and Sanders and Rafferty (2021) in the HR process book (Sanders et al., 2021), as well as a recently accepted meta-analysis on the role of HR strength in the bundles of HR practices and employee outcomes performance link (Bednall et al., 2021).

The co-variation principle of the attribution theory proposes that when people interpret behaviours or events, they often have access to multiple instances of the stimulus across time and situations. At such times, they employ a *covariation principle* to determine the cause of the stimulus based on three features: *distinctiveness, consistency*, and *consensus*. Distinctiveness refers to the extent to which a stimulus "stands out" in its environment, thereby capturing attention and arousing interest (Kelley, 1973, p. 102). Consistency refers to similarity across time and modalities. If the stimulus is the same in all situations, individuals perceive the situation as consistent. Consensus is the similarity of behaviour across different people. If many people perceive the situation in the same way, consensus is high. Depending on the information available, individuals attribute the behaviour or event to the *entity or stimulus* when they perceive the information as high distinctive, high consistent, and high consensual, to *context or time* when they perceive the information as high distinctive, low consistent and low consensual, or to the *person themselves* when they perceive the information as low distinctive, high consistent and low consensual.

In their Academy of Management Review paper, Bowen and Ostroff (2004) applied the covariation principle of Kelley's (1967, 1973) attribution theory to the domain of HR and developed a framework to explain *how* HR as a system 'can contribute to organizational performance by motivating employees to adopt desired attitudes and behaviours that, in the collective, help to achieve the organization's strategic goals' (Bowen and Ostroff, 2004, p. 204). To enhance the likelihood that employees interpret the messages conveyed by HR in a uniform manner, employees should perceive the content of HR as being distinctive, consistent and consensual. Bowen and Ostroff introduced the concept of '*Strength of the HR System*', which they define as: 'the features of an HR system that send signals to employees that allow them to understand the desired and appropriate responses and form a collective sense of what is expected'. While researchers have used various terms for this concept, including 'HR(M) (system) strength' and/or 'Strength of the HR System', I use the term 'HR strength' in this chapter.

Bowen and Ostroff used the three meta-features of distinctiveness, consistency and consensus as an organizing framework for nine specific characteristics relevant to the HR system (Ostroff and Bowen, 2016, p. 197). The meta-feature of *distinctiveness* comprises visibility, understandability of practices, relevance of the HR practices to strategic and individual goal achievement, and legitimacy of authority of the HR function. The meta-feature of *consistency* includes instrumentality by establishing an *unambiguous* perceived cause-effect relationship in reference to the HRM system's desired content-focused behaviours and associated employee consequences, validity in terms of consistency between the intention and the actuality of the practice, and alignment (vertical and horizontal) and stability over time. The meta-feature of *consensus* is composed of agreement among message senders and fairness of practices into the meta-feature of consensus. All these features and meta-features work in concert to deliver the HR message. Related to the co-variation model of the attribution theory (Kelley, 1967; 1973), when employees perceive HR as high distinctive, high consistent and high consensus they attribute HR to the entity (management) and can understand what is expected from them (see also Sanders and Yang, 2016).

The theoretical framework of Bowen and Ostroff (2004), however, focuses in addition to HR strength on *organizational climate*, defined as the shared interpretations of what is important and what behaviours are expected and rewarded. While organizational climate is assumed to be a crucial mediator that explains the HRM-organizational performance relationship, HR strength is considered necessary to emerge from individual perceptions of HRM (psychological climate) to the shared perceptions (organizational climate). In other words, an organizational climate in which employees possess a shared understanding of HR only emerges from individual perceptions when the HR strength is strong. Conversely, when an HR strength is weak, individual perceptions (psychological climate) tend to be idiosyncratic. Their model is presented in Figure 3.1.

While the construct of HR strength received a lot of attention, HR process researchers largely ignored the organizational climate aspectof the framework

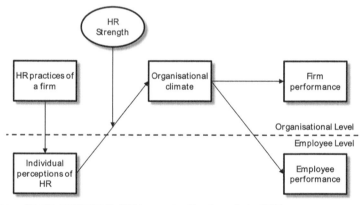

Source: Bowen and Ostroff, 2004; see also Sanders et al., 2021

Figure 3.1   The HR strength model

(see also Sanders et al., 2021). As research on organizational climate as elaborated on in the model of Bowen and Ostroff is very rare (with some exemptions: Sanders, Dorenbosch and De Reuver, 2008; Li, Frenkel and Sanders, 2011; Aksoy and Bayazit, 2014) and less related to attribution framework, I focus on HR strength in this review. Also, in comparison to the Bowen and Ostroff model most empirical researchers have interpreted the construct of HR strength in terms of employee perceptions and measured the construct and examined its effects at the individual level (see Ostroff and Bowen, 2016). Although Ostroff and Bowen agree that employee perceptions of HR strength is a 'meaningful construct' (p. 198), it is different from the original construct, namely a construct at the unit or organization level.

While Hewett et al. (2018) identified 15 qualitative and quantitative articles for their review on HR strength, and Wang et al. (2020) identified 24 articles, Bednall et al. (2021; see also Sanders et al., 2021, who identified 41 papers) identified 46 papers for their meta-analysis on the role of individual perceptions of HR strength. Given this number of papers we will not describe them in much detail. The majority of the studies Sanders et al. identified were conducted in Europe (19 studies; 41%; including seven studies in the Netherlands and four studies in the UK) and in Asia (20 studies; 47%; including 10 studies from mainland China). It is surprising that none of the empirical studies was conducted in the United States despite the original framework being proposed by American scholars. When linking the national cultural values with the research contexts, Sanders et al. find that the data were mainly collected in the countries with high uncertainty avoidance, high power distance, high future orientation, high collectivistic, high performance orientated, and high gender egalitarian cultures.

Consistent with Hewett et al.'s (2018) review, Wang et al. (2020) also detect a positive association between employee perceptions of HR strength and positive employee outcomes (e.g., knowledge sharing, innovation, innovative behaviour and performance) and a negative association with negative employee outcomes (e.g., turnover intentions and negative emotions). In addition, Wang et al. conclude that the studies that examine perceived HR strength as a mediator in the (bundle of) HR practices and outcome relationship 'are virtually non-existent' (p. 23), although some of the studies examine the effect of HR strength as a moderator (Sanders and Yang, 2016; Sanders et al., 2018; Sanders and Yang, 2016; Bednall et al., 2014; Bednall and Sanders, 2017).

However, in a meta-analysis on the role of perceived HR strength in the (bundles of) HR practices and outcomes relationship, Bednall et al. (2021) found more support for a mediation effect of perceived HR strength in this relationship in comparison to a moderation influence. These results suggest that perceived HR strength transfers the effects of (bundles of) HR practices on to employee outcomes instead of being independent of the bundles of HR practices. Even when accounting for study characteristics, like the operationalization of perceived HR strength, research study design (cross-sectional versus longitudinal or experimental designs), industry, sampling strategy, and publication status, these authors detected a consistent pattern on the mediation effect of perceived HR strength and an inconsistent pattern regarding the moderation effect of perceived HR strength.

Similar to the work on HR attribution, despite the very valuable work done on HR strength, there are still important topics that are largely neglected, and which still need to be effectively addressed in future research on HR attributions (Hewett et al., 2018; Wang et al., 2020; Sanders et al., 2021). Ostroff and Bowen (2016, p. 199) also notice that the field lacks a comprehensive and sophisticated measure of HR strength. As a result, it is not clear whether the inconsistencies across studies are due to the ambiguity of the theoretical framework or to the measurements and methodological issues empirical research used. In this way, it is difficult to systematically accumulate knowledge on the role and effects of HR strength.

In only a few studies HR strength is measured at the higher level (e.g., Cunha and Cunha, 2009; Katou et al., 2014) as was intended by Bowen and Ostroff (2004). This level of confusion may have arisen from the fact that HR strength is derived from an individual-level theory of attributions, namely Kelley's (1967, 1973) covariation model (see also Sanders and Yang, 2016). In their original work, Bowen and Ostroff use the covariation model (comprising distinctiveness, consistency and consensus) as an organizing framework to derive the nine proposed features of HR strength rather than a literal application of the Kelley model in an HR context. Sanders et al. (2021) argue that instead of forcing researchers to conceptualize HR strength in the same way and at the same level, it can be argued that multiple research lines related to the different levels can emerge. For instance, one stream of research, which can be seen as the current state of research, can focus on the individual perceptions of HR strength, while other research can focus on HR strength as a contextual variable at the team, unit or organizational level. While the first research stream can rely more, but not necessarily on the co-variation model of the attribution theory (Kelley, 1967; 1973), the second research stream may focus more strongly on organizational climate literature (Schneider, Salvaggio and Subirats, 2002), and include organizational climate (as the mean or inversed standard deviation) as the shared perceptions as a mediator between (bundles of) HR practices and individual and/or organizational outcomes. And a third stream can combine these two research streams and test the whole model as proposed by Bowen and Ostroff (2004).

While in the last two sections I presented an overview of the HR attribution and perceived HR strength research, in the following section we pay attention to the integration of these two research streams of the HR process research.

4.   An integrated model of HR attributions and perceived HR strength

As mentioned in the Introduction to this chapter, the existing research on HR attribution and perceived HR strength seems fragmented, developing different citation patterns without much cross-fertilization. In this last section of the chapter, I discuss research that attempts to integrate these two research streams within the HR process research, as well as some theoretical frameworks that can be used for further integration.

In the following I discuss two papers (Katou, Budhwar and Patel, 2021; and Guest et al., 2021), both published in the special issue of *Human Resource Management Journal*, which integrate HR attributions and perceived HR strength (see also Sanders et al., 2021). Both papers studied the pathway from HR practices to employee and organizational outcomes via mediators and moderators at different levels. They responded to the call (Sanders et al., 2017) to include the role of line managers in the HR attribution process. They also included aspects of organizational climate, conceptualized as the shared perceptions among employees and line managers which are largely neglected in HR strength research. For instance, Guest et al. added an agreement measure among employees of their HR attributions as a moderator in their model.

Katou, Budhwar and Patel propose and test an integrated multi-level and multi-path framework examining the impact of HRM content on organizational performance, through the serially mediating mechanisms of HR strength, line manager HR implementation, and employee HR attributions. Using a sample of 158 Greek private organizations with data from senior managers, line managers and employees, they conducted a multilevel path analysis. They found that between organizations, (1) HR strength fully mediates the relationship between HRM content and line manager HR implementation, (2) line manager HR implementation fully mediates the relationship between HR strength and employee HR attributions, and (3) employee HR attributions fully mediate the relationship between line manager HR implementation and organizational performance.

Guest et al. (2021) use signalling theory as an integrating mechanism for examining the role of HR attributions in the pathway from HRM to unit performance. A study of employees in 83 bank branches confirmed that strong HR signals, reflected in implementation of a coherent set of high commitment HR practices and consensus about their implementation, have a positive association with the HR attributions and attitudes of employees as signal receivers. They found no link with branch performance.

While both papers examine HR attribution as a mediator between HR content and (employee and) organization performance, Katou et al. added more mediators into their model, including HR strength and line manager implementation. On the other hand, Guest et al. considered boundary conditions of their model and included two (agreement) moderators. These two models advance our understanding of the complex relationship between HR content and outcomes, incorporating both HR attributions and perceived HR strength, and employees' and line managers' perceptions analyzed at different levels. We encourage researchers to continue these lines of research by testing multi-level models including both mediators and moderators to explore the 'how' and 'why' of the relationship between HR practices and outcomes.

In addition to the studies of Katou et al. (2021) and Guest et al. (2021), two theoretical frameworks may be helpful in further integrating HR attribution and perceived HR strength research. First, Kelley and Michela (1980) connected causal attribution theory to the co-variation model of attribution theory to identify distinctive, consistent and consensual information (Weiner, 1979) as one of the antecedents of causal attributions. In developing a model of the antecedents to attributions, Kelley and Michela (1980) argued that three categories of antecedents influence attributions. The first is *information* about the stimulus, including its features and the environmental context in which it exists. Within this information category Kelley and Michela connect the co-variation principle of the attribution theory with the causal attributions as they argue that by providing distinct, consistent and consensual information an individual can present themselves in a favourable manner to enhance their self-image and provide a form of self-protection as clear communications result in favourable employee perceptions. A second class of antecedents are *general beliefs* about causes and effects of the stimulus, which are based on prior and ongoing experiences (Jones and Davis, 1965). The final class of antecedent identified by Kelley and Michaela is individuals' *motivation* to make attributions.

Drawing on this model of Kelley and Michela (1980), Hewett et al. (2019) suggest that HR attributions are influenced by information (perceptions of distributive and procedural fairness), beliefs (organizational cynicism) and motivation (perceived relevance; see also section 2 of this chapter). They found that perceptions of fairness and cynicism are important for the formation of commitment attributions but less so for cost-saving or exploitation attributions. Fairness and cynicism also interact such that distributive fairness buffers the negative attributional effect of cynicism, and individuals are more likely to attribute fair procedures to external forces if they are cynical about their organization.

Also related to the work of Kelley and Michela (1980), Li (2021) argues that in addition to considering HR attribution as an important mediator in the perceived HR strength–outcomes relationship, the elaboration likelihood model (ELM) of information influencing provides a theoretical perspective to understand the process by which individuals may be influenced by the messages they receive. Li (2021) argues that HR professionals can be seen as the centre of communication flow from management to employees; and she integrates the ELM with the HR process approach. Specifically, according to the ELM, HR attributions can be viewed as the central route relating to communication quality; and perceived HR credibility (i.e., the extent to which HR professionals are perceived as credible by employees) can be viewed as the peripheral route relating to communication source credibility. It is contended that perceptions of HRM strength can improve both routes and ultimately alter employees' general attitudes at work. More research on the combination of the perceived HR strength and the elaboration likelihood model of information influencing is needed.

A second theoretical model that may be used to combine HR attributions and perceived HR strength can be found in the work of Martinko and Thomson (1998). They integrate the work on the co-variation model of attribution theory of Kelley (1967; 1973) and the achievement-motivation model of Weiner and his colleagues (Weiner, 1986). While Kelley focus on the attribution of distinctive, consistent and consensual information as one of the antecedents of causal attributions, Weiner and colleagues elaborate on the internal versus external attributions people make when experiencing success or failure. In addition to the locus of causality dimension (referring to the degree to which a person perceives that an outcome is caused by the person's own action), they distinguish the stability (whether or not the cause of the outcome changes over time) and the globality (the degree to which the cause of an outcome is generalizable across situation) dimensions. As Martinko and Thomson argue that the two models (Kelley vs Weiner) do not represent fundamentally different processes, these models representing the informational and attributional dimensions can be integrated. As a result, these scholars propose a direct relationship between Kelley's informational dimensions of consensus, consistency and distinctiveness, and Weiner's attributional dimensions of locus of stability, stability and globality, respectively.

They connect consensus information, which is concerned with how others behave in the same situation, to the locus of causality dimension (high consensus is attributed to the characteristics of the situation: external attribution); consistency is proposed to lead to attributions regarding the stability dimension (high consistency infers stable causes); and distinctiveness is proposed to be related to the globality dimension (high distinctiveness is unique for a particular situation). Given that strong HR strength is characterized by high distinctiveness, high consistency and high consensus, this refers to an external, stable and specific attribution (see Martinko and Thomson, 1998; Sanders and Yang, 2016).

With this integrated framework we can for instance elaborate on the influence of national cultural values of a country. For instance, while we know that in-group collectivism defined as 'the degree to which individuals express pride, loyalty, and cohesiveness in their organizations or families' (House et al., 2004) is one of the most significant cultural dimensions that distinguish the attributional differences across East Asians and West Europeans (Hofstede and Hofstede, 2005; Schwartz and Bilsky, 1994; Nisbett, 2003), it can be related to this integrated framework. Western Europeans (in general more individualistic countries) tend to attribute behaviour and performance in terms of dispositional or internal attributes; by contrast, East Asians (in general more collectivistic countries) tend to pay more attention to contextual or external attributes to explain behaviors and performance (e.g., Nistbett, 2003; Morris and Peng, 1994; Chiang and Birth, 2007).

External, stable and specific attributions may be pervasive in making sense of management styles. Given that perceived HR strength is an external, stable and specific attribution to making sense of HR signals (Martinko and Thomson, 1998), we thus believe that the effect of perceived HR strength on employee outcomes is more salient in countries high on power distance, high on in-group collectivistic and low on performance-orientation in comparison to countries low on power distance, low on in-group collectivistic and high on performance orientation countries' cultures and in low power distance cultures.

Employees in high power distance countries tend to believe that improved performance is unlikely without explicit intervention from their superiors, which leads employees to use external, stable and specific attribution to understand the management styles and their performance (Chiang and Birth, 2007). External, stable and specific attributions also play a more importance role in the collectivist cultures than in the individualistic cultures (Morris and Peng, 1994; Nisbett, 2003). The independent view of self leads employees in individualistic countries (low in-group collectivism) to focus on their own goals, develop their own abilities and solve their own problems; thus it is more likely that internal attributions are applied to make sense of the performance and management styles in high collectivistic countries. Finally, members in high performance-oriented countries believe through their own hard work and choice (internal attributes) that they can affect personal outcomes. This will facilitate an internal attribution to make sense of management styles.

In sum, despite the young age of the HR process field, the work on the two research streams, HR attributions and perceived HR (system) strength, has received a lot of attention in terms of various reviews and an edited book, published by Edward Elgar (Sanders et al., 2021). Until now, HR attribution and perceived HR strength has generally been studied in isolation. In this chapter, in addition to the review of the two main streams of research, I attempt to combine the two research streams.

When reflecting on the realm of the HR practices–outcome relationship over the past 30 years, Ostroff (2021; see also for the first three domains Ostroff and Bowen, 2016; Wang et al., 2020) identified four interrelated domains. First, the 'what' of HR practices (HR practices and systems related to the content approach of HR research. The second and third domains are related to the HR process research, namely the 'how' (the (perceived) HR system strength), and the 'why' (HR attributions) of HR. Finally, the 'who' can be identified: delivery agents of HR, like HR professionals and line management. I wish to echo Ostroff by saying that scholars should be encouraged to carefully consider the meaning of each construct, its nature and measurement, across levels of analysis so as to further clarify and make advancements in the role and effectiveness of HR in organizations.

References

Aksoy, E. (2015). *The influence of HRM as a process on absenteeism: exploring the influence of the meta-features of HRM system strength on absenteeism.* University of Twente.

Aksoy, E. and Bayazit, M. (2014). The relationships between MBO system strength and goal-climate quality and strength. *Human Resource Management,* 53 (4), 505–525.

Alfes, K., Shantz, A.D., Bailey, C., Conway, E., Monks, K. and Fu, N. (2019). Perceived human resource system strength and employee reactions toward change: Revisiting human resource's remit as change agent. *Human Resource Management,* 58 (3), 239–252.

Alfes, K., Veld, M., and Furstenberg, N. (2020). The relationship between perceived high-performance work systems, combinations of human resource well-being and human resource performance attributions. *Human Resource Management*, 31 (3), 729–752.

Appelbaum, E., Bailey, T., Berg, P. and Kalleberg, A.L. (2000). *Manufacturing Advantage: Why High Performance Work Systems Pay Off*. Cornell University Press.

Arthur, J.B. (1994). Effects of human resource systems on manufacturing performance and turnover. *Academy of Management Journal*, 37(3), 670–687

Bednall, T.C. and Sanders, K. (2017). Do opportunities for formal learning stimulate follow-up participation in informal learning? A three-wave study. *Human Resource Management*, 56 (5), 803–820.

Bednall, T.C., Sanders, K. and Runhaar, P. (2014). Stimulating informal learning activities through perceptions of performance appraisal quality and human resource management system strength: A two-wave study. *Academy of Management Learning and Education*, 13 (1), 45–61.

Bednall, T.C., Sanders, K., and Yang, H. (2021; in press) A meta-analysis on employee perceptions of Human Resource Strength: Examining the mediating versus moderating hypotheses. *Human Resource Management*, 61, 5–20.

Boon, C., Den Hartog, D.N and Lepak, D.P. (2019). A Systematic Review of Human Resource Management and their Measurement. *Journal of Management*, 45 (6), 2498–2537.

Bos-Nehles, A., Trullen, J. and Valverde, M. (2021). HRM system strength implementation: a multi-actor process perspective. In: K. Sanders, H. Yang and C. Patel (Eds.). *Handbook on HR Process Research*. (99–114). Edward Elgar.

Bowen, D.E. and Ostroff, C. (2004). Understanding HRM–Firm Performance Linkages: The Role of the 'Strength' of the HRM System. *Academy of Management Review*, 29 (2), 203–221.

Chacko, S. and Conway, N. (2019). Employee experiences of HRM through daily affective events and their effects on perceived event-signalled HRM system strength, expectancy perceptions, and daily work engagement. *Human Resource Management Journal*, 29 (3), 433–450 https://doi.org/10.1111/1748-8583.12236.

Chen, D. and Wang, Z. (2014). The effects of human resource attributions on employee outcomes during organizational change. *Social Behavior and Personality: An International Journal*, 42 (9), 1431–1444.

Chiang, F.F.T. and Birth, T.A. (2007). Examining the perceived causes of successful employee performance: an East-West comparison. *International Journal of HRM*, 18 (2), 232–248.

Connelly, B.L., Certo, S.T., Ireland, R.D. and Reutzel, C.R. (2011). Signaling Theory: A Review and Assessment. *Journal of Management*, 37 (1), 39–67.

Cunha, R. and Cunha, M.P. (2009). Impact of strategy, strength of the HRM system and HRM bundles on organizational performance. *Problems and Perspectives in Management*, 7 (1), 57–69.

Farndale, E. and Sanders K. (2017). Conceptualizing HRM system strength through a cross-cultural lens. *International Journal of Human Resource Management*, 28 (1), 132–148.

Fiske, S.T. and Taylor, S.E. (1991). *McGraw-Hill Series in Social Psychology*. *Social Cognition* (2nd ed.). McGraw-Hill Book Company.

Fontinha, R., José Chambel, M. and De Cuyper, N. (2012). HR attributions and the dual commitment of outsourced IT workers. *Personnel Review*, 41 (6), 832–848.

Guest, D.E., Rodrigues, R. and Oliviera, T. (2019). Trade Union Influence on HRM: The Role of External Attributions. *HR Process Research: Next Steps and New Avenues*. Academy of Management Annual Meeting, Boston, Mass., USA.

Guest, D., Sanders, K., Rodrigues, R. and Oliveira, T. (2021). Signalling theory as a framework for analysing HRM processes and integrating HR attribution theories: A conceptual and empirical analysis. *Human Resource Management Journal*, 31 (3), 796–818.

Gyekye, S.A. (2010). Occupational safety management: The role of causal attribution. *International Journal of Psychology*, 45 (6), 405–416.

Heider, F. (1958). *The Psychology of Interpersonal Relations*. Martino Publishing.

Heider, F. (1944). Social perceptions and phenomenal causality. *Psychological Review*, 51 (6), 358–374

Hewett, R. (2021). HR Attributions: A critical review and research agenda. In: K. Sanders, H. Yang and C. Patel (Eds.), *Handbook on HR Process Research* (pp. 7–26). Edward Elgar.

Hewett, R., Shantz, A. and Mundy, J. (2019). Information, beliefs, and motivation: The antecedents to human resource attributions. *Journal of Organizational Behavior*, 40(5), 570–586.

Hewett, R., Shantz, A., Mundy, J. and Alfes, K. (2018). Attribution theories in human management research: A review and research agenda. *International Journal of Human Resource Management*, 29 (1), 87–126.

Hofstede, G. (1984). The cultural relativity of the quality of life Concept. *Academy of Management Review*, 9, 389–398.

Hofstede, G. and Hofstede, G.J. (2005). *Culture and Organizations – Software of the Mind: Intercultural Cooperation and its Importance for Survival* (2nd Ed.). McGraw Hill.

House, R.J., Hanges, P.J., Javidan, M., Dorfman, P.W. and Gupta, V. (2004). *Culture, Leadership, and Organizations: The GLOBE Study of 62 Societies*. Sage.

Jones, E.E. and Davis, K.E. (1965). From acts to dispositions: the attribution process in person perception. *Advances in Experimental Social Psychology*, 2, 219–266.

Katou, A., Budhwar, P.S. and Patel, C. (2021). Line manager implementation and employee HR attributions mediating mechanisms in the HRM system – organizational performance relationship. A multilevel and multipath study. *Human Resource Management*, 31(3), 775–795.

Kehoe, R.R. and Collins, C.J. (2017). Human resource management and unit performance in knowledge-intensive work. *Journal of Applied Psychology*, 102 (8), 1222–1236.

Kelley, H.H. (1973). The processes of causal attribution. *American Psychologist*, 28 (2), 107–128.

Kelley, H.H. (1967). Attribution theory in social psychology. In D. Levine (Ed.), *Nebraska Symposium on Motivation* (192–238). University of Nebraska Press.

Kelley, H.H. and Michela, J.L. (1980). Attribution theory and research. *Annual Review of Psychology*, 31 (1), 457–501.

Khan, S.A. and Tang, J. (2016). The paradox of human resource analytics: being mindful of employees. *Journal of General Management*, 42 (2), 57–66.

Koys, D.J. (1988). Human resource management and a culture of respect: Effects on employees' organizational commitment. Employee Responsibilities and Rights Journal, 1, 57–68.

Lee, B.Y., Kim, T.-Y. and Gong, Y. (2019). Employee well-being attribution and job change intentions: the moderating effect of task idiosyncratic deals. *Human Resource Management*, 59 (4), 327–338.

Lepak D.P., Taylor, M.S., Tekleab, A. and Marrone, J. (2002). Firms' use of high investment HR systems to manage employees for competitive advantage: Differential use and implications for performance. Presented at the Annual Meeting for the Academy of Management, Denver, CO.

Li, X. (2021) Putting perceived HR credibility into the HRM process picture: insights from the elaboration likelihood model. In: K. Sanders, H. Yang and C. Patel (Eds.), *Handbook on HR Research* (83–98). Edwards Elgar.

Li, X., Frenkel, S.J. and Sanders, K. (2011). Strategic HRM as process: How HR system and organizational climate strength influence Chinese employee attitudes. *International Journal of Human Resource Management*, 22 (9), 1825–1842.

Martinko, M.J. and Thomson, N. F. (1998). A synthesis and extension of the Weiner and Kelley attribution models. *Basic and Applied Social Psychology*, 20 (4), 271–284. https://doi.org/10.1207/s15324834basp2004_4.

Martinko, M.J., Harvey, P. and Dasborough, M.T. (2011). Attribution theory in the organizational sciences: A case of unrealized potential. *Journal of Organizational Behavior*, 32 (1), 144–149.

Montag-Smit, T. and Smit, B. (2020). What are you hiding? Employee attributions for pay secrecy policies. *Human Resource Management Journal. Early View*, 31 (3) 704–728.

Morris, M.W. and Peng, K. (1984). Culture and cause: American and Chinese attribution for social and physical events. *Journal of Personality and Social Psychology*, 67, 949–971.

Nisbett, R. E. (2003). *The Geography of Thought: How Asians and Westerners Think Differently ... And Why*. Free Press.

Nishii, L.H. and Wright, P.M. (2008). Variability within organizations: Implications for strategic human resource management. In D.B. Smith (Ed.), *The People Make the Place: Dynamic Linkages between Individuals and Organizations* (225–248). Lawrence Erlbaum Associates Inc.

Nishii, L.H., Lepak, D.P. and Schneider, B. (2008). Employee attributions of the 'why' of HR practices: Their effects on employee attributions and behaviors, and customer satisfaction. *Personnel Psychology*, 61 (3), 503–45.

Osterman P. (1994). How common is workplace transformation and how adopts it? *Industrial and Labor Relations Review*, 47, 173–188.

Ostroff, C. (2021). Reflections on the HR landscape. In: K. Sanders, H. Yang and C. Patel (Eds.), *Handbook on HR Process Research*. (162–176). Edward Elgar.

Ostroff, C. and Bowen, D.E. (2016). Reflections on the 2014 Decade Award: Is There Strength in the Construct of HR System Strength? *Academy of Management Review*, 41 (2), 196–214.

Patel, C., Yang, H. and Sanders, K. (2021). Introduction to human resource management process. In: K. Sanders, H. Yang and C. Patel (Eds.), *Handbook on HR Process Research* (1–6). Edward Elgar.

Sanders, K. and Rafferty, A. (2021). Change within organizations: an attributional lens. In: K. Sanders, H. Yang and C. Patel (Eds.), *Handbook on HR Process Research* (27–45). Edward Elgar.

Sanders, K. and Yang, H. (2016). The HRM process approach: The influence of employees' attribution to explain the HRM-Performance relationship. *Human Resource Management*, 55, 201–17.

Sanders, K., Bednall, T.C. and Yang, H. (2021). HR Strength: Past, Current and Future Research. In: K. Sanders, H. Yang and C. Patel (Eds.), *Handbook on HR Process Research* (27–45). Edward Elgar.

Sanders, K., Dorenbosch, L. and De Reuver, R. (2008). The impact of individual and shared employee perceptions of HRM on affective commitment: Considering climate strength. *Personnel Review*, 37 (4), 412–25.

Sanders, K., Guest, D. and Rodrigues, R. (2017). Call for papers: The role of HR attributions in the relationship between HRM and outcomes. *Human Resource Management*, 31 (3), 694–703.

Sanders, K., Jorgensen, F., Shipton, H., Van Rossenberg, Y., Cunha, R., Li, X. and Dysvik, A. (2018). Performance-based rewards and innovative behaviors. *Human Resource Management*, 57 (6), 1455–1468.

Sanders, K., Nguyen, P.T., Bouckenooghe, D., Rafferty, A. and Schwarz, G. (2020). Unraveling the what and how of organizational communication to employees during the COVID-19 pandemic: Adopting an attributional lens. *Journal of Applied Behavioural Science*, 56 (3), 289–293.

Sanders, K., Shipton, H. and Gomes, J.F.S. (2014). Guest editors' introduction: Is the HRM process important? Past, current, and future challenges. *Human Resource Management*, 53 (4), 489–503.

Sanders, K., Yang, H. and Li, X. (2019). Quality enhancement or cost reduction? The influence of high-performance work systems and power distance orientation on employee human resource attributions. *The International Journal of Human Resource Management*. 32 (21), 4463–4490 .

Sanders, K., Yang, H. and Patel, C. (Eds.) (2021). *Handbook on HR Process Research*. Edward Elgar.

Schneider, B., Salvaggio, A.N. and Subirats, M. (2002). Climate strength: A new direction for climate research. *Journal of Applied Psychology*, 87 (2), 220–229.

Schuler, R.S. and Jackson, S.E. (1987). Linking competitive strategies with human resource management practices. *The Academy of Management Executive*, 1 (3), 207–219.

Schwartz, S. H. and Bilsky, W. (1987). Toward a universal psychological structure of human values. *Journal of Personality and Social Psychology*, 53 (3), 550–562 https://doi.org/10.1037/0022-3514.53.3.550.

Shantz, A., Arevshatian, L., Alfes, K. and Bailey, C. (2016). The effect of HRM attributions on emotional exhaustion and the mediating roles of job involvement and work overload. *Human Resource Management Journal*, 26 (2), 172–191.

Stanton, P., Young, S., Bartram, T. and Leggat, S.G. (2010). Singing the same song: Translating HRM messages across management hierarchies in Australian hospitals. *The International Journal of Human Resource Management*, 21 (4), 567–581.

Taylor, S.E. and Fiske, S.T. (1978). Salience, attention, and attribution: Top of the head phenomena. In Leonard Berkowitz (Ed.), *Advances in Experimental Social Psychology* (Vol. 11, 249–288). Academic Press.

Valizade, D., Ogbonnaya, C., Tregaskis, O. and Forde, C. (2016). A mutual gains perspective on workplace partnership: employee outcomes and the mediating role of the employment relations climate. *Human Resource Management*, 26 (3), 351–368.

Van De Voorde, K. and Beijer, S. (2015). The role of employee HR attributions in the relationship between high-performance work systems and employee outcomes. *Human Resource Management Journal*, 25 (1), 62–78.

Wang, Y., Kim, S., Rafferty, A. and Sanders, K. (2020). Employee perceptions of HR practices: A critical review and future directions. *The International Journal of Human Resource Management*, 31 (1), 128–173.

Weick, K.E., Sutcliffe, K.M. and Obstfeld, D. (2005). Organizing and the Process of Sensemaking. *Organization Science*, 16 (4), 409–421.

Weiner, B. (2018). *Keynote address.* The 3rd International Symposium on Attribution Theory., Tallahassee, FL, USA (16 March).

Weiner, B. (2008). Reflections on the history of attribution theory and research: People, personalities, publications, problems. *Social Psychology*, 39 (3), 151–156.

Weiner, B. (1986). *An Attributional Theory of Motivation and Emotion.* Springer-Verlag http://www.springer.com/gp/book/9781461293705.

Weiner, B. (1985). 'Spontaneous' causal thinking. *Psychological Bulletin*, 97 (1), 74.

Wong, P. T. and Weiner, B. (1981). When people ask 'why' questions, and the heuristics of attributional search. *Journal of Personality and Social Psychology*, 40 (4), 650–663 https://doi.org/10.1037/0022-3514.40.4.650.

Yang, J. and Arthur, J.B. (2019). Implementing commitment HR practices: line manager attributions and employee reactions. *International Journal of Human Resource Management* https://doi.org/10.1080/09585192.2019.1629986.

Zhang, Wei and Wang (2021) Team leaders' HR attributions and their implications on teams and employee-level outcomes. In: K. Sanders, H. Yang and C. Patel (Eds.), *Handbook on HR Process Research* (70–82). Edward Elgar.

4 Leveraging strategic human capital research themes in strategic HRM research

Clint Chadwick, Mengwei Li and Ilhwan Na

Introduction

There is no shortage of strategic human resource management (SHRM) empirical work, and no lack of SHRM research reviews, either. This research has flourished since the publication of the initial SHRM empirical studies, particularly Huselid's (1995) seminal study. It has become commonly accepted that systems of human resource (HR) practices, particularly high performance work systems (HPWS), are related to an array of individual, meso, and organizational level outcomes. Yet despite notable success along this main line of inquiry and the development of related research offshoots examining such topics as mediating mechanisms, employee attributions about managerial intent behind the implementation of HR practices, and the effects of HPWS on different facets of employee wellbeing, previous reviewers have noted a sense of stagnation in the SHRM research stream (e.g., Jackson et al., 2014). We suggest that this issue is primarily a theory problem that could benefit from cross-fertilization from other fields. Such cross-fertilization can broaden SHRM researchers' focus beyond HPWS to include other important topics linking HRM and performance (cf. Chadwick & Flinchbaugh, 2021). In this chapter, we will focus on potentially fruitful cross-fertilization for SHRM with ideas from the strategic human capital (SHC) research stream.

We will narrow our discussion of SHRM research opportunities that are suggested by the juxtaposition of these contrasting research streams to three topics: (1) the distinction between value capture and value creation in the pursuit of economic rents, (2) the relationship between HR practices and HC, particularly organizations' human capital resources (HCRs), and (3) the creation of HRM-related complementarities within organizations. We will begin with a brief review of the commonalities and differences between SHRM

Table 4.1   Summary of the review of the two disciplines

Criteria	SHRM	SHC
Dominant Base Discipline	Psychology	Economics
Key Assumptions	Organizational level HRM heterogeneity drives the success of organizations A bundle of HR practices can have greater influence than a simple aggregation of its component (i.e., horizontal fit) HR practices shape workers' "on the job" behavior to increase organization performance	Organizational level HC heterogeneity drives the success of organizations Workers' HC can be complementary to their peers' HC, to the capabilities of their organizations, and to other contingencies within and outside their organizations Workers have free will and perpetual ownership of their HC that must be actively managed
Basic Theoretic Perspectives	RBV Behavioral perspective Ability-motivation-opportunity HR system strength Social exchange/reciprocity HR attributions Configurational perspective	RBV/strategic factor markets HC theory Isolating mechanisms/Labor market frictions HC value creation/value capture
Cross-Fertilization Research Opportunities	HRM value creation vs. value capture HR practices' relationships with HC/HCRs HRM complementarities	

and SHC research and then describe testable research questions within each of these three cross-fertilization topics.

A brief comparative review of the two streams of research

In this section, we conduct a brief comparative review of the two streams of research, SHRM and SHC, by discussing each research stream's dominant base discipline, key assumptions, and basic theoretic perspectives in turn, as summarized in Table 4.1.

Dominant base discipline

SHC research had its genesis in human capital theory (HCT) as formulated by Becker (1964) and other economists to explain workers' labor market experiences. Strategy scholars have applied HCT logic to organizations to formulate accounts of competitive advantage through people, but in contrast to SHRM, which emphasizes HR practices, the focus in SHC is on a particular type of strategic asset, human capital (HC), and the implications of its unique characteristics on organizations' pursuit of competitive advantage. The SHC research stream thus finds its primary roots in the economics discipline, in contrast to SHRM, which grew out of the human resource management (HRM) and industrial and organizational (I/O) psychology research traditions that have their principal roots in psychology. Both streams of research emphasize the competitive effects of organizational level heterogeneity, the resource-based view (RBV) of organizations as a theoretic baseline, the emergence of collective constructs from disaggregated phenomena at lower levels of analysis, and, most fundamentally, an emphasis on human beings as a unique type of strategic asset. Nonetheless, given their different disciplinary underpinnings, both streams of research have developed these themes in very different ways. Of course, these are broad generalizations. SHRM researchers successfully employ economic logic, and SHC scholars incorporate psychological phenomena in their work as well, and both sets of researchers draw on a variety of research perspectives from their research traditions.

Key assumptions

Nevertheless, these different disciplinary starting points account for many of the differences in theoretic assumptions and emphases between these two research streams. SHRM scholarship begins with workers. HR practices can be defined as specific methods and procedures that organizations adopt to implement their principles and policies by shaping workers' behaviors on the job (Posthuma et al., 2013). The fundamental assumption of SHRM research is that organizational level heterogeneity in HR practices can drive differences in organizations' success, conditional on the other factors that impact organizational performance. In other words, SHRM researchers emphasize HR practices as antecedents to such outcomes as collective employee attitudes and turnover, organizational productivity, and organizational financial performance.

The second (and related) fundamental assumption of SHRM research is that "bundles" or systems of HR practices (MacDuffie, 1995) have a greater influence on organizational outcomes than a simple aggregation of HR practices would lead one to expect. These bundles of HR practices should be organized around an overarching logic that offers chances for synergistic interactions (Delery, 1998; Chadwick, 2010), a principle which is labeled "horizontal fit". Although a number of organizing logics for HR practice bundles are possible, SHRM scholars' favorite is an approach to employment relationships that emphasizes employee participation/discretionary effort, organizational investments in carefully acquiring and investing in and developing employees, and worker commitment to the organization, an approach most commonly labeled HPWS.

A variety of theoretic mechanisms have been proposed to connect HR systems with organizational performance. Most of them either explicitly or implicitly emphasize how HR practices ultimately shape workers' job behaviors in ways that enhance organizational performance. One consequence of this emphasis is an intermittent debate amongst SHRM scholars about the difference between intended HR practices (that is, HR practices as designed by top management) and realized HR practices (i.e., the HR practices in employees' lived experiences). Since realized HR practices are closer to workers' job behaviors, they are expected to be stronger determinants of organizational performance than intended HR practices (Van Beurden et al., 2021).

In contrast, the conceptual origin point for SHC scholarship is the labor market. Deviations from perfect competition in labor markets (known as market "frictions" or "imperfections") allow organizations opportunities to garner economics rents from HC (Campbell et al., 2012). Thus, SHC research links types of HC that are imperfectly traded in the labor market with organizational level outcomes. The assumption is that imperfect labor markets allow organizations to accumulate stocks of heterogeneous HC, which then give organizations an advantage vis-à-vis competitors. For this advantage to be meaningful, such heterogeneity must be persistent and in types of HC that have a meaningfully large impact on organizational level outcomes.

The second fundamental assumption of SHC research is that complementarities amongst organizations' stocks of HC and with other key competitive factors can yield greater effects on organizational outcomes than the simple summation of individuals' HC. Thus, organizational level HC resources (HCRs) can be qualitatively different constructs with a stronger relationship to organizational outcomes than are organizations' pools of individual level HC (Ployhart et al., 2014). This cross level "emergence" argument has obvious parallels to SHRM research, but with the emphasis switched from complementarities amongst HR practices to HC complementarities. More specifically, SHC studies focus on how workers' HC affects their deployment within organizations, their mobility across organizations, their productivity, and, ultimately, their organizations' performance.

Other foundational themes in SHC research are an emphasis on workers' free will and their perpetual ownership of their HC, characteristics that distinguish HC from other types of competitive assets (Chadwick, 2017; Coff, 1997). For instance, workers can voluntarily leave or transfer to another organization, taking their HC with them, and, on the job, need to be motivated to use their HC in ways that their organizations value. The specific means for doing the latter are familiar to SHRM scholars, and, in economic terms, require appealing to workers' utility functions in ways that address both financial and non-financial motivators, encompassing such issues as compensation, identification with the organization, perceived organizational support, equity to referent others, relationships with supervisors, and so forth. The challenges in addressing both issues are such that Chadwick (2017) observed: "For organizations, garnering rents from human capital is complex, with abundant opportunities for failure, and is a significantly different endeavor than is pursuing rents from other types of resources" (p. 500).

Basic theoretic perspectives

The most frequently cited theoretic perspective in both SHRM and SHC research is the RBV (Barney, 1991). RBV scholars posit that organizational resources and capabilities that satisfy certain criteria (value, rareness, inimitability, and non-substitutability, or VRIN) can be a source of sustained competitive advantage. Hence, advantages accrue to organizations that have better quality resources. SHRM researchers argue that a bundle of HR practices fulfills the VRIN criteria and thus can be a source of sustained competitive advantage (Jackson et al., 2014; Jiang et al., 2012). SHC researchers, on the other hand, emphasize the VRIN nature of HC, especially HCRs, and its relationship with organizational competitiveness (Campbell & Kryscynski, 2019).

More subtly, the RBV is a theory of strategic factor market imperfections, which are deviations from the ideal type of perfect competition. Absent imperfections, neither HR practices/bundles of HR practices nor HC/HCRs can maintain their VRIN characteristics (see Chadwick, 2017, for a detailed application of this logic to labor markets). While it is clear that the factor market for HC is the labor market, the "factor market" that applies to HR practices is largely implicit in SHRM research. One way to describe this "market" is as an informational clearinghouse for organizations' knowledge concerning HR practices' impact and implementation. "Imperfections" in this factor market would be barriers to the dissemination of effective HR practices, such as organizational or industry traditions, ambiguity about the performance effects of HR practices, differences of opinion amongst key stakeholders, HR practice implementation complexity and customization, managerial agency dilemmas, and so forth. Such factor market logic, though rarely articulated explicitly, is implied by SHRM scholars' arguments that cross-organizational HR practice heterogeneity is competitively meaningful and long lasting (Chadwick & Flinchbaugh, 2021).

As the RBV is a high level strategy theory, SHRM researchers have adopted other theoretic frameworks that are more proximate to workforces to detail the mechanisms through which HRM might affect organizational level out-comes. According to the behavioral perspective, HRM systems can contribute to organizational effectiveness by inducing required work behaviors from employees (Schuler & Jackson, 1987). A variant of the behavioral perspective, the AMO framework, posits more specifically that workforce performance is a function of employees' collective abilities, motivation, and opportunities to perform (Jackson et al., 2014). Thus, HRM systems can contribute to organizational performance by enhancing organizational workforces' AMO dimensions (Jiang et al., 2012). HR system strength theory (Bowen & Ostroff, 2004) describes how the gestalt of a theoretically integrated set of HR practices might lead to a strong organizational climate, under which employees receive a common meta-message about what is expected from the organization and thus pull together to achieve organizational goals. Social exchange theory (Blau, 1964) researchers argue that employees who are advantaged by HR practices that improve employee utility feel obligated to do more for their organizations in return (reciprocity). Thus, they are likely to have increased commitment to the organization and higher job performance, particularly discretionary effort. Employee attributions scholars (e.g., Nishii et al., 2008) suggest that the ways that employees perceive and interpret management's intentions behind the implementation of HR practices affects the job behaviors that those practices elicit. Consistent with the theoretic starting point in workers, at heart, these theoretic perspectives concern employees' relationships with each other, with their organizations, and most fundamentally, with their work and its meaning to them.[1]

The SHC literature, too, employs a variety of theoretic perspectives to link organizations' pools of HC with organizational performance. In addition to the RBV and strategic factor market theory, another fundamental ground for SHC research is HCT (Becker, 1964). Until recently, the SHC field has been largely preoccupied with HC-based competitive advantage stemming from workers' firm/organization-specific HC (FSHC), which is a central construct in HCT (Coff, 1997). FSHC seemed to neatly epitomize the labor market imperfection view, since FSHC is not tradable from organization to organization; in a sense, FSHC is the ultimate market imperfection because the factor market for FSHC, by definition, cannot exist (Chadwick, 2017).

However, a broader interest in labor market imperfections in addition to FSHC has gained greater attention from SHC scholars in recent years. For

---

[1]   An exception to this generalization is the configurational perspective on SHRM, as we describe later in the chapter.

example, Campbell et al. (2012) identified two categories of imperfections that can occur in labor markets: (1) "demand-side" mobility constraints that affect employers' demand for workers and (2) "supply-side" mobility constraints that influence workers' willingness to put themselves on the labor market. A related stream of SHC research has focused on maximizing organizations' HC rents (e.g., Chadwick, 2017) by differentiating between value creation and value capture (or value appropriation). Organizations' HC rents are the difference between their HC costs and the "use value" that their workers' HC provides. Organizations' actions that increase this difference can therefore boost the HC rents that organizations accrue. In contrast to SHRM, the theoretic through line in SHC theories is markets, specifically in how markets deviate from perfect competition, which some strategy scholars have suggested is at the heart of all organizational level economic rents, whether through HC or other strategic assets or actions (Mahoney & Qian, 2013).

Cross-fertilization research opportunities

This brief review of both streams of research suggests several research opportunities in SHRM that could be opened up by cross-fertilization with SHC. First, as a number of SHRM reviewers have observed, most of SHRM scholars' attention has been given to the potential benefits of HR practices, with the costs of implementing HR practices relatively under-researched (e.g., Gerhart & Feng, 2021). The SHC emphasis on economic rents puts a sharper point on this topic, suggesting the reducing HC costs (a form of "value capture") and HC value creation are distinct but related pursuits. Secondly, the emphasis in SHRM on mapping out mediators in the "black box" between HR systems and organizational performance has frequently included HC (Jiang et al. 2012). SHC scholarship suggests that we can add nuance to this relationship by matching different types of HR practices with different types of HC. Thirdly, insights from SHC work on HC complementarities is drawing some attention in SHC to differences between types of complementarities, and to the managerial capabilities to integrate HR practices and HC with each other and with other organizational resources and capabilities (Chadwick & Flinchbaugh, 2021).

Value creation, value capture, and human capital rents

SHRM researchers have long argued that bundles of HR practices help the organizations that implement them to achieve competitive advantage (e.g., Delery & Doty, 1996; Huselid, 1995; Kehoe & Collins, 2017), but the definition of "competitive advantage" in this work has been rather ambiguous. As

Chadwick and Cappelli (1999) observed some time ago, a common operational definition of SHRM's "strategic" orientation (and, implicitly, of competitive advantage) is simply to denote researchers' use of organizational level dependent variables such as productivity, market share, profitability, turnover, innovation, and so forth. A different conception of competitive advantage has achieved prominence amongst SHC researchers: the interplay between HC value creation and value capture. This topic offers SHRM researchers an opportunity to add greater precision and nuance to their discussions of competitive advantage by focusing on a particular type of organizational level performance, the accrual of HC rents (Chadwick & Flinchbaugh, 2021).

Strategy researchers in the RBV tradition have long observed that the ability of organizational resources (such as HC) to contribute to organizations' rents is the difference between what that resource costs an organization to acquire, utilize, and retain it and the extent to which the resource contributes to products that meet customers' needs in the market (Bowman & Ambrosini, 2000; Chadwick & Dabu, 2009). In perfect competition, there will be no difference between the value that a resource creates (labeled as "value in use" or "use value") and what the resource costs the organization. Thus, imperfections (deviations from perfect competition) in a resource factor market are essential to creating this gap, a type of economic rents. Moreover, a particular organization does not garner such rents unless it can leverage a factor market imperfection in a unique way; imperfections that affect organizations similarly do not yield organization specific rents (Chadwick, 2017).

In the RBV, organizations take advantage of their heterogeneous resource endowments to maximize rents from strategic resources. Hence, in RBV terms, "competitive advantage" is defined by the difference between the use values and the costs of the organization's strategic resources (see Figure 4.1). Accordingly, one route to increasing rents is to boost the use value of the organization's resources closer to their maximum potential use value, a process called *value creation*. However, it is not inevitable that a resource's full use value flows to the organization that employs it. Other stakeholders that have some control of this resource may be able to claim some of its use value for themselves (Bowman & Ambrosini, 2000); this is one reason why workers' perpetual ownership of their HC is a fundamental concern to SHC scholars (Chadwick, 2017; Coff, 1997).

Accordingly, another route to increasing organizational rents is reducing the amounts paid to other parties for the use of a strategic resource. Because this process primarily concerns stakeholders' relative bargaining power over the use value created by a resource, gains for one party ostensibly occur at the

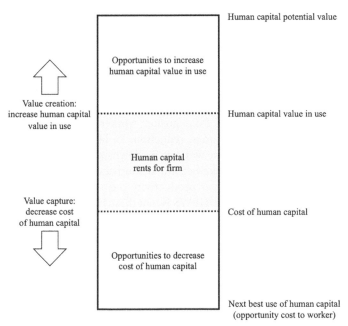

Source: Chadwick, 2017. Reprinted with permission of the Academy of Management

Figure 4.1   Theoretical depiction of organizations' human capital rents

expense of another stakeholder (Bowman & Ambrosini, 2000). Thus, this way of increasing organizational rents is labeled *value capture*. Stakeholders will bargain until their share of use value for a resource falls below the amount they would expect to receive from the next best alternative use of their resource, at which point they will shift their resource to that other use. For workers, the usual "next best" alternative use of their HC is the utility that they could derive from the financial and non-financial rewards of their second most favored employer.

For organizations' HC rents, value creation involves boosting the use value of a workforce's job behaviors closer to their highest potential use value, while value capture concerns reducing a workforce's wages and other costs to the organization, including the administrative costs of HRM (Chadwick, 2017). Most of SHRM researchers' reasoning to date about the contributions of HR practices to organizations' competitive advantages has emphasized the HC value creation point of view. AMO theoretic arguments about how workers are more capable, motivated, and enabled by job design to be more effective for their organizations, for instance, is an HC value creation argument (Gerhart & Feng, 2021). Similarly, SHRM researchers' "external fit" discussions about how contingencies enhance the performance effects of HR practices (e.g., Datta et al., 2005) also concern HC value creation.

However, as we noted above, the distribution of HC use value across stake-holders is a second essential determinant of the HC rents associated with HR practices. Some HR practices, for example, entail greater labor costs that may ultimately outweigh the gains from greater worker effectiveness (Cappelli & Neumark, 2001). At other times, reductions in labor costs (for example, through wage concessions from workers or downsizing) can reduce organ-izations' net HC rents if workers become demotivated and/or overwhelmed by job demands that reduce their productivity (i.e., reduce their use value). A strong HC rents argument for HPWS is that these HR systems may increase HC use value more than their incremental increase in HRM implementation costs, resulting in a net gain for the organization. Increasing organizations' HC rents, in other words, is a joint optimization problem where the combina-tion of these two distinct but related processes, HC value creation and value capture, maximizes the "gap" between the organization's HC use value and its HC costs. Thus, from an HC rents perspective, omitting HR practices' costs is not merely leaving out an interesting, fuller picture of SHRM's effects on organizations (Cappelli & Neumark, 2001). Rather, omitting costs makes it virtually impossible for us to determine whether HR practices are reducing or adding to organizations' competitive advantages in terms of HC rents.

Applying value creation and value capture to SHRM

Perhaps the most immediately applicable opportunity of these points for new SHRM scholarship lies in using the value creation/value capture distinction to decompose the aggregated effects of HR systems into the HC rents effects of specific HR practices. This would be a different categorization of HR practices than the traditional HRM domains (e.g., job design, recruitment, selection, training, development, and compensation) or the three AMO (ability-enhancing, motivation-enhancing, opportunity-enhancing) categories (Jiang et al., 2012) that are typically employed in SHRM. Rather, when discuss-ing competitive advantage and HRM, we suggest categorizing HR practices according to the two different paths to HC rents that we have been discussing, namely, the relative magnitudes of *value-creating* and *value-capturing* charac-teristics of individual HR practices, and considering both of those characteris-tics simultaneously.

The essence of this categorization is that the strategic value of HR practices does not lie solely in either increasing HC use value or decreasing HC costs. Instead, HC rents emerge from the interplay between value creation and value capture that we suggest applies to all individual HR practices. Considering both value creation and value capture together for each HR practice suggests some routes to competitive advantage that lie beyond the usual HPWS paradigm. For instance, an organization may not necessarily have to use "high-performance" HR practices to increase its HC-related competitive advantages (Toh et al., 2008) if the use value of implementing an HR practice exceeds the costs associated with its implementation, including both changes in compensation paid to workers and the HR practices' administrative costs (Chadwick, 2017). In light of their linkage with HC rents, then, HR practices that are typically considered to be "technical" or "transactional" HRM (Huselid et al., 1997) can also be "strategic" HR practices.

Let's consider some specific examples. Various pay for performance (PFP) plans are a commonly employed type of value-creating HR practice that, by design, also incur high implementation costs; the more that worker performance increases, the more, in many cases, the organization pays its employees, as those costs are scaled to worker performance. Extensive research suggests that most types of PFP have powerful enough effects on employees' work motivation and behavior to be worth their implementation costs (e.g., Rynes et al., 2005), but that will not be true in all circumstances. For example, Nyberg et al. (2016) showed that merit pay and bonus pay, in general, are both positively associated with individual performance, but that these relationships are moderated by several contextual factors such as the characteristics of employees, job, organizations, and pay systems.

In a similar vein, researchers on the organizational level have found that the performance effects of organizations' pay dispersion (a consequence of PFP plans) may be moderated by task interdependence (Shaw et al., 2002) or the strategic orientation of the organizations (Tenhiälä & Laamanen, 2018). Such evidence suggests that the value capture/value creation interplay could inform organizations' choices from the menu of possible PFP practices that best enhance HC rents in their specific circumstances. As an extreme example, consider the case of implementing financial incentives in professions such as firefighting where workers' intrinsic motivation to rescue people from hazardous situations is high. Perhaps in this circumstance, the resources that the organization is spending on value creation could be better spent on employment security (e.g., seniority-based pay) that rewards employees' investments in increasing their firm- and task-specific skills (i.e., pay for skill) and enhances their psychological safety than on financial incentives for task behaviors that workers are already motivated to perform. As another example, the high incentive compensation paid to "star" employees who have a lot of marketability may closely track their use value, which helps the organization accomplish its mission but can yield little increase in organizations' HC rents. HC rents are more likely to accrue to organizations from workers whose labor markets are more imperfect.

More recently, some SHC researchers have introduced a new perspective for achieving HC-based competitive advantage via incentives that "provide more utility to workers in the focal organization than similar incentives available at other employers", referred to as firm-specific incentives (FSIs; Kryscynski et al., 2021, p. 388). While all incentive plans share the intent of motivating employees to create more use value, they vary in their ability to ultimately create and capture the value that employees create. FSIs take advantage of heterogenous organizational resources to offer context-specific incentives that maximize the gap between use value and implementation cost by offering workers utility that cannot be imitated by competitors. For example, employees at Disney receive benefits on free access to its world-class amusement parks and discounts on its hotels, restaurants, and merchandise (Kryscynski et al., 2021). Although these specific benefits are, in principle, equally available to workers in other organizations, only Disney can offer these perks regularly at a low or near zero cost.

The relationships between HR practices and HC

To summarize the argument in the preceding section, organizations' HC rents are a joint product of value creating and value capturing processes, and specific HR practices can affect the interplay between these related processes differently. In other words, while more HPWS practices may be generally better for organizations than less HPWS practices (which is one way to interpret the broadly positive effects of HPWS that SHRM scholars have documented), sustainable HC rents for organizations lie in HR practices that leverage labor market imperfections to widen the gap between HC use value and HC costs in ways that are hard for their competitors to imitate (Chadwick, 2017). Similarly, Campbell and Kryscynski (2019) recently pointed SHC scholars towards how HR practices affect HC: "Most of the advantages we ascribe to human capital as a strategic asset may actually reside in the HR system" (2019, pp. 165–166). Accordingly, we posit that the type of VRIN that matters most to HC rents stems from *uniquely valuable organization specific combinations of HR practices and stocks of HC* (cf. Chadwick & Flinchbaugh, 2021). In other words, connections between these two constructs are a fundamental issue for SHRM research.

Discussions of the relationship between HR practices and HC are not absent from the SHRM literature. Generally speaking, the existing discussion can be classified into three categories. In keeping with the majority of SHRM research, scholarship in the first category takes a holistic view of HR systems and employs them as antecedents to organizations' stocks of HC as part of a causal chain that concludes with outcomes at the individual, meso, and organizational level. For example, at the organizational level, Takeuchi et al. (2007) reported that HPWS generate a high level of collective HC and encourage a high degree of social exchange within an organization, which, in turn, are positively related to the organization's overall performance. The second type of SHRM linking HR practices and HC draws on the AMO framework (Appelbaum et al., 2000) to differentiate amongst HR practices. In a meta-analysis, Jiang et al. (2012) found that skill-enhancing HR practices were more positively related to HC than were motivation-enhancing practices and opportunity-enhancing practices. The third category of this research approaches the HRM-HC relationship more subtly by arguing that the HR practices applied to different groups of employees in an organization should reflect the strategic value and uniqueness of different employees' HC. Specifically, Lepak and Snell (1999) suggested that only when HC is both valuable and unique should organizations develop HC internally through commitment-based (i.e., HPWS) HR systems.

In sum, while there is a considerable amount of existing research exploring connections between HR practices and HC, we suggest that most of these treatments could be expanded by incorporating an HC rents perspective. SHC scholars posit that different types of HC have different effects on HC rents, depending on how their characteristics impact value creation and value capture. Attention to such differences may therefore enrich current findings in SHRM research regarding HC. For example, HC can be divided into generic, industry-specific, occupation/task-specific, and firm/organization-specific categories (e.g., Becker, 1964). Furthermore, some SHC researchers view social capital as an additional category of HC which they label "relation-based HC" (Nahapiet & Ghoshal, 1998). As the SHRM research just mentioned implies, these important differences can be masked when HC is treated as a generic construct. FSHC, for example, is inherently strong with respect to value capture since it is, in RBV terms, intrinsically inimitable and non-substitutable. The question of whether it is also rare and has high use value may vary across various contextual characteristics, including organizations' HR practices (Chadwick, 2017). If different types of HC can have different causal paths to performance, then a richer conception of HC can help to map out the frequently noted "black box" of causality between HR practices and organizational performance in greater detail.

Applying linkages between HRM and HC to SHRM

We highlight two specific research questions that could help to further uncover the linkages between HR practices and HC. The first research question is: "How do HR practices influence organizations' accumulation of different types of HC?" For illustration, we consider the implications of general HC and FSHC (Becker, 1964), as this distinction has drawn the most attention in SHC research. The dual HR systems literature (Kehoe & Collins, 2017) suggests that different HR systems, each of which serves a different purpose with respect to different types of HC, can coexist in the same organization. This is similar in spirit to Lepak and Snell's (1999) groundbreaking work, though their focus was on how different types of HC required distinct types of HR practices for different groups of employees. We suggest that this causality can be reversed to inform an examination of how HR practices can engender different types of HC in organizations.

For example, to increase generic HC in organizations, staffing practices could focus on getting the most competent job candidates on such generalized characteristics as intelligence. Tuition reimbursement programs can also improve employees' general HC by fostering schooling and/or obtaining certificates. In addition, a number of organizations have established corporate universities (such as Apple Campus, Disney University, Deloitte University, etc.) or integrate massive open online courses (MOOC) into their training programs to cultivate employees' general skills and to develop leadership (Passarelli, 2014). It is also common for organizations to tie a proportion of salaries to education degrees/certificates/learning outputs to reward employee investment in their general HC.

On the other hand, different HR practices can be employed to increase the level of FSHC in organizations. Rather than simply focusing on employees' current HC level, organizations in the staffing process could put more weight on employees' demonstrated propensity to make investments in FSHC (Morris et al., 2017). Similarly, organizations can highlight more organization-specific content such as organization cultures or internal networks during their training. In the evaluation process, organizations may tie workers' pay to organization-specific training investments. Communication channels and employee participation programs that focus on exchanging internal information and addressing particular on-the-job problems can also increase the level of FSHC. Note that, while HR practices that enhance general HC and those that enhance FSHC are different in this discussion, this distinction is typically subsumed in the common operationalizations of HPWS (cf. Posthuma et al., 2013).

Additionally, recent developments in the SHC literature suggest that employees' perceptions of the firm specificity of their HC is a distinct phenomenon that has a unique causal mechanism which may or may not be aligned with the objective FSHC that is the traditional focus of SHC researchers. For instance, Raffiee and Coff (2016) found that the amount of on-the-job training that employees had received, a traditional FSHC measure, correlates poorly with employees' perceived FSHC. Similarly, organizational commitment and tenure are negatively related to employee perceptions of their HC's firm specificity. Such findings offer an avenue for organizations to broaden value capture from employees by using HR practices to influence employees' perceptions of their HC's firm specificity as well as their actual amount of FSHC. In other words, the traditional SHC question about how to induce employees to invest in FSHC might differ from how to prompt employees to *perceive* that they have FSHC. Moreover, in predicting worker behaviors, workers' perception of FSHC may matter more than whether FSHC objectively exists.

The second research question that we highlight is: "How can HR practices facilitate HCR emergence?" Only recently have SHC scholars started to examine organizational factors that influence HCR emergence (e.g., Eckardt et al., 2021). However, no SHRM research, to date, has yet explained how HR practices might engender HCRs that broaden the gap between HC value in use and HC costs. Ployhart and Moliterno (2011) proposed that individual knowledge, skills, abilities, and other characteristics (KSAOs) transform into unit level HCRs through an emergence-enabling process that includes behavioral, cognitive, and affective states. Arguably, HR practices can play an essential role in enabling each state, though different HR practices may vary in their emphases in the HCR emergence process.

In the behavioral process, HR practices can align individual behaviors with unit goals. Consistent with the behavioral perspective in SHRM (Schuler & Jackson, 1987), HR practices (HPWS) may facilitate the behavioral process of HCR emergence by providing employees with necessary resources, incentives, and opportunities to display desirable behaviors that aggregate into elements of strategic routines and capabilities. In the cognitive process, HCR emergence may be enhanced by HR practices that build and maintain a strong organizational climate that aligns workers' conceptions of how their work fits together to meet organizational goals (e.g., Bowen & Ostroff, 2004). For example, Jiang et al. (2015) found that service-oriented HR practices can build a common understanding among individual workers by building a service climate and cultivate homogeneity in their KSAOs by creating collective customer knowledge. In the affective process, HR practices can create an emotional bond amongst employees that aids in HCR emergence. An example is relationship-oriented HR practices, which Kehoe and Collins (2017) found fostered interpersonal relationships and social interactions in the organization, which, in turn, increase knowledge flows both within and across the unit.

In addition, HR practices may also accelerate the HCR emergence process by increasing task complexity (Ployhart & Moliterno, 2011). In particular, involvement-oriented HR practices have been found to enable and reward an interdependent and dynamic group-based workflow, creating a strong social linkage among employees (Wood & Ogbonnaya, 2018). Note that we recognize the possibility that a set of HR practices can have crossover influence on multiple dimensions of HCR emergence, but our point is that different HR practices have their unique emphasis and can be differentiated when we examine specific emergence processes.

The creation of HRM-related complementarities within organizations

Complementarities have been defined as "the beneficial interplay of the elements of a system where the presence of one element increases the value of others" (Ennen & Richter, 2010, p. 207; cf. Milgrom & Roberts, 1992). To date, mapping out complementarities empirically is still rare in SHRM research (Gerhart & Feng, 2021), but doing so is another way forward in fleshing out the "black box" of causality in SHRM. RBV scholars point to resource complexity as a key avenue by which inimitability and non-substitutability can persist, and complementarities are quite complex, particularly as the number of elements in a system increase. Thus, it is primarily in complementarities that VRIN arguments about HR systems can be sustained (cf. Wright et al., 2001).

Both the SHRM literature and SHC literature have had rich discussions of complementarities, but each stream of research looks at this topic through a different lens. SHC researchers have considered HC complementarities at different levels of analysis and in different combinations (Ployhart et al., 2014). "Within level" HC complementarities refer to interactions between different types of HC at the same level of analysis. For example, Witt et al. (2002) reported that individual worker personality traits such as conscientiousness and agreeableness interact with each other to jointly influence individual performance. Additionally, different levels of HC can also complement each other. For instance, Crocker and Eckardt (2014) showed that the relationship between individual level HC and individual performance is impacted by complementary functional and managerial unit level HC resources. As we described in the previous section, SHC researchers suggest that HC may also combine across levels to create collective HC or HCRs (Ployhart & Moliterno, 2011).

Other complementarities research in SHC explores how contextual factors moderate HC's effects on organizational performance across different levels of analysis. For example, Wolfson and Mathieu (2018) found that individuals' specific competencies interact with situational characteristics to predict variance in their performance over time, beyond that accounted for by their general competencies' direct effects. Moreover, these effects are accentuated to the extent that teammates' competencies aligned with individual competencies in a given situation. Some organizational level SHC studies also explore the complementarities between HCRs and other organizational level resources vis-à-vis organizational performance. For example, Riley et al. (2017) reported that HC investments are more impactful when combined with complementary assets of R&D, physical capital, and advertising investments. In a recent paper, Wolfson and Mathieu (2021) showed that situational characteristics and social capital resources (SCRs) function as complements to influence SCRs' impact on performance.

These treatments of complementarities in SHC mirror similar broad categorizations of complementarities in the SHRM literature, but with HR practices in place of types of HC in the latter. In SHRM, complementarities are a foundational rationale for the HR systems point of view. SHRM scholars argue that the effects of HR practices on performance are interrelated with those of the organization's other HR practices. Consequently, examining the performance effects of HR practices individually is incomplete and likely to be biased by the omission of other HR practices that co-vary with those under study. In contrast, systems of HR practices may have synergistic effects on performance, such that their effects should be considered in aggregated bundles. Such complementarities amongst HR practices within an organization's HR system are labeled as "internal/horizontal fit", while interactions with contingency factors (both within and outside the organization, but which are outside the HR system) are "external/vertical fit". Inspired by SHC research, we believe that there are several HRM complementarities questions that can be explored in different ways than we generally see in the existing SHRM literature.

Applying SHC perspectives to HRM complementarities

For example, some observers (e.g., Delery, 1998; Chadwick, 2010) have noted that the majority of SHRM scholars' discussions of internal fit focus, implicitly and sometimes, explicitly, on interactions between HR practices that have beneficial effects on various outcomes. Note, for example, the wording in Ennen and Richter's (2010) definition cited above: "*the beneficial interplay ... where the presence of one element increases the value of others*" (p. 207, emphasis added).[2] However, it can be fruitful to broaden our view of complementarities to include both beneficial and deleterious effects and to acknowledge that those effects may vary across different types of outcomes. In this vein, Brymer and Hitt (2019) recently described different scenarios of discomplementarity, noncomplementarity, and complementarity within HCRs. Specifically, Brymer and Hitt (2019) argue that when relationships deteriorate in organizations, one party can take advantage of another party's interest to be a free rider (what they call "exploitative discomplementarity"). In another case, when both parties impede each other's efforts, the total value created in organizations would even be less than the value that each party could create by utilizing their HC independently (what they call "pugilistic discomplementarity").

Analogously, some HR practices may be functionally redundant (noncomplementarity) when they serve the same purpose with respect to a particular organizational outcome (cf. Chadwick & Flinchbaugh, 2021; Delery, 1998). In such cases, organizations that are not sensitized to this redundancy may over-invest in such HR practices (Kaufman, 2010). This is an example of the classic "substitution effect" that is frequently observed in strategy research. Our previous discussion of value creation and value capture can define this point with greater nuance. Redundant HR practices waste organizational resources that could have been allocated elsewhere, and thus largely affect value capture. As such, HR practice redundancy should be manifest in organizational level, financial dependent variables that reflect investment returns such as return on investment (ROI), return on assets (ROA), and profitability.

Alternatively, some combinations of HR practices may create "deadly combinations" (discomplementarity) in which they work at cross purposes and therefore reduce HC value creation (Delery, 1998). For example, a cross-functional team paired with an individual performance-based pay system can create confusion in employees and induce them to work at cross purposes, and thus decrease organizational level productivity. In instances of deadly combina-

---

[2]   This positive view of complementarities still also predominates amongst SHC researchers, but not entirely, as we describe.

tions, labor productivity and other dependent variables that measure the efficacy of employees' job behaviors, such as innovation performance and market share, would be more likely to help us detect such effects, inasmuch as this is principally a value creation phenomenon.

Both redundancy and deadly combinations are types of "complementarities" that degrade organizational outcomes, if the definition of complementarities is expanded to denote interactions between HR practices that modify their independent effects (positive or negative) on a particular outcome of interest. Utilizing similar logic to outline a positive view of such complementarities, Chadwick (2010) proposed two specific forms of HRM complementarities, which he labeled as "efficient complementarities" (the flipside of redundancy) and "virtuous overlaps" (the opposite of deadly combinations). Interestingly, Meuer (2017) empirically tested this distinction using a fuzzy-set qualitative comparative analysis (fsQCA) approach and found evidence for both types of complementarities in HPWS, suggesting that this difference described by Brymer and Hitt (2019) is empirically relevant to SHRM.

A complex complementarities argument can also be applied to external HR system fit. While external fit complementarities have received a strong amount of empirical support in SHRM research, there have also been numerous published and unpublished failures to find significant external fit evidence. Some observers argue that common approaches to contingencies (external fit) oversimplify the complexity in organizations' interactions with their environments by only considering linear relationships with single contingencies at a time (Ennen & Richter, 2010). As we noted earlier, the configurational perspective in SHRM takes both horizontal and vertical fit into consideration by considering "how the *pattern* of multiple independent variables is related to a dependent variable rather than with how individual independent variables are related to the dependent variable" (emphasis in original) (Delery & Doty, 1996, p. 804). In other words, a configurational approach allows for different configurations of HR practices to be equally effective (equifinality), rather than testing for a single optimal combination. While this perspective is more generalizable, it has also been more difficult to theorize and examine empirically. Consequently, empirical evidence for this perspective is relatively rare in SHRM research, but may be spurred by the advent of more complex configurational methodologies such as fsQCA (cf. Meuer, 2017).

A second SHRM complementarities research question that is suggested by SHC research is, "How does managerial HC influence complementarities between HR practices?" We consider top managers, HR managers, and line managers in answer to this question because of their pertinence to different aspects and processes of HRM complementarities. Specifically, top managers shape HR philosophy and policies and determine the amount of integration across HRM activities necessary to support organizational processes and capabilities. HR managers play a role in translating HR policies into specific practices and delivering the HR practices to subunits and departments (Chadwick, Super, & Kwon, 2015). Line managers help realize HR practices for employees in their on-the-job work experiences, connecting upper management's intent to frontline employees and shaping employee perceptions towards management and the organization. We propose that the extent to which HR practices are complementary has much to do with managers' HC at each of these three levels in the organization (Steffensen et al., 2019). However, current SHRM research on managers is, at present, unsystematic, with few discussions on their roles in shaping HRM complementarities (Jo & Chadwick, 2019).

SHC research on managerial influence suggests new ways forward on this question. Specifically, resource orchestration theorists (Sirmon et al., 2007) suggest that it is not resources per se but managers' capabilities at structuring, bundling, and leveraging resources that create organizational competitive advantages in the long term. In smaller organizations where the hierarchical levels of management are condensed, the same managers can influence the performance of their units both by applying their HC to the tasks at hand and by using their ability to coordinate organizational activities. As the scale of the organizations grows, management tasks and responsibilities become dispersed and the strategic importance of coordinating people management both vertically and horizontally increases correspondingly, while the importance of managers' abilities to personally perform organizational activities will lessen.

Additionally, in dynamic environments, the need for managers to continuously adapt their organizations' HR practices should also be greater. Dynamic capabilities theory (Teece et al., 1997) highlights how organizations create rents through sensing, seizing, and reconfiguring resources in a changing environment. Following this research line but highlighting the role of senior managers, Helfat and Martin (2015) propose that organizations whose managers have superior dynamic managerial capabilities are able to adapt and change more successfully. Accordingly, to the extent that these capabilities vary across organizations, managerial HRM capabilities (of which the capabilities of various groups of managers are key components) are another dimension of strategic action for SHRM researchers to explore.

An example of such managerial HRM capabilities, "acqui-hiring", involves accessing desirable HC by acquiring small organizations. This is an important strategic choice at the discretion of top managers, who aim to adjust their

HC base and complement other organizational resources when dynamic environments allow little time for internal development (Chatterji & Patro, 2014). Presumably, some organizations become more skilled than others at making and executing such choices successfully, a skill that can improve with experience. To cite another example, some organizations are better skilled at building HCRs externally through specialized pipelines and well-developed selection tools, while other organizations do a better job of maintaining HCRs through internal training and development programs (cf. Brymer, et al., 2019). Moreover, adaptions like altering evaluation methods or replacing training programs also require HR managers' role in rebundling HR practices; it is up to HR managers to figure out the best configuration of HR practices to maintain HR systems' internal and external complementarities as their organizations' environments change. Furthermore, when organizations experience change, line managers with superior management skills and leadership can make organizational goals complementary to employee goals and create positive employee attributions towards newly implemented HRM (Nishii, et al., 2008). In short, organization-specific managerial HRM capabilities to orchestrate HR practices may be bigger determinants of long term HRM effectiveness in dynamic environments than the specific HR practices that exist at any one point in time (Chadwick & Flinchbaugh, 2021) – a testable proposition.

Conclusion

As our preceding discussion has emphasized, the possibilities for enriching SHRM research with perspectives from SHC have great potential. In this chapter, we have focused on the interplay between value creation and value capture, on the linkages between HR practices and different types of HC, and on the possibilities for expanding SHRM scholars' views of complementarities both within and outside of HR systems. Other possibilities for cross-fertilization between SHRM and SHC, and, more broadly, between SHRM and strategy and with other types of organizational research outside of strategy are too plentiful to explore in this chapter. For instance, the strategy field's concept of managerial discretion (Wangrow et al., 2015) can enrich SHRM researchers' view of managers' roles in implementing and modifying HR practices. We also note that the third foundational discipline of management research, sociology, offers many additional opportunities to broaden and deepen the SHRM research conversation. Moreover, such fertilization can run in both directions. SHRM scholarship, for instance, has much to offer SHC researchers' interests in how HR practices can shape HCRs. In many ways, despite nearly three decades of research and theory, we have only begun to explore how HRM influences outcomes of interest for individuals and the organizations where they work.

References

Appelbaum, E., Bailey, T., Berg, P. and Kalleberg, A. L. (2000). *Manufacturing Advantage: Why High Performance Work Systems Pay Off*. Cornell University Press.

Barney, J. (1991). Firm Resources and Sustained Competitive Advantage. *Journal of Management, 17*(1), 99–120.

Becker, G. S. (1964). *Human Capital: A Theoretical and Empirical Analysis with Special Reference to Education* (3rd ed.). University of Chicago Press.

Blau, P. M. (1964). *Exchange and Power in Social Life*. Transaction Publishers.

Bowen, D. E. & Ostroff, C. (2004). Understanding HRM–Firm Performance Linkages: The Role of the "Strength" of the HRM System. *Academy of Management Review, 29*(2), 203–221.

Bowman, C. & Ambrosini, V. (2000). Value Creation Versus Value Capture: Towards a Coherent Definition of Value in Strategy. *British Journal of Management, 11*(1), 1–15.

Brymer, R. A. & Hitt, M. A. (2019). Agonistic relations, social capital, and (dis) complementarity in the emergence of human capital resources. In *Handbook of Research on Strategic Human Capital Resources*. Edward Elgar Publishing.

Brymer, R., Chadwick C., Hill, A., & Molloy, J. C. 2019. Pipelines and Their Portfolios: A More Holistic View of Human Capital Heterogeneity Via Firm-Wide Employee Sourcing. *Academy of Management Perspectives, 33*(2): 207–233.

Campbell, B. & Kryscynski, D. (2019). What are we isolating? Why human capital-based competitive advantage may not be so much about human capital. In A. Nyberg & T. Moliterno (Eds.), *Handbook of Research on Strategic Human Capital Resources* (157–168). Edward Elgar Publishing.

Campbell, B. A., Coff, R., & Kryscynski, D. (2012). Rethinking Sustained Competitive Advantage from Human Capital. *Academy of Management Review, 37*(3), 376–395.

Cappelli, P. & Neumark, D. (2001). Do "High-Performance" Work Practices Improve Establishment Level Outcomes? *Industrial and Labor Relations Review, 54*(4), 737–775.

Chadwick, C. (2010). Theoretic insights on the nature of performance synergies in human resource systems: Toward greater precision. *Human Resource Management Review, 20*(2), 85–101.

Chadwick, C. (2017). Toward a More Comprehensive Model of Organizations' Human Capital Rents. *Academy of Management Review, 42*(3), 499–519.

Chadwick, C. & Dabu, A. (2009). Human Resources, Human Resource Management, and the Competitive Advantage of Organizations: Toward a More Comprehensive Model of Causal Linkages. *Organization Science, 20*(1), 253–272.

Chadwick, C. & Flinchbaugh, C. (2021). Searching for Competitive Advantage in the HRM-Firm Performance Relationship. *Academy of Management Perspectives, 35*(2), 181–207.

Chatterji, A. & Patro, A. (2014). Dynamic capabilities and managing human capital. *Academy of Management Perspectives, 28*(4), 395–408.

Coff, R. (1997). Human Assets and Management Dilemmas: Coping with Hazards on the Road to Resource-Based Theory. *Academy of Management Review, 22*(2), 374–402.

Coff, R. (1999). When Competitive Advantage Doesn't Lead to Performance: The Resource-Based View and Stakeholder Bargaining Power. *Organization Science, 10*(2), 119–133.

Crocker, A. & Eckardt, R. (2014). A Multilevel Investigation of Individual- and Unit level Human Capital Complementarities. *Journal of Management, 40*(2), 509–530.

Datta, D. K., Guthrie, J. P., & Wright, P. M. (2005). Human Resource Management and Labor Productivity: Does Industry Matter? *Academy of Management Journal, 48*(1), 135–145.

Delery, J. E. (1998). Issues of fit in strategic human resource management: Implications for research. *Human Resource Management Review, 8*(3), 289–309.

Delery, J. E. & Doty, D. H. (1996). Modes of Theorizing in Strategic Human Resource Management: Tests of Universalistic, Contingency, and Configurational Performance Predictions. *Academy of Management Journal, 39*(4), 802–835.

Eckardt, R., Tsai, C. Y., Dionne, S. D., Dunne, D., Spain, S. M., Park, J. W., Cheong, M., Kim, J., Guo, J., & Hao, C. (2021). Human capital resource emergence and leadership. *Journal of Organizational Behavior, 42*(2), 269–295.

Ennen, E. & Richter, A. (2010). The Whole Is More Than the Sum of Its Parts – Or Is It? A Review of the Empirical Literature on Complementarities in Organizations. *Journal of Management, 36*(1), 207–233.

Gerhart, B. & Feng, J. (2021). The Resource-Based View of the Firm, Human Resources, and Human Capital: Progress and Prospects. *Journal of Management*, 1–24.

Helfat, C. E. & Martin, J. A. (2015). Dynamic managerial capabilities: Review and assessment of managerial impact on strategic change. *Journal of Management, 41*(5), 1281–1312.

Huselid, M. A. (1995). The Impact of Human Resource Management Practices on Turnover, Productivity, and Corporate Financial Performance. *Academy of Management Journal, 38*(3), 635–672.

Huselid, M. A., Jackson, S. E., & Schuler, R. S. (1997). Technical and Strategic Human Resource Management Effectiveness as Determinants of Firm Performance. *Academy of Management Journal, 40*(1), 171–188.

Jackson, S. E., Schuler, R. S., & Jiang, K. (2014). An Aspirational Framework for Strategic Human Resource Management. *Academy of Management Annals, 8*(1), 1–56.

Jiang, K., Chuang, C.-H., & Chiao, Y.-C. (2015). Developing Collective Customer Knowledge and Service Climate: The Interaction Between Service-Oriented High-Performance Work Systems and Service Leadership. *Journal of Applied Psychology, 100*(4), 1089–1106.

Jiang, K., Lepak, D. P., Hu, J., & Baer, J. C. (2012). How Does Human Resource Management Influence Organizational Outcomes? A Meta-analytic Investigation of Mediating Mechanisms. *Academy of Management Journal, 55*(6), 1264–1294.

Jo, J. & Chadwick, C. (2019). Human Capital Resource Orchestration: The Strategic Value of Functional Managers in Resource Orchestration. *Academy of Management Proceedings, 2019*(1), 13410.

Kaufman, B. E. (2010). SHRM theory in the post-Huselid era: Why it is fundamentally misspecified. *Industrial Relations: A Journal of Economy and Society, 49*(2), 286–313.

Kehoe, R. R. & Collins, C. J. (2017). Human resource management and unit per-formance in knowledge-intensive work. *Journal of Applied Psychology*, *102*(8), 1222–1236.

Kryscynski, D., Coff, R., & Campbell, B. 2021. Charting a path between firm-specific incentives and human capital-based competitive advantage. *Strategic Management Journal*, *42*(2): 386–412.

Lepak, D. P. & Snell, S. A. (1999). The Human Resource Architecture: Toward a Theory of Human Capital Allocation and Development. *Academy of Management Review*, *24*(1), 31–48.

MacDuffie, J. P. (1995). Human resource bundles and manufacturing performance: Organizational logic and production systems in the world auto industry. *Industrial and Labor RelationsReview*, *48* 197–221.

Mahoney, J., & Qian, L. (2013). Market frictions as building blocks of an organizational economics approach to strategic management. *Strategic Management Journal*, *34*, 1019–1041.

Meuer, J. (2017). Exploring the complementarities within high-performance work systems: A set-theoretic analysis of UK organizations. *Human Resource Management*, *56*(4), 651–672.

Milgrom, P. & Roberts, J. (1992). *Economics, Organization & Management*. Prentice-Hall.

Morris, S., Alvarez, S., Barney, J.B., & Molloy, J.C. (2017). Firm-specific human capital investments as a signal of general value: Revisiting assumptions about human capital and how it is managed. *Strategic Management Journal*, *38*(4): 912–919.

Nahapiet, J. & Ghoshal, S. (1998). Social Capital, Intellectual Capital, and the Organizational Advantage. *Academy of Management Review*, *23*(2), 242–266.

Nishii, L. H., Lepak, D. P., & Schneider, B. (2008). Employee attributions of the "why" of HR practices: Their effects on employee attitudes and behaviors, and customer satisfaction. *Personnel Psychology*, *61*(3), 503–545.

Nyberg, A. J., Pieper, J. R., & Trevor, C. O. (2016). Pay-for-Performance's Effect on Future Employee Performance. *Journal of Management*, *42*(7), 1753–1783.

Passarelli, A. (2014). Harnessing the Power of a Massive Open Online Course (MOOC): Inspiring Leadership Through Emotional Intelligence. *Academy of Management Learning & Education*, *13*(2), 298–300.

Ployhart, R. E. & Moliterno, T. P. (2011). Emergence of the Human Capital Resource: A Multilevel Model. *Academy of Management Review*, *36*(1), 127–150.

Ployhart, R. E., Nyberg, A. J., Reilly, G., & Maltarich, M. A. (2014). Human Capital Is Dead; Long Live Human Capital Resources! *Journal of Management*, *40*(2), 371–398.

Posthuma, R. A., Campion, M. C., Masimova, M., & Campion, M. A. (2013). A High Performance Work Practices Taxonomy: Integrating the Literature and Directing Future Research. *Journal of Management*, *39*(5), 1184–1220.

Raffiee, J. & Coff, R. (2016). Micro-foundations of firm-specific human capital: when do employees perceive their skills to be firm-specific? *Academy of Management Journal*, *59*(3), 766–790.

Riley, S. M., Michael, S. C., & Mahoney, J. T. (2017). Human capital matters: Market valuation of firm investments in training and the role of complementary assets. *Strategic Management Journal*, *38*(9), 1895–1914.

Rynes, S. L., Gerhart, B., & Parks, L. (2005). Personnel Psychology: Performance Evaluation and Pay for Performance. *Annual Review of Psychology*, *56*(1), 571–600.

Schuler, R. S. & Jackson, S. E. (1987). Linking Competitive Strategies with Human Resource Management Practices. *Academy of Management Perspectives, 1*(3), 207–219.

Shaw, J. D., Gupta, N., & Delery, J. E. (2002). Pay dispersion and workforce performance: moderating effects of incentives and interdependence. *Strategic Management Journal, 23*(6), 491–512.

Sirmon, D. G., Hitt, M. A., & Ireland, R. D. (2007). Managing Firm Resources in Dynamic Environments to Create Value: Looking Inside the Black Box. *Academy of Management Review, 32*(1), 273–292.

Steffensen, D. S., Ellen, B. P., Wang, G., & Ferris, G. R. (2019). Putting the "Management" Back in Human Resource Management: A Review and Agenda for Future Research. *Journal of Management, 45*(6), 2387–2418.

Takeuchi, R., Lepak, D. P., Wang, H., & Takeuchi, K. (2007). An Empirical Examination of the Mechanisms Mediating Between High-Performance Work Systems and the Performance of Japanese Organizations. *Journal of Applied Psychology, 92*(4), 1069–1083.

Teece, D. J., Pisano, G., & Shuen, A. (1997). Dynamic capabilities and strategic management. *Strategic Management Journal, 18*(7), 509–533.

Tenhiälä, A. & Laamanen, T. (2018). Right on the money? The contingent effects of strategic orientation and pay system design on firm performance. *Strategic Management Journal, 39*(13), 3408–3433.

Toh, S. M., Morgeson, F. P., & Campion, M. A. (2008). Human Resource Configurations: Investigating Fit with the Organizational Context. *Journal of Applied Psychology, 93*(4), 864–882.

Van Beurden, J., Van De Voorde, K., & Van Veldhoven, M. (2021). The employee perspective on HR practices: A systematic literature review, integration and outlook. *International Journal of Human Resource Management, 32*(2), 359–393.

Wangrow, D. B., Schepker, D. J., & Barker, V. L. III. (2015). Managerial discretion: An empirical review and focus on future research directions. *Journal of Management, 41*: 99–135.

Witt, L. A., Burke, L. A., Barrick, M. R., & Mount, M. K. (2002). The Interactive Effects of Conscientiousness and Agreeableness on Job Performance. *Journal of Applied Psychology, 87*(1), 164–169.

Wolfson, M. A. & Mathieu, J. E. (2018). Sprinting to the finish: Toward a theory of Human Capital Resource Complementarity. *Journal of Applied Psychology, 103*(11), 1165–1180.

Wolfson, M. A. & Mathieu, J. E. (2021). Deploying Human Capital Resources: Accentuating Effects of Situational Alignment and Social Capital Resources. *Academy of Management Journal, 64*(2), 435–457.

Wood, S. & Ogbonnaya, C. (2018). High-involvement management, economic recession, well-being, and organizational performance. *Journal of Management, 44*(8), 3070–3095.

Wright, P. M., Dunford, B. B., & Snell, S. A. (2001). Human resources and the resource based view of the firm. *Journal of Management, 27*(6), 701–721.

5 An expanded model of HR strategy, social capital, and firm performance: the moderating effects of organizational contingencies and resource orchestration

Christopher J. Collins

Following the logic of the resource-based view of the firm, strategic HR scholars have argued that systems of HR practices can lead to competitive advantage when they create employee-based resources that are rare, valuable, and difficult to imitate (Collins & Smith, 2006; Wright & Ulrich, 2017). Increasingly, this approach has led scholars to focus on social or relational capital resources because these employee-based resources are embedded within the organizational context making them firm-specific and difficult to transfer, and therefore more likely to lead to sustained competitive advantage relative to human capital resources (Coff & Kryscynski, 2011; Collins & Kehoe, 2017). Indeed, a growing number of empirical studies have shown that collective employee social capital resources – defined as firm- or group-level employee social networks and relationships and norms for how employees will work together and support one another in an organizational setting – are one important set of employee-based resources that mediate the relationship between HR strategies and organizational performance (e.g., Collins & Smith, 2006; Kehoe & Collins, 2017; Shaw et al., 2005).

This growing body of research has provided initial insights as to the social/relational path between HR systems and firm performance; however, additional research is needed to better understand the complexity of these relationships. To date, the extant research has tended to examine simple direct relationships between a single HR system and collective employee social capital and simple direct relationships between these social capital resources and firm performance. Importantly, prior research has often failed to address the theoretically and practically important questions of when (i.e., under what conditions) investment in a system of HR practices leads to superior firm performance through social capital (Collins, 2021; Collins & Kehoe, 2017). First, current empirical research examining the relationship between HR systems and collective employee social capital has not accounted for the concept of vertical fit in strategic HR – the perspective that the effectiveness of a system of HR practices is contingent on other internal and external factors (Baird & Meshoulam, 1988; Delery, 1998). Second, the extant research on HR and social capital has also not incorporated recent work in strategy literature on resource orchestration which argues that valuable organizational resources may only lead to higher firm performance when firms are able to effectively mobilize, recombine, and deploy these resources to create competitive advantage in a dynamic environment (Greer, Lusch, & Hitt, 2017; Hitt et al., 2011).

In this chapter, I draw on extant literatures on vertical fit resource orchestration to more completely model the complex nature of how a system of high commitment human resource (HCHR) practices may lead to firm competitive advantage and performance through collective employee social capital (see Figure 5.1). First, I quickly review the extant literature on HR and social capital to establish the theoretical pathways between an HCHR system, collective employee social capital, and firm performance. Second, I draw on the vertical fit perspective to identify key contingency factors that may affect the extent to which HR systems may create an internal climate that fosters collective social capital resources. Third, drawing on the emerging literature on resource orchestration, I identify organizational factors that may enhance or limit the extent to which firms are able to put these social capital resources to productive use for competitive advantage and higher firm performance. Finally, I discuss opportunities for future empirical research to enhance our understanding of the complex relationships between HR systems, collective employee social capital, and firm performance.

Theoretical background

Social capital perspective of HR systems and competitive advantage

The field of strategic HR has gained momentum over the last four decades as more practitioners and academics have come to believe that HR systems are one set of organizational practices or decisions that are key to understanding organizational competitive advantage and firm performance (Jackson, Schuler, & Jiang, 2014; Wright & Ulrich, 2017). Central to this emerging

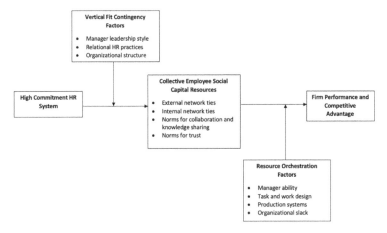

Figure 5.1   Moderated model of relationships between HR, social capital, and firm performance

body of research, scholars have argued that a coherent set of HR practices that align to the underlying philosophy of an overarching HR strategy work together to convey and reinforce a consistent signal to employees about the employer-employee relationship and provide clear guidance as to how the firm will look to develop and support employees and what the firm expects from employees in return (Bowen & Ostroff, 2004; Tsui et al., 1997). Because different HR systems are based on strategic choices regarding how to attract, develop, and motivate a set of employees, each unique system of HR practices is composed of different sets of mutually reinforcing HR practices that shape a unique climate that leads to the emergence of different employee-based resources across each HR system (Bowen & Ostroff, 2004; Jackson et al., 2014).

Importantly, firms can choose from a wide array of HR strategies that vary in terms of overall philosophical approach for managing the employee-employer relationship and direct employee actions and behaviors (Baron, Burton, & Hannan, 1996; Jackson et al., 2014; Tsui et al., 1997). Because different HR strategies create different internal climates that shape unique employee outcomes, they likely result in the emergence of different patterns of employee social capital (Collins & Kehoe, 2017; Kehoe & Collins, 2008). For example, a bureaucratic HR strategy, which includes HR practices that focus on a philosophy of command and control, works to shape an organizational climate that supports social networks where leaders are the key central nodes for team communication and decision making and strong internal team relationships based on followership of the team leader (Collins & Kehoe, 2017). In contrast, an engineering HR strategy – a system of HR practices focused on attracting and retaining highly skilled employees from the external labor market by offering challenging and exciting work and managing employees through peer influence and control (Baron et al., 1996) – supports the development of an organizational climate fostering social capital norms of high trust, productive task conflict, and collaboration and the development of cross-functional network ties (Kehoe & Collins, 2008). While these more general HR strategy approaches to managing employees lead to climates that may support the emergence of collective employee social capital, more targeted HR strategies may also support the development of these employee-based resources. For example, employee networks and norms for working together may be shaped by more targeted HR systems that increase employee motivation and opportunities to develop specific, targeted relationships or internal team norms around collaboration or how to work together (Gittell, Seidener, & Wimbush, 2010; Kehoe & Collins, 2017).

While firms can theoretically develop unique clusters of collective employee social capital outcomes through the choice of different HR strategies and underlying systems, the vast majority of empirical work in this area has focused on HCHR system practices. In prior research, scholars have generally defined the HCHR system as a combination of HR practices that demonstrate the firm's long-term commitment to and high level of investment in employees (Collins & Smith, 2006; Kehoe & Collins, 2017). Specific practices included in the HCHR systems have varied across studies, typical HR practices within an HCHR system include recruitment and selection practices that ensure new employee fit to the firm's culture and norms, high levels of on-going investment in employee training and development to enable employees to continue developing firm-specific capabilities, building internal labor markets to provide employees with career growth and progression, rewards and incentive pay tied to unit and overall organizational performance, and a focus on providing employees with job autonomy and involvement in decision making (Chang et al., 2014; Kehoe & Collins, 2017). In return for the high-level of investment and commitment demonstrated by the organization, employees are expected to reciprocate by continuing to stay with the firm (i.e., low levels of voluntary turnover), developing firm-specific resources (i.e., human and social capital), and exerting greater effort to support organizational strategy and activities that support organizational performance (Arthur, 1994; Tsui et al., 1997).

Scholars have argued that an HCHR system can shape the ability, motivation, and opportunity for employees to build social capital (Collins & Smith, 2006; Gittel et al., 2010), where social capital is defined as the social network ties, norms, and behaviors that enable employees to effectively work together towards productive organizational performance (Nahapiet & Ghoshal, 1998). Strategic human resource management (SHRM) scholars have argued that an HCHR system creates a context where employees have high motivation to develop firm-specific relationships, trusting and supportive relationships with colleagues, and greater collaboration and cooperation with one another (Chang et al., 2014; Collins & Smith, 2006; Kehoe & Collins, 2017). For example, practices such as high investment in employees' learning and hiring for fit to organizational culture create a climate of reciprocity which fosters supporting and trusting relationships between employees (Kehoe & Collins, 2008). Internal career movement and job rotations create the opportunity for employees to build larger internal social networks (Collins & Smith, 2006; Gittell et al., 2010). Further, shared goals and incentives create higher motivation for employees to collaborate and cooperate (Chang et al., 2014; Collins & Smith, 2006). Indeed, there is growing empirical evidence that employee social capital variables mediate the relationship between a system of HCHR practices and higher firm performance. For example, prior studies have demonstrated a positive and significant relationship between an HCHR system and the size and strength of employees' network ties (Collins & Clark, 2003); internal relationships for knowledge sharing (Kehoe & Collins, 2017); and the climate for collaboration and trust between employees within an organization (Collins & Smith, 2006).

Because research on the relationship between a system of HCHR practices and social capital is more developed than the relationships between social capital and alternative HR systems, I focus the following sections on how organizational contextual factors may affect the relationships in the mediated model of HCHR, social capital, and firm performance. In the sections below, I develop a more complete model that may help to explain both when an HCHR system is more likely to lead to higher levels of employee social capital and when this valuable employee-based resource is more likely to lead to organizational competitive advantage and higher firm performance. As noted in the discussion section below, my hope is that the focus on building out a model in the context of HCHR will help motivate research that helps us to more fully understand the complex relationships between HR strategies, social capital, and firm competitive advantage.

Vertical fit and the relationship between HR systems and social capital

Importantly, the concept of vertical fit in strategic HR has been the key perspective through which scholars have examined the question of when a system of HR practices is likely to lead to competitive advantage (Baird & Mesholoum,

1988; Delery & Doty, 1996). Given the long history and prominence of the concept of vertical fit in strategic HR research, a surprisingly small number of empirical studies have tested these ideas (Chadwick et al., 2013; Jackson et al., 2014). Most theoretical research on vertical fit has focused on the fit between HR strategies and business strategies, but empirical research has provided mixed support for proposed interactions between HR and business strategies (Wright & Ulrich, 2017). A more limited set of studies have begun to examine the fit between HR strategies/systems and other organizational contextual factors (e.g., culture, industry, firm history) and firm performance, again with mixed support (Jackson et al., 2014). More recently, Collins and colleagues (e.g., Collins, 2021; Kehoe & Collins, 2017), have argued that prior research on vertical fit in strategic HR may be mis-conceptualized because it has not accounted for the mediated, resource-based view of strategic HR. That is, because HR practices lead to firm competitive advantage by building and retaining valuable employee-based resources, the fit of HR strategies and other organizational factors are most likely to impact the resulting organizational climate and signal to employees about important required capabilities and behaviors (Collins, 2021).

Indeed, this newer perspective on vertical fit in HR fits with early work on structural contingency theory which suggests the choices that firm leaders make regarding organizational systems and structure must effectively support one another because they are all part of a larger system of organizational factors that shape employee behaviors and outcomes (Drazin & Van de Ven, 1985; Tushman, 1979). Importantly, the emergence of firm-level employee-based resources is dependent on the extent to which employees across the firm receive consistent signals regarding expected capabilities, norms, and behaviors (Li et al., 2018; Nishii et al., 2008). Therefore, it is likely that the effect of a system of HCHR practices on employee social capital is contingent on the extent to which other aspects of the broader employee management system support and reinforce the messages, signals, and directions regarding the development of social capital that are driven by this particular set of HR practices (Collins, 2021). Below, I examine a number of organizational contextual factors that may work to support an HCHR strategy to enhance the creation of collective employee social capital.

Leadership behaviors

Extant research suggests the behaviors exhibited by leaders play a signifi-cant role in shaping employee outcomes by setting a clear tone regarding cultural norms and providing visible signals to employees of goals, vision, and expectations of the organization (Bass, 1985; Podsakoff, MacKenzie, & Fetter, 1993). Similarly to HR systems, leaders' behaviors provide employees strong contextual cues on the employer-employee relationship, influencing employees' understanding of what to expect from the organization and what is expected of them in return (Rousseau, 1995). Because both HR systems and leadership behaviors provide signals and salient cues as to expected behaviors, work norms, and cultural expectations, fit between these two aspects of the overall employee management system can enhance the creation of desired employee-based resources (Collins, 2021). Employees are more likely to have an unambiguous understanding of desired behaviors and consequences when they receive consistent messages from multiple sources of information on the employee psychological contract, but may be confused about expectations when different sources are not aligned with the same messages or signals (Rousseau, 1995).

Transformational leadership is one of the most frequently studied forms of leadership behaviors (Colbert et al., 2008). Transformational leadership is comprised of four primary behaviors – inspirational motivation, intellectual stimulation, idealized influence, and individual consideration (Bass, 1985). Individually and collectively, the four behaviors of transformational leaders would seem to reinforce the messages and signals of an HCHR system that leads to employee social capital. For example, idealized influence and individual consideration behaviors demonstrate transformational leaders' commitment to building employee capabilities and providing support which in turn create a climate of mutual liking, respect, and concern for other employees within the organization (Podsakoff et al., 1993). Importantly, this type of climate will help to shape the environment of relationship building and trust created by practices within an HCHR system. In addition, through inspirational motivation, transformational leaders communicate higher level organizational goals and objectives building stronger employee affiliation to the company and increasing employee motivation to work together to achieve collective outcomes (Bass, 1985; Colbert et al., 2008). This set of behaviors should work to reinforce and support the collective orientation, trust, and collaboration supported by HCHR practices such as performance management and rewards tied to firm- or group-level outcomes. These transformational behaviors encourage a climate of teamwork and working together, which overlap and reinforce the messages communicated by an HCHR system that enhances collaboration and helping relationships between employees. Idealized influence behaviors build a climate of support and a safe environment, which supports employee trust in one another and motivation to share and exchange knowledge between one another (Colbert et al., 2008), again supporting the climate for social capital created by a system of HCHR practices.

Importantly, when multiple aspects of the complete employee management system send consistent signals of the climate and expectations for employee behaviors, employees are more likely to have clarity on what is expected and norms for how to behave leading to more consistent development of employee-based resources (Delery, 1998). When employees perceive congruence between espoused values displayed by the leader and inferred values derived from practices within an HR system, they should view the combined set of signals as stronger and have a clear understanding of expected norms and behaviors (Bowen & Ostroff, 2004; Rousseau, 1995). In this case of social capital, the practices in an HCHR system and transformational leadership should have a positive synergistic effect because they send mutually reinforcing messages which create greater clarity for employees regarding norms and expectations regarding relationship building and expectations for trust and collaboration between employees. Thus, leaders' transformational behaviors could be a critical resource that enables firms to more consistently orchestrate the development of employee social capital resources that emerge from a system of HCHR practices.

Additional HR systems

Early work in the field of strategic HR focused on generic, high performance HR systems that are meant to shape broad human capital, higher intentions to stay with the company, and higher employee motivation to contribute to organizational goals (Jackson et al., 2014; Wright & Ulrich, 2017). More recently, however, strategic HR scholars have pointed to the need to look at more focused HR systems that focus on impacting employee ability, motivation, and opportunity to build specific employee-based resources (Kehoe & Collins, 2017; Jackson et al., 2014). For example, researcher have begun to look at HR systems that are narrower in focus and specifically targeted towards employee outcomes such as employee network ties (Collins & Clark, 2003), occupational safety (Zacharatos, Barling, and Iverson, 2005), and customer service orientation (Liao et al., 2009). Further, recent research suggests that leaders are likely to simultaneously implement both a generic and more tailored system of HR practices to manage the same group of employees (Kehoe & Collins, 2017). Following the work on resource orchestration, it is important to understand how an HR system with a narrower focus would help to reinforce and orchestrate the social capital outcomes tied to a system of HCHR practices.

In the context of social capital, scholars have begun to study a network-enhancing or relational system of HR practices that is intended to shape employees' abilities, motivation, and opportunities to build network ties and trusting relationships with others (Collins & Clark, 2003; Kehoe & Collins, 2017). The practices within this system include targeted training and feedback on how to develop work relationships, frequent social events and activities to build relationships with other employees within and outside immediate work groups, meetings and technology to share information and exchange ideas across geographically dispersed units, and workspace design that enables employees to meet one another and more easily collaborate (Collins & Clark, 2003; Kehoe & Collins, 2017). As with transformational leadership, the practices within this more targeted HR system should help to reinforce and support the climate for social capital creation enabled by a system of HCHR practices.

For example, practices such as within- and cross-unit knowledge sharing meetings create opportunities for employees to meet other employees and a context to build trust and reciprocity between employees that should enable greater collaboration and stronger network ties (Collins & Clark, 2003; Luthans & Youssef, 2004). Similarly, workspace designs that enable employees to 'bump' into new employees and support frequent interactions and group work create both the opportunity to build new internal network ties and for employees to more frequently collaborate and cooperate with one another. Similarly, company sponsored social events create opportunities for employees to meet other employees and build stronger relationships and potentially lead to shared goals and interests and to work together and collaborate (Gittel et al., 2010; Leana & Van Buren, 1999). The combination of practices creates greater opportunities to build networks and develop trusting and collaborative working relationships, which should work to reinforce the climate of cooperation and relationship development that was motivated by implementing a system of HCHR practices. Specific training on how to build and maintain network ties and relationships should help create greater abilities to develop social network connections and provide the abilities that match with the higher motivation to develop social capital that is supported by an HCHR system (Collins & Clark, 2003). Finally, company-wide meetings to celebrate successes and share information create an environment of trust and reciprocity between employees (Collins & Smith, 2006) that again reinforces the climate for social capital created by HCHR.

Organizational structure

To effectively manage employees, firm leaders also make choices on organizational structure and design (Drazin & Van de Ven, 1985; Hage, 1999). Organizational structure is one of the means through which companies look to effectively coordinate and control employee behaviors, resulting from choices regarding the distribution of authority and decision-making power, organization of tasks, and the connection and relationships between departments and functional units in an organization (Hage, 1999). As with HR systems and leadership, choices in organizational structure send signals to employees about expected norms and behaviors and create different opportunities for employees to develop relationships and work together in a collaborative manner (Burns & Stalker, 1994; Nahapiet & Ghoshal, 1998). Given the potential overlap with signals of expected behaviors and support for the creation of social capital, choices regarding structure may be another important contingency that impacts the orchestration and development of social capital outcomes that may emerge from a system of HCHR practices. An organic organizational structure is one form of structure that would seem to support the climate for social capital created by a system of HCHR practices. The organic structure is characterized by low levels of centralization and formalization leading to greater levels of employee empowerment and more frequent use of horizontal communication between employees and groups within the firm (Burns & Stalker, 1994; Hage, 1999). These aspects of an organic structure would create motivations and opportunities for employees that reinforce the social capital that emerges from an HCHR system.

For example, flatter organizational structures and employee empowerment demonstrate trust and support of employees (Hage, 1999), potentially reinforcing norms of reciprocity, trust, and collaboration that may result from the implementation of HCHR practices. Further, flat structures and higher levels of horizontal communication create more opportunities for employees to connect and meet other employees and share ideas and information with a wider array of colleagues (Burns & Stalker, 1994; Nahapiet & Ghoshal, 1998). These opportunities, combined with the motivational climate that emerges from a system of HCHR practices, should lead to the development of greater employee network ties across more parts of the organization. The reduction in power differences fostered by an organic structure should also enhance trust between employees and increase the potential for collaboration and cooperation (Hage, 1999; Zamuto & O'Conner, 1992), again reinforcing the social capital outcomes tied to an HCHR system. Finally, just as with an HCHR system, lower levels of formalization also support the movement of employees across departmental boundaries, resulting in more social connections across employees and promoting a climate of collaboration (Burns & Stalker, 1994; Hage, 1999). By creating opportunities and motivation for employees to meet and interact with a wider array of colleagues, reducing power differences, and increasing employee empowerment, an organic system works synergistically to reinforce the messages and signals of an HCHR system.

Combined with the above, I argue that transformational leadership, a relational HR system, and an organic organizational structure are all important contingencies that may affect the extent to which a system of HCHR practice can work to shape a climate that develops, reinforces, and retains collective employee social capital within a firm.

Examining when social capital leads to competitive advantage

In addition to moderating the relationship between HCHR practices and collective employee social capital, organizational contextual factors may also limit or enhance the extent to which the employee resources that emerge from this system lead to competitive advantage and higher firm performance (Collins, 2021). Following the resource-based view (RBV) perspective, resources that are valuable, rare, and difficult to imitate are the building blocks of competitive advantage (Barney, 1991; Peteraf, 1993). Recent work, however, has pointed to the orchestration of resources as being essential for strategy execution and the creation of competitive advantage (Greer et al., 2017; Hitt et al., 2011). From this perspective, attracting, developing, and retaining valuable and rare employee social capital resources is necessary but insufficient for creating competitive advantage; firms must also be able to manage, coordinate, and deploy these resources effectively in order to achieve competitive advantage (Eisenhart & Martin, 2000; Kor & Mahoney, 2005). Thus, to fully understand vertical fit in strategic HR, I argue that scholars must also identify key organizational resources and capabilities that enable resource orchestration of the collective employee social capital which emerges from an HR system. Examining resource orchestration is particularly important in the context of employee-based resources because these resources are tied to individual employees and are not the property of the organization (Coff & Kryscynski, 2011; Hitt et al., 2011).

Strategy scholars have argued that organizational leaders play a key role in identifying how to effectively manage, bundle and recombine, and deploy resources in order to ensure firms can put resources to productive use and sustain resource advantages over a period of time (Hansen et al., 2004; Eisenhart & Martin, 2000; Sirmon et al., 2007). In dynamic environments, managers are essential for identifying resource complementarities and new resource combinations to pursue new business opportunities and business strategies or models, and respond to shifts in the marketplace (Augier & Teece, 2009). Further, leaders directly and indirectly impact the extent to which firms can put employee-based capabilities to productive use for competitive advantage (Greer et al., 2017; Hitt et al., 2011). Specifically, leaders' capabilities (abilities and insights based on accumulated knowledge and experience), their ability to create and manage organizational slack, and their choices regarding organizational design can all impact the extent to which employee-based resources such as social capital can lead to firm performance.

Leaders' manager capability

Managerial capability – the combination of knowledge, knowhow, and insights build-up through experiences and education – is a critical resource that enables firms to more effectively utilize physical, financial, and human resources (Greer et al., 2017; Penrose, 1959). Differences in leaders' firm- and industry-specific experience and education lead to varying abilities to spot market trends opportunities and deploy organizational resources to take advantage of these opportunities (Holcomb et al., 2009; Penrose, 1959). Further, leaders with greater managerial capabilities based on firm-specific experience may better understand how to extract more value from existing resources and identify new ways to recombine these resources to create new forms of competitive advantage (Greer et al., 2017; Sirmon et al., 2007).

While directly measuring leaders' managerial capabilities is difficult, prior research has linked multiple proxy measures of capability (i.e., observable characteristics of managers) to resource orchestration. For example, greater firm- and industry-specific experience can increase leaders' tacit knowledge of and understanding of existing resources (Hitt et al., 2011; Holcomb et al., 2009), thus enabling leaders to more effectively organize and recombine these resources for competitive advantage (Kor & Mahoney, 2005). Leaders with greater firm- and industry-specific experience also develop a stronger set of network ties and industry knowledge that enable them to develop deeper insights into market patterns and potentially identify how to leverage organizational resources to pursue opportunities or mitigate threats (Carpenter et al., 2004; Holcomb et al., 2009). Further, deeper firm-specific experience and knowledge may be particularly important with respect to employee social capital because these resources are captured in the minds and relationships of employees, making them more complex to understand and manage (Collins & Smith, 2006; Gittell et al., 2010). Deeper knowledge of where these resources exist and how they work within an organization is likely to be enhanced to the extent that leaders have spent more time in the organization and had more opportunities to interact with the employees to whom they are tied. For example, leaders with greater firm-specific experience are likely to have built relationships with more employees and have had the chance to observe more employee working patterns which should enable these managers to better understand the social dynamics between employees and where social capital resources exist. Similarly, greater firm-specific experience may also help leaders more effectively to deploy and coordinate employee social capital against current or new strategic directions (Hitt et al., 2011).

Leaders' formal education is another proxy of managerial capability and has been linked to their ability to help drive organizational success. Education provides a unique set of experiences and insights that enhance executives' abilities to evaluate organizational resources and understand their usefulness for pursuing market opportunities (Hitt & Tyler, 1991). In particular, formal education enhances CEOs' absorptive capacity for integrating new internal and external experiences to which they are exposed (Cohen & Levinthal, 1990). Researchers have used education as a proxy for cognitive ability and argued that higher levels of education should enable CEOs to make better strategic decisions about resources (Wally & Baum, 1994). Education has also been seen as an indicator of executives' openness and learning orientation enabling leaders to potentially see existing resources in new ways or identify new market opportunities that are a fit to the existing social capital resources of the organization (Thomas et al., 1991). Collectively, the above arguments suggest that leaders' manager capability – knowledge and insights based on experience and education – are critical contextual factors that enable firms to more effectively orchestrate the deployment and recombination of the social capital resources that emerge from a system of HCHR practices.

Leaders' management of organizational slack

Leaders may also impact the ability of firms to effectively orchestrate employee-based resources based on the extent to which they create and manage organizational slack – the excess pool of resources beyond what an organization needs to produce a given level of output. Extant research suggests that organizational slack can be used to cushion against external pressures or potentially support entrepreneurial or innovation activities (Bourgeois, 1981; Nohria & Gulati, 1996). Further, organizational slack enables firms to potentially recombine or redistribute other organizational resources, creating the strategic flexibility to respond to rapidly changing environments or pursue new opportunities (Nohria & Gulati, 1996; Hitt et al., 2011). Organizations with greater slack also have more time and financial buffers to enable them to be more proactive in searching for environmental opportunities and to experiment with resource recombinations to pursue these opportunities (Cyert & March, 1963; Sirmon et al., 2007).

As with managerial capabilities, how managers allocate and maintain slack may play a particularly important role in the orchestration of employee-based resources. For example, employees need time and space in order to put their network ties to use in ways that may lead to the development of new ideas (Collins & Smith, 2006) or to capture and integrate knowledge from their broad social network ties (Nahapiet & Ghoshal, 1998). Further, employees are less likely to put network ties to productive use and less likely to reach out to their network ties to pursue new work activities if they are stretched too thin to accomplish existing tasks (Lawson, 2001). Employees need free time and the support of additional organizational resources in order for collaborative efforts to lead to innovation or to collaborate and combine or apply their collective knowledge to new tasks and activities (Nohria & Gulati, 1996). Based on these studies, there is some initial evidence that leaders may enhance the effectiveness of social capital resources to the extent that they create and deploy organizational slack to support work groups that have higher levels of social capital.

Organizational design

Leaders' choices regarding organizational design – including task/work design and supporting production and technology systems are also impact the ability of firms to orchestrate resources for productive use. Early work on structural contingency theory suggests that firms make a variety of choice regarding how to structure work and tasks and in the production and technology systems that support work and productivity (Drazin & Van de Ven, 1985; Hage & Aiken, 1969). Importantly, when these choices reinforce one another and when employee capabilities and behaviors match the requirements and demands of these choices, firms are more likely to achieve higher performance (Fry & Slocum, 1984; Van de Ven & Delbecq, 1974). In the context of vertical fit in strategic HR, employee-based resources that emerge from an HR system may be more likely to lead to competitive advantage and higher firm performance when they match with key aspects of how the work has been structured (Kehoe & Collins, 2008; Chung & Jackson, 2013). In contrast, firms will underperform to the extent that there is a mismatch between employee capabilities and the choices firms have made regarding production or technology systems (Snell & Dean, 1992) or the design for how work gets done (Chung & Jackson, 2013).

There is some early evidence to suggest that leaders' choices regarding job/ task design and product/technology system impact the ability of firms to put employee social capital to productive use. For example, researchers have found that HCHR systems lead to higher performance in companies that have implemented production systems which require greater collaboration and social interactions between employees (MacDuffie, 1995; Snell & Dean, 1992). Further, strong employee relationships, higher trust, and greater collaboration are more beneficial for firms that have chosen production systems that require higher levels of coordination and where procedures are less routine (Gittell et al., 2010). The impact of social capital on firm outcomes may also be contingent on work and task design. For example, Chung and Jackson (2013) found that task routineness moderated the relationship between research teams' social capital – measured as internal and external networks – and team performance. Similarly, the impact of collaboration, strong internal ties, and trust may have differing levels of impact on firm performance depending on how firms are attempting to drive innovation (Kehoe & Collins, 2017). Collectively, the extent to which potentially valuable employee social capital resources can lead to competitive advantage seems to be contingent on the extent to which they fit organizational choices regarding job/task design and production/technology.

Discussion

My goal in this chapter was to push research in new directions in order to help us better understand the complex relationships between HR strategies, collective employee social capital, and firm competitive advantage and performance. Early empirical research has provided support for the notion that HR strategies lead to competitive advantage through creating an organizational climate that fosters collective employee social capital (i.e., employee relationships and social norms for working together) that enable firm productivity, creativity, and innovation (Collins & Smith, 2006; Kehoe & Collins 2017). However, the simple direct, mediated relationships between HR, social capital, and firm performance ignores the true complexity of how choices in HR strategies may lead to firm competitive advantage (Collins, 2021; Collins & Kehoe, 2017). Indeed, past research has largely ignored the theoretical belief that there are contingencies that likely impact both the relationship between HR systems and collective employee social capital and between these employee-based resources and firm competitive advantage and performance.

Drawing on recent research on vertical fit in SHRM, I argued that the relationship between an HR strategy and social capital is likely to be dependent on a range of organizational factors that reinforce or contradict the signals sent to employees by the coherent set of HR practices underlying the HR strategy. To elucidate this argument, I developed specific rationale for how leader behaviors, specific HR systems, and organizational structure are likely to moderate the relationship between an HCHR system and the emergence for collective employee social capital. To further enhance our understanding of when and how HR strategies lead to competitive advantage through collective employee social capital, I also argued that scholars must identify the organizational contextual factors that may enhance or limit the extent to which these potentially valuable employee-based resources lead to competitive advantage. Drawing on extant literature on resource orchestration, I argued that leadership capabilities, organizational slack, and organizational structure and design moderate the relationship between the social capital resources that emerge from an HCHR strategy and firm competitive advantage and firm performance. Overall, this leads to a more complex model of the mediated relationship between an HCHR strategy, collective employee social capital, and firm competitive advantage and performance in which the size and strength of these relationships is dependent on other organizational factors.

I believe that this more complex model leads to multiple avenues for new research in strategic HR more broadly, and research opportunities on the mediating role of collective employee social capital more specifically. First, there are numerous alternative HR strategies from which firms can choose to manage employees, and these firms may implement different strategies to manage different groups of employees within the same organization. Further, the coherent set of HR practices underlying alternative HR strategies shape different climates and provide employees with different signals as to required capabilities and behaviors leading to the emergence of different forms of social capital across alternative HR strategies. It is, therefore, critical that future research more completely identifies the specific social capital outcomes that are likely to emerge from different choices in HR strategies. This future research should look at how different HR approaches may affect specific social network outcomes (e.g., size, strength, centrality) and norms for working together (e.g., collaboration, trust, competition). In addition, additional theoretical and empirical research is needed to identify whether some HR strategies are more effective than others for building and retaining different combinations of social capital outcomes. While there are a few studies that have examined direct relationships between a single HR strategy and a specific set of outcomes, I am not aware of any empirical work that has compared the relative effectiveness of multiple HR strategies across an array of different collective employee social capital outcomes.

Second, empirical work is needed to test the theoretical relationships that I have proposed in this chapter. While I have laid out specific theoretical rationale for how certain leadership characteristics and choices regarding organizational structure, design, and specific HR systems may serve as contingency factors, there is little to no empirical research testing any of these relationships. It would also be important to examine the robustness of these relationships across different types of employees (e.g., knowledge-based workers versus more manually focused roles) and industry and geographic settings. In addition, it will be important to examine how these organizational contextual factors may affect the relationship between HCHR practices and specific forms of collective employee social capital to understand whether there are different effects across different types of social capital (e.g., relationship networks vs. relational norms).

Third, I have really just begun to scratch the surface on contingency factors that may moderate the relationship between HR strategics and forms of collective employee social capital. Additional theoretical work is needed to identify other organizational factors that may provide supporting or conflicting signals that enhance or reduce the effect of HR strategies on collective employee social capital. For example, researchers might examine whether other forms of manager leadership behaviors (e.g., entrepreneurial leadership) or organizational systems (i.e., technology, communications) may help to enhance the likelihood that employees have the ability, motivation and opportunity to effectively create social capital. Alternatively, future research should also examine the impact of these leadership factors on the relationship between other forms of HR systems (e.g., general high performance work system, customer service HR system) and the employee-based resources that they are expected to attract, develop, and retain.

Finally, even though prior research has argued that resource orchestration may be particularly critical for employee-based resources as these resources inherently sit within employees rather than being owned by the firm (e.g., Coff, 1997; Collins, 2021), I could not find empirical work that has examined the question of when social capital resources that emerge from an HR system are more likely to lead to firm competitive advantage. As above, one immediate area for future research would be to test the specific relationships that I articulated in this chapter. In addition, future research should identify and empirically test how other organizational factors might enhance or limit the extent to which organizations can effectively utilize collective employee social capital for competitive advantage and higher firm performance. For example, it might be interesting to examine how physical assets, other forms of employee-based resources (e.g., human capital), or leadership behaviors might moderate the relationships between employee social capital and firm performance.

In conclusion, this chapter provides several implications for strategic HR scholars to expand our view and understanding of the complex relationships between HR strategies, collective employee social capital, and firm competitive advantage and performance. I looked to provide a new perspective on when an HCHR strategy can lead to higher firm performance. Specifically, I drew on strategic HR research on vertical fit to articulate how organizational contextual factors – leadership behaviors, a specific HR system, and job/task design – can enhance the likelihood that an HCHR system can lead to the emergence of collective employee social capital. Second, drawing on recent work on resource orchestration, I argued that contextual factors – leadership capabilities, organizational slack, organizational design – may affect the extent to which the social capital that emerges from an HCHR system may lead to firm competitive advantage and higher performance. In total, these arguments suggest that strategic HR scholars need to develop and test a more complex set of relationships to fully understand how HR strategies lead to firm competitive advantage through collective employee social capital.

References

Arthur, J. B. (1994). Effects of human resource systems on manufacturing performance and turnover. *Academy of Management Journal*, 37, 670–87.

Augier, M. & Teece, D. J. (2009). Dynamic capabilities and the roles of managers in business strategy and economic performance. *Organization Science*, 20, 410–421.

Baird, L. & Meshoulam, I. (1988). Managing two fits of strategic human resource management. *Academy of Management Review*, 13, 116–128.

Barney, J. (1991). Firm resources and sustained competitive advantage. *Journal of Management*, 17, 99–120.

Baron, J. N., Burton, M. D., & Hannan, M. T. (1996). The road taken: Origins and evolution of employment systems in emerging companies. *Industrial and Corporate Change*, 5, 239–275.

Bass, B. M. (1985). *Leadership and Performance Beyond Expectations*. New York: Free Press.

Bourgeois, L. J. (1981). On the measurement of organizational slack. *Academy of Management Review*, 6, 29–39.

Bowen, D. E. & Ostroff, C. (2004). Understanding HRM-financial performance linkages: the role of the 'strength' of the HRM system. *Academy of Management Review*, 29, 203–221.

Burns, T. & Stalker, G. M. (1994). The Management of Innovation. London: Tavistock.

Carpenter, M. A., Geletkanycz, M. A., & Sander, W. G. (2004). Upper echelons research revisited: Antecedents, elements, and consequences of top management team composition. *Journal of Management*, 30, 749–778.

Chadwick, C. C., Way, S. A., Kerr, G., & Thacker, J. W. (2013). Boundary conditions of the high-investment human resource systems-small firm labor market productivity relationship. *Personnel Psychology*, 66, 311–343.

Chang, S., Jia, L., Takeuchi, R., & Cia, Y. (2014). Do high-commitment work systems affect creativity? A multilevel combinational approach to employee creativity. *Journal of Applied Psychology*, 99, 665–680.

Chung, Y. & Jackson, S. E. (2013). The internal and external networks of knowledge-intensive teams: The role of task routineness. *Journal of Management*, 39, 442–468.

Coff, R. W. (1997). Human assets and management dilemmas: Coping with hazards on the road to resource-based theory. Academy of Management Review, 22(2), 374–402.

Coff, R. & Kryscynski, D. (2011). Drilling for micro-foundations of human capital-based competitive advantages. *Journal of Management*, 37, 1429–1443.

Cohen W. M. & Levinthal, D. A. (1990). *Absorptive capacity: a new perspective on learning and innovation. Administrative Science Quarterly*, 35, 128–152.

Colbert, A. E., Kristoff-Brown, A. L., Bradley, B. H., & Barrick, M. R. (2008). CEO transformational leadership: The role of goal congruence in top management teams. *Academy of Management Journal*, 51, 81–96.

Collins, C. J. (2021). Expanding the resource-based view model of strategic human resource management. *International Journal of Human Resource Management*, 32(2), 331–358.

Collins, C. J. & Clark, K. D. (2003). Strategic Human Resources Practices and Top Management Team Social Networks: An Examination of the Role of HR Practices in Creating Organizational Competitive Advantage. *Academy of Management Journal*, 46, 740–752.

Collins, C. & Kehoe, R. (2017). Examining strategic fit and misfit in the management of knowledge workers. *ILR Review*, 70, 308–335.

Collins, C. J. & Smith, K. G. (2006). Knowledge exchange and combination: The role of human resource practices in the performance of high-technology firms. *Academy of Management Journal*, 49, 544–560.

Cyert, R. C. & March, J. G. (1963). *A behavioral theory of the firm*. New York: Prentice Hall.

Delery, J. E. (1998). Issues of fit in strategic human resource management: Implications for research. *Human Resource Management Review*, 8, 289–309.

Delery, J. E. & Doty, D. H. (1996). Modes of theorizing in strategic human resource management: Tests of universalistic, contingency, and configurational performance predictions. *Academy of Management Journal*, 39, 802–835.

Drazin, R. & Van de Ven, A. H. (1985). Alternative forms of fit in contingency theory. *Administrative Science Quarterly*, 30, 514–539.

Eisenhart, K. M. & Martin, J. A. (2000). Dynamic capabilities: What are they? *Strategic Management Journal*, Special Issue, 21 (10–11), 1105–1121.

Fry, L. W. & Slocum J. W. (1984). Technology, structure and work group effectiveness: A test of a contingency model. *Academy of Management Journal*, 27, 221–246.

Gittell, J. H., Seidener, R. A., & Wimbush, J. (2010). A relational model of how high-performance work systems work. *Organization Science*, 21, 490–506.

Greer, C. R., Lusch, R. F., & Hitt, M. A. (2017). A service perspective for human capital resources: A critical base for strategy implementation. *Academy of Management Perspectives*, 31(2), 137–158.

Hage, J. (1999). Organizational innovation and organizational change. *Annual Review of Sociology*, 25, 597–622.

Hage, J. & Aiken, M. (1969). Routine technology, social structure, and organization goals. *Administrative Science Quarterly*, 14, 366–376.

Hansen, M. H., Perry, L.T., & Reese, C. S. (2004). A Bayesian operationalization of the resource-based view. *Strategic Management Journal*, 25(13), 1279–1295.

Hitt, M. A., Ireland, R. D., Sirmon, D. G., & Trahms, C. A. (2011). Strategic entrepreneurship: Creating value for individuals, organizations, and society. *Academy of Management Perspectives*, 25(2), 57–75.

Hitt, M.A., & Tyler, B. B. (1991). Strategic decision models: Integrating different perspectives. *Strategic Management Journal*, 12(5), 327–51.

Holcomb, T. R., Holmes, R. M., & Connelly, B. L. (2009). Making the most of what you have: Managerial ability as a source of resource value creation. *Strategic Management Journal*, 30, 457–85.

Jackson, S. E., Schuler R. S., & Jiang, K. (2014). An aspirational framework for strategic human resource management. *Academy of Management Annals*, 8, 1–56.

Kehoe, R. R. & Collins C. J. (2008). Exploration and exploitation strategies and the equifinality of HR systems. In J. Martocchio (Ed.), *Research in Personnel and Human Resources Management*, 27, 149–176. Greenwich, CT: JAI Press.

Kehoe, R. R. & Collins, C. J. (2017). Human resource management and unit performance in knowledge-intensive work. *Journal of Applied Psychology*, 102, 1222–1236.

Kor, Y. Y. & & Mahoney, J. T. (2005). How dynamics, management, and governance of resource deployments influence firm-level performance. *Strategic Management Journal*, 26, 489–496.

Lawson, M. B. (2001). In praise of slack: Time is of the essence. *Academy of Management Executive*, 15(3), 125–135.

Leana, C. R. & Van Buren, H. J. (1999). Organizational social capital and employment practices. *The Academy of Management Review*, 24, 538–555.

Li, Y., Wang, M., Van Jaarsveld, D. D., Lee, G. K., & Ma, D. G. (2018). From employee-experienced high-involvement work system to innovation: An emergence-based human-resource management framework. *Academy of Management Journal*, 61, 2000–2019.

Liao, H., Toya, K., Lepak, D. P., & Hong, Y. (2009). Do they see eye to eye? Management and employee perspectives of high-performance work systems and influence processes on service quality. *Journal of Applied Psychology*, 94, 371–391.

Luthans, F. & Youssef, C. M. (2004). Human, social, and now positive psychological capital management: Investing in people for competitive advantage. *Organizational Dynamics*, 33 (2), 143–160.

MacDuffie, J. P. (1995). Human resource bundles and manufacturing performance: Organizational logic and flexible production systems in the world auto industry. *Industrial and Labor Relations Review*, 48(2), 197–221.

Nahapiet, J. & Ghoshal, S. (1998). Social capital, intellectual capital, and the organizational advantage. *Academy of Management Review*, 23, 242–266.

Nishii, L. H., Lepak, D. P., & Schneider, B. (2008). Employee attributions of the "why" of HR practices: Their effects on employee attitudes and behaviors, and customer satisfaction. *Personnel Psychology*, 61(3), 503–545.

Nohria, N. & Gulati, R. (1996). Is slack good or bad for innovation? *Academy of Management Journal*, 39, 1245–1264.

Oh, H., Chung, M., & Labianca, G. (2004). Group social capital and group effectiveness: The role of informal socializing ties. *Academy of Management Journal*, 47(6), 860–875.

Penrose, E. (1959). *The Theory and Growth of the Firm*. New York: Oxford University Press.

Peteraf, M. A. (1993). The cornerstones of competitive advantage: A resource based view. *Strategic Management Journal*, 14, 179–191.

Podsakoff, P. M., MacKenzie, S. B., & Fetter, R. (1993). Substitutes for leadership and the management of professionals. *The Leadership Quarterly*, 4(1), 1–44.

Rousseau, D. (1995). *Psychological Contracts in Organizations: Understanding Written and Unwritten Agreements*. Washington, D.C.: Sage.

Shaw, J. D., Duffy, M. K., Johnson, J. L., & Lockhart, D. E. (2005). Turnover, social capital loses, and performance. *Academy of Management Journal*, 48, 594–606.

Sirmon, D. G., Hitt, M. A., & Ireland, R. D. (2007). Managing firm resources in dynamic environments to create value: Looking inside the black box. *Academy of Management Review*, 32, 273–292.

Snell, S. & Dean J. (1992). Integrated manufacturing and human resource management: A human capital perspective. *Academy of Management Journal*, 35, 467–504.

Thomas, A. S., Litschert, R. J., & Ramaswamy, K. (1991). The performance impact of strategy-manager alignment: an empirical investigation. *Strategic Management Journal*, 12, 509–522.

Tsui, A. S., Pearch, J. L., Porter, L. W., & Tripoli, A. M. (1997). Alternative approaches to the employee-organization relationship: Does investment in employees pay off? *Academy of Management Journal*, 40, 1089–1121.

Tushman, M. L. (1979). Work characteristics and sub-unit communication structure: A contingency analysis. *Administrative Science Quarterly*, 24, 82–98.

Van de Ven, A. H. & Delbecq, A. L. (1974). A task contingent model of work-unit structure. *Administrative Science Quarterly*, 19(2), 183–197.

Wally, S., & Baum, J. R. (1994). Personal and structural determinants of the pace of strategic decision making. *Academy of Management Journal*, 37, 873–896.

Wright, P. M. & Ulrich, M. D. (2017). A road well traveled: The past, present, and future journey of strategic human resource management. *Annual Review of Psychology and Organizational Behavior*, 4, 45–65.

Zacharatos, A., Barling, J., & Iverson, R. D. (2005). *High-performance work systems and occupational safety. Journal of Applied Psychology*, 90, 77–93.

Zammuto, R. F. & O'Connor, E. J. (1992). Gaining advanced manufacturing technologies benefits: the role of organizational design and culture. *Academy of Management Review*, 17, 70.

PART II

Variety in HRM forms

6   The liquid workforce

Peter Cappelli and Minseo Baek

Introduction

Readers with an interest in policy are well aware of the fact that in recent years, jobs have gotten worse, at least for the average worker and especially for those at the bottom. Real wages adjusted for inflation have declined (Donovan and Bradley, 2019) and job insecurity has increased especially for employees in positions that had been seen as lifetime in larger companies (Lee, Huang and Ashford, 2018). Retirement income is less secure as we have moved from pensions, where payments are guaranteed, to defined contribution plans, where returns are uncertain (Zelinsky, 2004). Hours of work for white collar employees who are exempt from wage and hour laws has increased steadily (Fuentes and Leamer, 2019), and evidence of the negative effects of workplace stress and insecurity on employee health continues to accumulate (Ganster and Rosen, 2013).

There is no accepted explanation as to why this has happened. Economists' arguments, not surprisingly, point to factors that have lowered the market price of labor, such as low-wage Chinese competitors or technology that may reduce the need for labor (Acemoglu *et al.*, 2016). These factors explain relatively little of the overall decline in job quality. What they have in common is that they see the employer as a black box with no decisions to make because market wages are falling.

When we look at the workplace, though, we see employers making use of new practices over time that cut labor costs (Goldstein, 2012). The most important of these has been with the very notion of employment and jobs themselves. There is no doubt that pushing work out of the organization and its internal labor markets and into competitive labor markets with temps and outsourcing defined broadly has been a major factor in shifting work from good jobs to worse, lower-paying jobs (Bernhardt *et al.*, 2016). This includes not only off shoring to lower-wage countries, but also within the US, as David Weil's identification of 'the fissured workplace' has demonstrated (Weil, 2014).

117

Outsourcing that drives work down to low-wage, individual contractors exists even in the hi-tech world of Silicon Valley (Hyman, 2018).

Arguably more important than outsourcing in recent years is the move to what we refer to as the liquid workforce, a phenomenon that has not been considered in any detail in the academic literature. The idea here is that employers basically turn over the basic task of talent management – getting the right workers in the right jobs at the right time – to vendors who in turn rely on the outside labor market to give their employer clients what they need when they need it. The 'liquid' notion comes from the idea that the client asks those vendors to turn up the supply when demand is up and dial it back down when demand falls so that the employer always has just the right amount of labor that they need. As we will see below, the largest component of that workforce is leased employees who are brought in from other organizations to staff jobs that used to be held by the organization's own employees.

As to the connection to business strategy and overall business performance, the notion of a liquid workforce provides a substantial advantage when business needs change because it eliminates the talent management challenge. They cannot be short of talent that would hinder business expansion in this conceptualization, nor could they have too much talent that would lead to costly layoffs. All that is pushed onto vendors and, ultimately, the labor market. Employers do not need to plan or anticipate what their needs for talent will be, developing talent to meet those needs. They simply wait to see what they need and have vendors provide it. Nor do they have to worry about having too many employees should business decline. The vendors just take it away when it is no longer needed.

The question is whether this conceptualization of the liquid workforce is actually true. We first describe the nature and extent of this new workforce, especially the complexity of how it operates. Then we consider how likely it is that the approach delivers on its promise of providing cost and flexibility benefits for employers.

Employment practices as a choice

Despite the talk of 'gig' work, all but about 6 percent of people in the work-force are employees, a number that has barely budged in recent decades.[1] Employment is still what matters. Getting the right number of those employees in the right place at the right time – the practical and common definition of talent management – remains the fundamental task for employers (Cappelli, 2008).

There have been two basic approaches for doing so (Cappelli and Keller, 2014). The first is to internalize it, hire and then develop employees to fit various roles, deciding how broad and interchangeable their capabilities are, adjusting the speed of development along with retraining, creating career paths aligned with that development, and so forth. That is the model developed in the US after WWII and what is still described in textbooks. The second is to external-ize it, relying on the labor market to fill positions whenever they become vacant or whenever we need different ones. These two choices also echo the famous question about what constitutes the boundary of a firm, what should be done inside and outside.[2]

There is no doubt that some employers, especially smaller ones, always used the latter approach (DeVaro, 2020), but there is also little doubt that larger employers have moved away from the former (Cappelli, 1998). Employers lay off employees more quickly than in previous generations and do so all the way up through the executive levels (Todd, 2019). They also do so not just when business is down but when companies want to cut old approaches, dropping the employees associated with those approaches, and hire new employees to move into new ones (Sucher and Gupta, 2018). The dream of being able to do this seamlessly – cut off workers as soon as there is nothing for them to do, start new ones up as soon as there is – has come to fruition in the promise of a liquid workforce.

---

[1] Self-reported data from the US Current Employee Survey actually shows a decline over the last 20 years to 6.3 percent of the US workforce. Administrative data, such as those filing IRS 1099 forms for non-employee compensation, have risen over this period, to 11.3 percent in 2012, the most recent reported data, but a majority of those filings are for transient experiences, such as selling on eBay (see Abraham et al., 2018 for a summary). Outside the US, the numbers are greater: more than 15 percent of workers are self-employed independent contractors in industrial-ized countries (OECD, 2018).

[2] For the classic account, see Coase, 1937. For the application to employment and the transaction cost focus, see Williamson, 1981.

When we look at corporate practices that help explain this churning, Charles Handy (2007) described a model of a flexible workforce where there was a 'core' employee group that was protected from the ups and downs of business needs (and layoffs) by a 'periphery' of contractors and non-employee workers whose ranks would rise and fall with changes in demand. In 1984, John Atkinson broadened the story by noting that while it was possible to be flexible in the manner that Handy described – 'numerical flexibility' – it was also possible to be flexible by being able to redeploy cross-skilled employees to meet changing needs (Atkinson, 1984). Cappelli and Neumark (2004) looked at which path US companies were actually taking, though they found them pursing both aspects of flexibility at the same time. That included retraining and using temps but also layoffs of regular employees, contrary to what the periphery models suggested.

Uber and its business model allowed for numerical flexibility on a permanent basis and created a shock wave that went far beyond the ride-sharing industry. Here was a perfect liquid workforce that was only paid when there was something right at that moment that they needed to do. Otherwise, they waited, with no pay, and at no cost to Uber. The idea that companies could have a workforce that only had to be paid right when they needed it – turn it on then turn it off – was extremely attractive to employers.

It was not possible in existing companies to move completely to contractors, but the idea of keeping employment and wages down and making up the inevitable staffing gap with Uber-like workers who did not get paid when there was nothing to do sounded extremely attractive. Recruitment Process Outsourcing vendors jumped on that model. They use the term 'full cycle' engagement to describe their ideal arrangement, where they manage the balance of hiring, layoffs, and especially non-employee workers to ensure that the client has just the minimum number of workers needed to get the work done each day even when business goes up and down.

The overall goal is to cut employment costs as much as possible and optimize, more specifically minimize, the number of employees needed. The conceptual appeal of these ideas to leaders focused on cost control and accustomed to optimization thinking is very powerful. It is much the same way in which MBA students might be taught to handle supply chain problems in production operations.

The new liquid workforce model relies heavily on non-employee workers. If you threw a dart into any large organization, there is a good chance you would hit someone working there who was not an employee of that organization.

They could be employees of staffing firms working for the client on a contract, individual independent contractors, employees of a vendor who has taken over some function like running the cafeteria, or some other arrangement. An important aspect of this new liquid workforce is that it does not look at all like a typical workforce. But neither does it look like the 'gig' workers at Uber.

The liquid workforce infrastructure.

The main manifestation of the liquid workforce idea is not independent contractors or even 'gig' workers (however they are defined). It involves workers who are employees of other organizations, such as staffing firms, vendors, and so forth. The term for this used by the Bureau of Labor Statistics now is 'leased employees' – those employed by vendors but working at a client's location for at least a year (US Department of Labor, 1996). The size of that 'liquid' workforce is considerable. In 2001, Cappelli and Keller asked in a Census survey how many workers who were not their employees were performing work in establishments on a peak day, and the answer was already about 20 percent (Cappelli and Keller, 2013). More recent estimates come from a variety of sources and suggest a substantial increase since then. For example, a survey of corporate budgets found that non-employee workers accounted for 32 percent of the total budgeting for labor (Ardent Partners, 2017). A survey by Kelly Services found that 27 percent of their client's workforces were made up of these workers[3] while Ernst & Young's client survey reported businesses expecting it to be 30 percent of their workforce in 2020 (Ernst & Young, 2017). Consider the food and hospitality company Aramark, which has contracts covering 89 percent of the Fortune 500 companies and 2,000 healthcare facilities using over two million workers to do so. It has only 215,000 of its own employees.[4]

It would be a monumental task to negotiate, monitor compliance, and enforce individual contracts for almost one-third of one's workforce. Instead, employers turn to vendors to do this for them. Here is where the liquid workforce becomes remarkably complex, and the administrative challenges of navigating through it appear to be quite challenging.

---

[3]   Contributing to the confusion, Kelly refers to these workers as 'free agents,' but they appear to actually be non-employees of the client: Kelly Services, 2017.

[4]   This information comes from the company's website.

At the apex of this model with the largest companies are what used to be referred to as temporary help agencies with prominent names like Adecco, Randstadt, and Manpower. This industry had only 20,000 employees in 1956, focused on clerical and factory jobs, and stepping in for workers on vacation or who were off work with illnesses. By 1990, it had one million employees – 1 percent of the labor force, and 2.7 percent by 2000 where it has more or less remained (see, e.g., Luo, Mann and Holden, 2010). Outside the US, the numbers are considerably larger as temp operations were one of the few ways to get around the long-term commitments of regular employment (Kentley Insights, 2021). Companies have their own internal temp operations as well, which are referred to as 'on call workers.' These are employees, but they only work on the days when they are needed. The numbers here are equal in size to the temp industry (Abraham and Houseman, 2022). This is still only about 5 percent of the workforce, though, so it will take a few more steps to get close to the 30 percent of the corporate workforce.

We know a fair bit about how temporary help operates and how employers use it. Clients of temp agencies stopped reporting some decades ago that temp workers per se were cheaper, but they may help keep labor costs down, especially in tight labor markets where it is hard to fill positions. Rather than raising wages to attract applicants to fill open vacancies, which would then have to be increased for existing workers as well, the clients engage agencies to fill their vacancies with non-employees who can be paid more without raising the wages for all employees.[5] In other words, price discrimination: We effectively have two wage scales, one for the employees who are embedded in the company and the other for workers who move across employers to staff vacancies, which is facilitated and kept separate by agencies.

A context where this is a permanent feature is nursing, where hospitals and other healthcare providers routinely use 'travel nurses' who come into staff long-term vacancies. Estimates put the revenues of travel nurse companies at $5.3 billion, a non-trivial amount. The average gross profit margin of those companies was 26 percent despite paying travel nurses significantly more per hour than staff nurses (Staffing Industry Analysts (SIA), 2019). In other words, per nurse, it is considerably more expensive to use travel nurses. It is not the case that staffing requirements for nurses are especially variable such that supplemental nurses are needed to manage the uncertainty.

---

[5] Nothing in the law prohibits employers from paying otherwise equivalent workers doing the same work differently unless the pattern appears driven by demographic patterns protected by non-discrimination laws and regulations. It is the likely reaction from those paid less that stops most employers from doing so.

Why don't healthcare providers just raise their wages to fill their vacancies rather than keep paying the higher costs of travel nurses? Because they want to avoid raising wages for all their nurses, which they would likely have to do. Similar arrangements are also used for doctors, IT professionals, and indeed any standardized job where an experienced person could walk in and perform it proficiently.[6] An analysis within individual companies found that where temporary help was more expensive than employees – as with travel nurses and doctors – it still prevented the employer from having to raise wages for all employees in those roles in order to fill standing vacancies (Houseman, Kalleberg and Erickcek, 2003). Temps could be paid more than regular employees and still hold down average labor costs.

The plethora of vendors

Staffing agencies that began in temporary help have branched out to include 'professional' staffing firms with a white-collar focus, such as accounting, and 'commercial' firms that provide a full range of workers to clients.[7] These vendors in the talent acquisition segment account for almost half of the roughly $500 billion human capital industry, as noted above. The biggest of the staffing companies provide temporary help, leased employees, and in some cases direct hires like Adecco and Manpower. Their gross profit margins are 25 percent (Wallins, 2020), not bad for a reasonably simple business with few barriers to entry.

Among the lesser-known categories, 'managed service providers' (MSPs) may be the most important player in the liquid workforce. They sound like outsourcers but are more accurately described as 'vendors on premises' because they do the work at their client locations. That work is central to their client's operations, and they work extremely closely with the client's employees. They take over outsourced functions, typically in IT as with managing data centers. They differ from what is now referred to as 'on-demand outsourcing,' which provides services as requested and bills for those services in response to need, in that they are there permanently.

---

[6]   Survey of Temporary Physician Staffing Trends (2017) *Staff Care*.
[7]   This descriptive material comes from Staffing Industry Associates, North American Staffing Industry Company Survey 2019.

To illustrate, a company that uses outside legal counsel might have an arrangement where the outside law firm responds to requests from the company and bills the client for that work. This would be an on-demand outsourcer. If the client has the outside law firm on retainer, however, the firm does whatever legal work the client requires for one set fee, like a managed service provider and similar to the old Health Maintenance Organizations (HMOs) in healthcare: you pay one fee, and they take care of all your health needs. Another difference is that the MSP is typically doing the work in your location, often working alongside other functions. The on-demand outsourcer may do the work elsewhere or come to your site to do it.

Although the MSP industry is mainly in IT and fields that intersect IT, it is a big industry, creating more than $250 billion in revenue. IBM appears to be the largest provider, but five of the 10 largest of these companies are based in India, and much of the work is 'offshored' there (EM360, 2019). (It is not a coincidence that those five also dominate the list of H1-B visa users in the US.) It is not a highly concentrated industry, though, and beyond the top 10, it is unlikely that anyone outside the IT industry will have heard of the next 500 in size.

IT work in many and perhaps most companies is now deeply integrated in the finance function, customer relationships, supply chains, and so forth. Starting with enterprise resource planning systems, IT is also seen as the backbone of companies because it integrates so many parts of the operation (Thompson, 2020). MSPs therefore reflect something about the claim that organizations are 'hollowed out' with central aspects of their work done by someone else. In this case, the work is still done onsite but by workers employed by another organization.

SOW or 'statement of work' providers are vendors who manage specific projects and the contractors who perform them for clients. A master supplier or master vendor, in contrast, takes charge of all of the non-employee workers, often subcontracting out client work to other vendors who supply the contractors, temps, and individual workers. They are like a general contractor at a building site.

'Payrolling' is similar to 'professional employee organizations,' where the vendor becomes the employer of record, except in this context it is directed at seasonal workers, contractors and project-based work, and direct-hire temps rather than one's own employees. 'Direct to consumer' arrangements are what are most appropriately referred to as gig work, where there is an electronic platform like Uber that matches contract workers to clients, taking a fee in the process. Aside from Uber and Lift, the vendor 'Task Rabbit' may be the best-known of these arrangements. They match providers and clients for household tasks and handyman projects like fixing window screens.

The biggest of these gig operations by far, however, are in the domestic support business – home healthcare, house cleaning, babysitting, etc. The largest of the platforms, Care.com, claims 34 million 'members,' evenly split between clients and individual providers, yet it is an extremely decentralized industry with thousands of platforms (Mateescu and Ticona, 2020). Collectively, these gig companies dwarf the ride-sharing industry.

Finally, 'Master Suppliers' are vendors who take over and organize one of these channels, typically temporary help. They create and manage networks of smaller vendors, essentially subcontractors, to provide all the temp workers for larger clients.

These human capital vendors have also moved into providing hires for regular employment (SIA, 2019). Most temp arrangements also allow clients to pay a fee and hire the temp workers into permanent jobs, essentially to try them out first – 'temp-to-perm' or contract-to-hire. They are an important source of regular employees. A recent survey of companies with more than 1000 employees found that 10 percent of their temp agency workers were turned into regular, full-time employees (see SIA, 2017), therefore constituting a much more substantial share of total hiring. These 'direct hire' offerings operate like retained and contingent search where the vendor recruits candidates, and the client makes the hiring decision. Last but not least, recruitment process outsourcers are vendors that take over the entire recruiting function, in some cases including hiring, for their clients.

Even a startup operation with little or no human resource function can quickly jump into this world of alternative work using vendors to dial up a solution to a project, bring in a work group one week to handle a new task and a different group the next week to handle another. Vendors in this industry are now advertising a 'worforce-as-a-service' business, where the client needs virtually no employment infrastructure or human resources of any kind. They just ping the vendor who delivers the type of workers needed, perhaps going a step further and scoping out for the client what workers and how many the client needs, and then delivering and managing them.[8] Behind the scenes, there is

---

[8] For an example of this claim, see https://www.workmarket.com/blog/workforce
-service-arrived#gsc.tab=0.

likely a stack of vendors – master vendor overseeing a statement of work provider who manages one-off-projects, a payrolling firm that manage long-term temps, a sea of small temp agencies providing the temps, etc.

A new development tracked by Staffing Industry Analysts is the 'Hiring Platform' model, a kind of automated staffing firm in the direct hire market. These vendors maintain a database of candidates, much like an executive search firm might, that provides assessments and vetting of candidates that clients might want. Data science-driven matching algorithms tell clients which candidates are the best fit for their openings. Like executive search firms, they charge a fee based on the annual starting salary of a candidate they place. The big difference is that the process is automated and therefore much cheaper than the traditional arrangement (Nurthen, 2020).

The PEO model

It is also possible for a company to outsource its own employees. Professional employer organizations (PEOs) will take over the legal obligations for the company's own employees, becoming the 'employer of record,' leasing the company's own workers back to it. Initially, PEOs were a regulatory dodge: If a company's regular employees were technically 'employed' by someone else and leased back to the company, it was possible for the company to provide much more generous healthcare and retirement benefits to those who remained employees, mainly the executives.

That loophole was closed in the 1980s, but other advantages remained (Katz, 1999). PEOs were seen as a way to avoid litigation costs: If the government took legal action against a company as an employer, or indeed if the employees sued, the PEO as the employer of record was liable, not the company. Many PEOs were small operations, and if they were hit by a big lawsuit, they would simply fold up into bankruptcy. As they got bigger, they were no longer willing to take on that liability. Now they take out Employment Practices Liability Insurance, the costs of which is built into their charges. What kind of legal challenges they will absorb or indemnify their employer clients against is a negotiated topic. Taking on legal risk is no longer a compelling reason for using them, however. About 3.7 million workers are employed by PEOs, which makes them larger than the temp industry (NAPEO, 2021).

The PEO takes responsibility for most of the administrative aspects of employment, such as payroll processing, managing benefits, filing employment taxes, and so forth and may be more efficient at doing so than the original employer. That employer, now the 'client,' would not have the authority to supervise and direct those workers, who are now employed by the PEO. But they typically decide to become a 'co-employer' along with the PEO in order to do so. With that decision, they share liability for employment-related violations and litigation.

The main benefit from using PEOs for the client, according to its industry group, is that it eliminates the need to hire HR people. It shifts that cost from the 'employment' column to 'current expenses.' On the other hand, the clients are still paying for HR, just not one they control. It also breaks the control the organization has over direct relationships with employees, including supervisory relationships. Employers pay for this service, of course, from 2 to 12 percent of payroll (NAPEO, 2021).

There are other costs as well, associated with the fact that human resources delivered by a PEO is an arm's-length arrangement that almost by definition has to offer standardized and bare-bones content. To illustrate, consider a typical employment relationship where an employee is having performance problems that lead to some kind of an impasse with the immediate supervisor. We would hope that an on-site HR manager might be able to offer an objective and professional opinion, step in if the conflict becomes personal, and figure out if the supervisor might be at fault and need some help. It is difficult to see how anything like that could happen with a 1-800 phone number to a call center handling HR issues for 100 companies. It is just not possible in that circumstance for even an experienced representative to know enough about the culture of an organization, the history of the relationship between supervisor and subordinate, and so forth to work out the problem.

PEOs also set the rules for issues like dismissing employees and employee discipline and pick the insurance carriers and other providers of services for employees across their clients. No doubt it is possible for a client to customize some of those attributes for their workers, at a price, but the client loses considerable control over the running of their organization because the PEO both sets the rules and administers them. If we think it is important to have distinctive ways of competing, then we need distinctive management practices and cultures to support that. Certainly, there are small employers who could not afford to have any human resources presence in the absence of a PEO, and others would have objectively bad human resources. But for others, outsourcing it is not without costs.

The costs of the liquid workforce

Is it cheaper for a client to push all these human resource tasks out to vendors? It would be surprising if paying the overheads, insurance, and other charges of vendors as well as the wages of the employees they provide is much cheaper than employing those workers directly, remembering that even though a company may have eliminated some of its own HR staff, it is still paying for it via the vendors.

There are two other claims for this approach, though, that are not about up-front cost savings.

The first, the basic idea that outsourcing something makes it easier to do and cheaper because real expert vendors will be better at it, bumps up against the complexity of the vendor market and the transactions within it. That begins with the fact that clients have to negotiate an agreement with each vendor and then also manage the contract that results. To manage the plethora of vendors in the liquid workforce space, clients have had to create a new administrative function, 'vendor management.' It has its own industry certifications for managers tasked with handling vendors and its own professional associations to help those managers keep pace with what the vendors are doing. Perhaps not surprisingly, there are now vendors to whom a company can outsource the management of the other vendors to whom it has outsourced the actual work.[9] The notion that we save resources by not having to handle the administrative functions we outsource is mitigated at least somewhat by having to create another administrative function to manage those outsourced arrangements.[10]

Vendor management is far from a perfect solution, however. An Ernst & Young survey finds that the respondents in 21 percent of the organizations surveyed say they do not even know who has primary responsibility for recruiting their liquid workforce, and 25 percent do not know who has primary

---

[9]   For a 'pros and cons' discussion of outsourcing vendor management, see Overby, 2016.

[10]   Most companies now have software to assist the process – Vendor Management Solutions or VMS. The survey data above indicates that it is the most used 'vendor' in the liquid workforce panoply. The main task of the software is to take a client's work needs – e.g., we need five workers with these attributes – and distribute them across the various vendors with whom it works to see who can fill them. The software keeps track of who has delivered what, which requisitions are unfilled, and provides data and analysis measuring the performance of different vendors, mainly time to fill vacancies.

responsibility for managing them. For those who do know, only 20 percent say that HR is responsible.[11] Vendor management functions typically negotiate the contract with the vendors, but line managers seem to be responsible for managing the contracts: the IT department is responsible for its non-employees, as in the finance department for its, and so forth. Their managers have to specify how many, what kind, and when they are needed and, of course, someone has to 'manage' these workers from outside.

Lauren Weber's account in the *Wall Street Journal* of what is required just to manage one type of contractors – programmers – in the computer gaming industry should give one pause. Each contract, therefore each contractor, has to be 'managed' by a current employee to make certain that the person is actually doing what needs to be done (Weber, 2017). That task is typically added to the list of things that regular employees have to do. It well may make sense to have the managers who are responsible for the work to be the ones managing those non-employee workers. But it also hides much of the administrative costs of using them by pushing their supervision onto line managers. Unless clients of liquid workforce vendors outsource all their hiring and staffing, they must maintain at least some of those capabilities and infrastructure.

Then consider the mass of contracts involved in a typical liquid workforce. Let's assume the client has a vendor management function whose job it is to set out the requirements for vendors. An operating division may engage a master supplier agreement with a big vendor, the equivalent of a general contractor in construction, who will fight out an agreement with our vendor management function. The master supplier will in turn engage a number of 'statement of work' subcontractors to find particular sets of workers with unique skills, just as the general contractor engages subcontractors. The statement of work vendors have their own subcontractors, often overseas firms scanning LinkedIn and other online sources to find contract workers or potential leased employees.

Each one of these contracts and sets of vendors has its own principle-agent incentive issues, and each has its own infrastructure and administrative costs.

---

[11] Most companies have a 'vendor management office,' which oversees contracts per se and in recent years has concentrated on the financial risk such contracts might pose. Forrester Research provides one of the few estimates of its use from a 2011 survey finding that 47 percent of companies had one https://www.forrester.com/Building+And+Enhancing+A+VMO+That+Will+Change+Your+Company/-/E-EVE2581. No doubt the tasks these offices perform vary, but they seem focused on drafting and negotiating the contracts rather than managing them.

At the extreme, vendors often find that it is not in their interest to meet the demands of a particular client – something bigger comes along and demands their resources – or they may find that a deal is not profitable and want to renege on it. Yes, they have contracts, but contracts do not guarantee compliance: paying the damages and moving on is standard advice, which is rarely in the client's interests.

The bigger issue behind contract disputes of all kinds is with interpreting the requirements of the contract. This is a much bigger challenge in the liquid workforce model because what is being delivered is workers, and they are about as non-standard as one could get. Clients have an interest in getting the very best workers sent to them by the vendors – experienced, conscientious, easy to work with. Such workers also cost the vendor more to engage. The vendors have the opposite interest, to deliver workers who are cheaper for them to hire, other things being equal, that improves their margins, and those workers tend to be less experienced, less conscientious, more difficult to work with, and so forth. Then there is the quirky issue of 'fit.' A client may not like a worker sent to perform particular tasks, but if they want them replaced, the vendor has to find something else for that worker to do as well as find a suitable replacement. They do not want to have workers just 'sitting on the bench' waiting for an assignment. Even if the vendors want to deliver exactly the workers the client wants, those workers may not be available when the client wants them.

The construction business has some clear similarities with the liquid workforce model. Construction management companies are the equivalent of the vendor management overseeing architects and general contractors, who then in turn oversee their own contracts with subcontractors. In this industry, big projects inevitably end up with some or all of the parties in court claiming contract violations (Eccles, 1981).

Unlike commercial construction, legal fights among the hierarchy of contractors in the liquid workforce appear to be relatively rare, so industry insiders say, possibly because they hash out extremely specific and restrictive contracts covering all contingencies. It is also the case that these parties hope to be together for many years, much longer than a building project, so their interest in fighting to the death over disputes is muted. It is also easier to 'fix' problems: 'you sent me worthless workers' is easier to resolve (replace them) than 'you poured the wrong type of concrete.'

Next, we come to the 'flexibility' part of the liquid workforce claim, specifically that it is easy to dial up and down the size and composition of the workforce by just having the supplier do it. But clients pay for that ability, and how much of that ability they actually have depends on the contract they negotiate. It is possible that the vendor may be able to move leased employees to some other client should a client want its workforce dialed down, but that is not always the case. The factors that lead to layoffs are often common across clients of these vendors, in which case the vendor is also stuck with excess labor and the costs of having them. Employers do not seem to have much difficulty in dialing down their own employee workforce with layoffs, which does make one wonder how much better the liquid approach could be on that dimension. The problem is just as acute with dialing up a workforce: companies often do that at the same time as other clients, making it impossible for the vendor to make everyone happy. In short, clients cannot simply have their vendors bring them more or fewer workers without paying a price for doing so.

The first constraint in making these adjustments for the client is that everything is subject to the contractual operating agreement: if the adjustments are not already outlined in the agreement, any change has to be renegotiated. Renegotiations have costs, not just the time and effort to engage them but 'hold-up' costs: If a vendor is in the middle of a project for a client, and the client wants to change it, the option of starting over with another vendor is unpalatable, so the client's vendor can charge the client a lot to make changes. It is the same problem a client faces in making changes to an agreement with building contractors working on a client's home. When there is a hierarchy of vendors, each of which has operating costs that have to be paid for, each one having a contract that has to be negotiated, the administrative costs will be considerable. In other words, the more flexibility the client wants to secure, the more they have to pay for it at the beginning of the agreement.

Oliver Williamson's Nobel Prize-winning work outlined why organizations would not want to operate this way, with a mass of contracts that have to be negotiated and renegotiated, especially for workers whose skills are idiosyncratic and their performance is not a given. The flexible nature of employment is much better suited to these problems that generate transaction costs – conflicts, monitoring agreements for compliance, negotiations and potential delays in negotiating them, and so forth (Simon, 1951).

What we know about organizational effectiveness is also that it takes some time for groups to learn to work together, even if the individual participants are skilled and experienced. The idea that we can throw a group of strangers together and get a well-functioning team is simply not true. Especially when we are performing similar tasks repeatedly – building hospitals, writing particular insurance, dealing with the same customers – we get better at it over time. These are the conclusions from organizational learning, especially about the tacit knowledge that comes from experience, where that knowledge can be very specific (Huckman and Pisano, 2006). Surgery teams, for example, develop knowledge specific to the pairings of individual doctors and staff: change them up, and outcomes get worse. Established teams will therefore beat new teams, other things being equal. The idea that we can change up vendors, bring in new workers, and just expect them to be effective sounds like an assumption necessary in optimization models, and it is a myth.

One of the best of the surveys asking companies why they use a liquid work-force was carried out by the Economist Intelligence Unit (2019).[12] The survey focuses specifically on gig workers where the definition is a little imprecise but it seems to include non-employee workers, and there may be differences in the US (75 percent of the respondents) and UK employers (25 percent) who responded to the survey. But flexibility leads the way in their answers.

What the respondents meant when they said that flexibility was their moti-vation for using these practices is less clear. A revealing statistic is that 32 percent of the respondents agree that their company cannot meet its strategic objectives without these gig workers, while 48 percent were unsure. Strategic objectives are plans for the future, which means that these companies are building plans that require these alternative workers. In other words, they are not used simply to meet unforseen demands. That means that the companies are setting their own staffing levels below what they believe will be necessary to operate their businesses, which creates the need for a permanent, alternative workforce.

Whether this approach is actually cheaper is a very difficult question of inter-nal accounting for the companies to answer as it depends on what is included in the costs. The respondents reported unique problems with using these workers that were not present with their own employees. Eighty percent of the respondents in this survey reported that it required a different approach to manage these liquid workers than their own employees. They also agreed that using them took more management resources (58 percent) and involved more risk (55 percent). Twenty-nine percent of the respondents report that the ben-efits of using these workers were offset by the additional administrative costs,

---

[12]   The term 'gig' is not defined in the survey. While it includes individual con-tract workers, the responses indicate that staffing agencies are the most impor-tant source for finding these workers. The fact that over 58 percent of responding companies say that more than 20 percent of the workforces are made up of these workers suggests that the answers include a broad definition of non-employee workers.

vs. 23 percent who did not agree; 31 percent said that the benefits were offset by the additional risk, vs. 26 who did not agree (in both cases the remaining responses were 'neutral' and 'don't know').

Remarkably, given what we know about the difficulty in making teams work, 71 percent of the respondents reported that they bring in these gig workers as individuals and then assemble them into teams managed by their own employees.

Management challenges

Where vendors are the employer of record of the liquid workforce, the workers onsite for clients are only partially responsible to the client even when the client is a co-employer. All the practices that employers can use to motivate and engage their regular employees, from compensation and benefits to organizational culture to effective supervisors, are largely off the table with the liquid workforce because those practices are driven by the vendor or the PEO if there is one. What that means in practice is that the organization where these workers do their jobs has largely given up on managing them. The 'borrowed servant' doctrine in employment law allows the client to direct the work being performed by those liquid workforce workers, but that does not include the broader practices of management, such as rewarding employees, setting performance targets and measuring them, and so forth.[13]

What it means for employees to have these 'split' authority structures is not well known. There is an older literature on 'boundary spanners' such as sales employees who spend more time with clients than with their own employer, highlighting the difficulties when obligations conflict (Tushman, 1977), and an equivalent literature on 'dual allegiance' for unionized employees who had obligations to their union and to their employer (Sherer and Morishima, 1989). What it means, especially for 'leased' employees who work full time and for more than a year onsite and who are employed by an organization that arguably has more power over them but that they see less, remains unexplored.[14]

---

[13]   State laws govern the application of common law era borrowed servant doctrines as well as whether the client becomes a 'dual employer.' The main relevance in employment law is who the employee can sue and who is responsible if they are injured on the job.

[14]   The one exception to this conclusion is the several studies examining employee commitment of temp workers, which has been reported to be as high as for regular

Assuming that the liquid workforce model means the transfer of some jobs from one organization to a vendor, the net effect depends on what the jobs are like in each organization. For some tasks, such as accounting, law, and management consulting, outsourcing means pushing those jobs to professional service firms. It is true that doing so eliminates the possibility that accountants, lawyers, and strategic planners will ever get to be operating executives in those corporations, but they may well be better paid accountants, lawyers, and consultants with more autonomy than if they had been in the corporations.

The changes that get the most attention and that involve more employees are at the bottom of the corporate pay scales – janitors, food service workers, gardeners, and so forth. In the corporations, employees in those jobs had similar benefits to other employees in part encouraged to do so by IRS regulations and laws like the Affordable Care Act, which prohibit having fancier healthcare benefits for some employees and not others. A janitorial service that only does that work might be less likely to offer benefits like healthcare to its employees or have compensation systems that tie janitor pay at least in part to the pay of higher paid employees. When a bank or other large corporation outsources its janitorial work, it is quite likely that the individuals doing that work will be paid less and have less access to benefits.

The other consequence is that career paths become more limited. It was possible to work one's way up from the shop floor at companies like UPS when virtually all positions were filled from within by people who began as loaders or drivers (Hoover, 2018). But even if every manager position was filled that way, there were only so many lower-level employees and so few open manager positions that it was hard to describe it as a reasonable career path. As a contemporary example, Walmart fills 75 percent of its store manager positions from the hourly workforce, a commendable number. But there are roughly 470 employees per store manager, and given turnover rates, the base rate probability of any new store associate becoming a store manager is likely more than 1000 to one.[15]

One way to see whether the liquid workforce jobs are worse than the jobs for regular employees in the client organizations is that we regularly and routinely see workers move from temp or staffing roles into permanent jobs at

<hr>

employees. The complication with those studies, however, is that we cannot tell if the temps are independent contractors or leased employees of agencies.

[15]   See, e.g., https://corporate.walmart.com/newsroom/company-facts.

their clients, as noted above, but we do not hear of staffing companies hiring employees of their clients into their jobs.[16]

The decision to move toward a Liquid Workforce model also creates clear path dependence that makes it difficult to go back even if circumstances change, an irony for the cause of flexibility. Consider a company in the late 1980s that made a decision to bring in workers from a staffing agency to take over some function such as clerical tasks in a division. To recognize some immediate cost savings, once it makes that move, it cuts the recruiters, trainers, and HR staff from that division.

Suppose years later it decides that the cost gap between its internal pay and what it is paying the vendors has disappeared. What does it do to go back to having employees? It would have to bring back some recruiters, some trainers, develop and put in place management systems for the employees, and hire human resource people to run them. These are 'switching costs' that make it difficult to change back. Given its financial accounting system, costs would all need to be offset by revenue the year they are incurred because they count as current expenses, even though they are an investment in the future. A thoughtful observer might wonder whether some of those costs could be outsourced. It is possible. For example, RPO firms could staff the business for the company, but the more parts the company outsources, the more it defeats the reason for moving back to employees.

Public policy also facilitates the liquid workforce approach with immigration practices. There are at least 23 different categories under which foreign workers can come to the US for temporary work, bringing in about one million workers per year on temporary assignments. These include separate programs to bring in fashion models (which Melania Trump made famous), entertainers, athletes, and the best-known H1-B (for college-level jobs) and H-2B (for shorter or peak-load employment) visas and other kinds of immigration categories allowing foreign workers to fill jobs in the US. Employers interested in accessing these workers have to promise that they will pay market wages. They only have to assert that they could not find US workers for these jobs if they hope to bring in foreign workers permanently.[17]

---

[16]   According to the 2016 Workforce Solutions Buyers Survey, the median temp-to-perm conversion ratio among large contingent workforce buyers was 10% for North American companies. http://cwstrategies.staffingindustry.com/temp-to-perm-conversion-ratio/.

[17]   For details, see H-1B Specialty Occupations, DOD Cooperative Research and Development Project Workers, and Fashion Models. US Citizenship and

Although these workers are employees, they are not like US employees in that the employer who sponsors them can make them pay a penalty if they quit, in which case they must return to their home country unless they can find a new employer to take them on before they leave their original employer (US Department of Labor, 2021).

Virtually all of the H1-B visas are for IT workers and most all of those bring in workers from India.[18] Although they are sometimes confused with the super smart temporary workers (those are O-1 Visas), these workers typically perform mid-level tasks that hundreds of thousands of US workers are also carrying out. The biggest employers are disproportionately Indian firms or those with Indian outsourcing operations where the H1-B temps perform tasks for US clients and then continue to do so when they return to India. Cognizant Technology alone employs roughly 10 percent of all H1-B workers (Costa and Hira, 2020).

There are many issues about these programs – is it really true, for example, that employers could not find workers to do these jobs even in the Great Recession? – but perhaps the biggest is that they hold the labor market back from adjusting. In the 1960s, for example, the program was used mainly to bring in nurses. As a result, nursing wages were held down, which reduced the incentive to expand nursing education, and made it less attractive for US workers to enter the field (Masselink and Jones, 2014).

Effects on employees

There are two bodies of research evidence on the effects of using these alternative workforces, one with a psychology base, one with an economics base. Of course they ignore each other, but they reach a quite similar conclusion – that the effects are not positive for organizations.

Immigration Services, Washington, D.C. https://www.uscis.gov/working-in-the-united-states/temporary-workers/h-1b-specialty-occupations-dod-cooperative-research-and-development-project-workers-and-fashion.

[18] According to the 2020 H-1B visa report that lists the top H-1B visa sponsors by NAICS Industry, the top two industries were 'Computer systems design and related services (313,857 Labor Condition Application (LCA)s for H1B Visa)' and 'Management, scientific, and technical consulting services (44,393 LCAs).' https://www.myvisajobs.com/Reports/2020-H1B-Visa-Category.aspx?T=IN.

The complication in knowing is that the decision to use temps or staffing firms is not random. Something about companies causes some to use them and some not, so sorting out the effect of that decision per se on outcomes is quite difficult. The psychology studies look within companies, which gets around that problem a bit. They uniformly find negative effects on the temps themselves, that is, being second-class citizens in their organizations (see, e.g., Boyce *et al.*, 2007). More interesting are the results that using temps depresses the job-related attitudes of regular employees, such as commitment to the organization by making them see themselves more like temps. Turnover rises as well (Broschak and Davis-Blake, 2006). A similar study found that this mechanism also reduces overall productivity and service quality of stores (Eldor and Cappelli, 2021). The research in economics finds negative relationships with productivity and declines in innovation (Cappellari, Dell'Aringa and Leonardi, 2012; Kleinknecht, van Schaik and Zhou, 2014). Finally, a recent study undermines the notion that getting rid of temps is easy, showing that even when temps come to the end of their contract – when they and everyone knows they are leaving – their departure still has negative effects on organizational performance (De Stefano, Bonet and Camuffo, 2019).

Many of the factors that appear to be associated with a good employment relationship have to do with the notion of 'social exchange': by taking care of its employees a company creates a sense of obligation that would make its employees feel like looking after the company's interests, which is especially important when employees are not being supervised and have discretion over how to behave (Settoon, Bennett and Liden, 1996).

The idea of social exchange plays out in several of these contemporary psychological concepts, all of which have been studied and documented many times. The relevant fact about them is that it is very difficult to imagine how a client would have the ability to generate that reciprocity and sense of obligation with workers who are not their employees because they simply do not control much that happens to them.

The idea of *perception of organizational support* (POS) and the considerable evidence for it is that where employees feel that the organization both supports them and recognizes that they are contributing, they feel the need to reciprocate. A distinction from the general idea of social exchange is the fact that if the employer recognizes and appreciates the employee's performance, then the employee perceives that they are already in a social exchange relationship: I contribute, you support me, and so forth (the seminal article here is arguably Eisenberger *et al.*, 1986).

Leader-member exchange is the notion first that the more important relationship in organizations is an interpersonal one between supervisors and their subordinates and second that the relationship is established over time, in part through an exchange of information flowing from the subordinate about things like what they are seeing in the workplace and support of various kinds flowing from the supervisor to the subordinate. The better those relationships are, the better job performance will be (see Graen and Scandura, 1987).

What these concepts articulate is the variety of ways in which employers can influence the behavior and job performance of their employees. They also contradict the notion that work is a simple economic exchange with the employer, where employees want to do as little as possible and want to get out of it as much as possible. There is no leader-member exchange relationship between the client and the liquid workforce vendors.

Psychological contract describes expectations that the employee has of what the employer will do for them and what is expected of them in return. In the liquid workforce, it is difficult to see that the workers have much of any expectations of what the client will do for them and, in turn, little expectation that they owe the client anything. Everything is contractual, which means that discretionary effort is largely irrelevant. The modest good news in this context is that the downside when those expectations are not met – 'violations' and more severe 'contract' breaches that lead to negative responses from employees, withdrawal of discretionary effort all the way to sabotage[19] – are likely to be irrelevant when liquid workforce workers have no expectations of anything from their employer.

Conclusion

The evidence about the extent to which employers make use of vendors and through them access the liquid workforce might also be seen as a proxy for the lack of internal flexibility in moving current employees around. The more difficult it is to rearrange employees – move them physically from declining jobs to expanding ones, retrain them for such new positions, and so forth – the

---

[19] Although the notion that expectations mattered to employees has been known arguably since work began, thinking clearly about what happens when those expectations are violated was articulately most clearly by Denise Rousseau (1995) *Psychological Contract in Organizations: Understanding Written and Unwritten Agreements*. Newbury Park, CA: Sage.

more we might expect employers to rely on the liquid workforce as an alternative. It is something of a joke but nevertheless true that many companies use LinkedIn profiles to learn about the capabilities of their *current* employees. Getting current employees released from their managers to work on pressing projects has become more difficult in recent years as authority has been decentralized and local managers are accountable for their own profit-and-loss, which means that it costs their performance to release employees. In other words, it is worth considering to what extent the interest in the liquid workforce approach is a push away from current practices instead of a pull toward the former.

The net advantages of using the liquid workforce approach as opposed to relying on flexibility from within the firm are simply not obvious. That leaves us with the question as to why so many employers are using it. One explanation is that few employers have any serious ability to assess the actual costs and benefits. Instead, they rely on what sounds persuasive. The optimization logic behind the idea of a liquid workforce solving the otherwise challenging problems of talent management has great appeal. The tremendous marketing campaigns of the vendors who constitute the liquid workforce approach are no doubt persuasive as well. Another explanation, noted above, is that many employers cut back their capabilities to develop talent and manage it in any sophisticated manner when the supply of talent in the market was abundant – first in the 1980s layoff period, especially following the Great Recession, with the brief exception of the dot.com years. Trying to rebuild the capacity to have internal flexibility is a considerable challenge. Many employers may be stuck on the current trajectory even if they do not want to be on it.

Another explanation looks to financial accounting. Shifting jobs from employees to vendors moves costs from the 'wage and salaries' category, which investors punish, to a 'business services' category. With respect to internal accounting and actual costs, many of the costs of the liquid workforce are hidden. If we added, say, 30 percent more employees to our organization, the human resource administrative costs would rise sharply, but if we move 30 percent of our jobs to non-employee arrangements, with vendors setting them up, the human resource administrative costs decline. Those costs show up elsewhere, in business services, but not in wages and salaries. Some of the costs are also pushed onto existing employees. Rather than have recruiting handled by $75 000/year recruiters, we push most of those tasks onto hiring managers who might make double or triple that amount. Those managers struggle to get their own work done as a consequence and likely do a poor job of recruiting and hiring, but the change appears as a cost reduction of $75 000.

Ironically, the notion that financial accounting sees employees as fixed costs actually appears to be more relevant to the non-employee workers of the liquid workforce than it does to the actual employees of the organization because they are governed by actual contracts that place restrictions on adjusting employment levels.

References

Abraham, K. G., Haltiwanger, J. C., Sandusky, K. and Spletzer, J. R. (2018). Driving the gig economy. Unpublished paper, National Bureau of Economic Research.

Abraham, K. G. and Houseman, S. N. (2022) 'Contingent and Alternative Employment: Lessons from the Contingent Worker Supplement, 1995–2017'.

Acemoglu, D. *et al.* (2016) 'Import competition and the great US employment sag of the 2000s', *Journal of Labor Economics*, 34, 141–198.

Ardent Partners. (2017) The State of Contingent Workforce Management 2017–2018.

Atkinson, J. (1984) 'Manpower strategies for flexible organisations', *Personnel Management*. 16(8), 28–31.

Bernhardt, A. *et al.* (2016) 'Domestic outsourcing in the United States: a research agenda to assess trends and effects on job quality'. Upjohn Institute Working Paper.

Boyce, A. S. *et al.* (2007) '"Temporary worker, permanent loser?" A model of the stigmatization of temporary workers', *Journal of Management*. Sage Publications, 33(1), 5–29.

Broschak, J. P. and Davis-Blake, A. (2006) 'Mixing standard work and nonstandard deals: The consequences of heterogeneity in employment arrangements', *Academy of Management Journal*. Academy of Management Briarcliff Manor, 49(2), 371–393.

Cappellari, L., Dell'Aringa, C. and Leonardi, M. (2012) 'Temporary employment, job flows and productivity: A tale of two reforms', *The Economic Journal*. Oxford University Press, 122(562), 188–215.

Cappelli, P. (1998) *New Deal at Work*. Harvard Business School Press, Boston.

Cappelli, P. (2008) 'Talent management for the twenty-first century', *Harvard Business Review*, 86(3), 74.

Cappelli, P. H. and Keller, J. R. (2013) 'A study of the extent and potential causes of alternative employment arrangements', *ILR Review*. SAGE Publications, 66(4), 874–901.

Cappelli, P. and Keller, J. R. (2014) 'Talent management: Conceptual approaches and practical challenges', *Annu. Rev. Organ. Psychol. Organ. Behav.* Annual Reviews, 1(1), 305–331.

Cappelli, P. and Neumark, D. (2004) 'External churning and internal flexibility: evidence on the functional flexibility and core-periphery hypotheses', *Industrial Relations: A Journal of Economy and Society*. Wiley Online Library, 43(1), 148–182.

Coase, R.H. (1937) 'The nature of the firm', *Economica*, 4(16), 386–405.

Costa, D. and Hira, Ron. (2020) H-1BVisas and Prevailing Wage Levels. EPI May 4. https://www.epi.org/publication/h-1b-visas-and-prevailing-wage-levels/.

De Stefano, F., Bonet, R. and Camuffo, A. (2019) 'Does losing temporary workers matter? The effects of planned turnover on replacements and unit performance', *Academy of Management Journal*. Academy of Management, 62(4), 979–1002.

DeVaro, J. (2020) 'Internal hiring or external recruitment?', *IZA World of Labor.*

Donovan, S. A. and Bradley, D. H. (2019) 'Real Wage Trends, 1979–2018', *Washington DC: Congressional Research Service.*

Eccles, R. G. (1981) 'The quasifirm in the construction industry', *Journal of Economic Behavior & Organization.* Elsevier, 2(4), 335–357.

Economist Intelligence Unit. (2019) Sourcing and Managing Talent in a Gig Economy. London.

Eisenberger, R. *et al.* (1986) 'Perceived organizational support', *Journal of Applied Psychology.* American Psychological Association, 71(3), 500.

Eldor, L. and Cappelli, P. (2021) 'The use of agency workers hurts business performance: An integrated indirect model', *Academy of Management Journal.* Academy of Management, 64(3), 824–850.

EM360 Tech. (2019) Top 10 Managed Service Providers. https://em360tech.com/tech-news/top-ten/top-10-managed-service-providers.

Ernst & Young. (2017) *Gig Economy – Global Contingent Workforce Study.*

Fuentes, J. R. and Leamer, E. E. (2019) *Effort: The unrecognized contributor to US income inequality.* National Bureau of Economic Research.

Ganster, D. C. and Rosen, C. C. (2013) 'Work stress and employee health: A multidisciplinary review', *Journal of Management.* Sage Publications, 39(5), 1085–1122.

Goldstein, A. (2012) 'Revenge of the managers: Labor cost-cutting and the paradoxical resurgence of managerialism in the shareholder value era, 1984 to 2001', *American Sociological Review.* Sage Publications, 77(2), 268–294.

Graen, G. B. and Scandura, T. A. (1987) 'Toward a psychology of dyadic organizing,' *Research in Organizational Behavior.* JAI Press, Inc.

Handy, C. (2007) *Understanding Organizations.* Penguin.

Hoover, G. (2018) 'Jim Casey: The Unknown Entrepreneur Who Built the Great UPS'. American Business History Center.

Houseman, S. N., Kalleberg, A. L. and Erickcek, G. A. (2003) 'The role of temporary agency employment in tight labor markets', *ILR Review.* SAGE Publications, 57(1), 105–127.

Huckman, R. S. and Pisano, G. P. (2006) *The Firm Specificity of Individual Performance: Evidence from Cardiac Surgery, Management Science.* INFORMS: Institute for Operations Research.

Hyman, L. (2018) *Temp: The Real Story of What Happened to Our Salary, Benefits, and Job Security.* Penguin.

Katz, B. E. (1999) 'What a PEO can do for you', *Journal of Accountancy.* American Institute of Certified Public Accountants, 188(1), 57.

Kelly Services, 'From Workforce to Workfit' (2017). https://www.kellyservices.us/us/siteassets/united-states---kelly-services/files/b2b-files/white-paper_new-narrative_040518_singlepgs.pdf.

Kentley Insights. (2021) *Staffing and Temp Agencies Global Market Size & Growth Report.*

Kleinknecht, A., van Schaik, F. N. and Zhou, H. (2014) 'Is flexible labour good for innovation? Evidence from firm-level data', *Cambridge Journal of Economics.* Oxford University Press, 38(5), 1207–1219.

Lee, C., Huang, G.-H. and Ashford, S. J. (2018) 'Job insecurity and the changing workplace: Recent developments and the future trends in job insecurity research', *Annual Review of Organizational Psychology and Organizational Behavior.* Annual Reviews, 5, 335–359.

Luo, T., Mann, A. and Holden, R. (2010) 'The expanding role of temporary help services from 1990 to 2008', *Monthly Lab. Rev.* HeinOnline, 133, 3.

Masselink, L. E. and Jones, C. B. (2014) 'Immigration policy and internationally educated nurses in the United States: A brief history', *Nursing Outlook.* Elsevier, 62(1), 39–45.

Mateescu, A. and Ticona, J. (2020) 'Invisible work, visible workers: visibility regimes in online platforms for domestic work', *Beyond the Algorithm: Qualitative Insights for Gig Work Regulation.* 57–81.

NAPEO. (2021) 'PEO Industry Statistics'. https://www.napeo.org/what-is-a-peo/about-the-peo-industry/industry-statistics#:~:text=PEOs%20provide%20services%20to%20175%2C000,is%20estimated%20at%20%24270%20billion.

NAPEO. (2021) 'What Does Employee Management Leasing Cost?' https://www.netpeo.com/faqs/what-does-employee-management-leasing-cost/.

Nurthen, J. (2020) *Introduction to Hiring Platforms.* Staffing Industry Associates (SIA). December 15.

Organisation for Economic Co-operation and Development (OECD) Staff. (2018) *The Future of Social Protection: What Works for Non-Standard Workers?.* Paris: OECD.

Stephanie Overby. (2016) 'Should You Outsource Vendor Management?' *CIO Magazine*, March 21.

Settoon, R. P., Bennett, N. and Liden, R. C. (1996) 'Social exchange in organizations: Perceived organizational support, leader–member exchange, and employee reciprocity', *Journal of Applied Psychology.* American Psychological Association, 81(3), 219.

Sherer, P. D. and Morishima, M. (1989) 'Roads and roadblocks to dual commitment: Similar and dissimilar antecedents of union and company commitment', *Journal of Labor Research.* Springer, 10(3), 311–330.

Simon, H. A. (1951) 'A formal theory of the employment relationship', *Econometrica: Journal of the Econometric Society.* JSTOR, 293–305.

Staffing Industry Analysts. (2017) 'Contingent Workforce Strategies 3.0.' cwstrategies.staffingindustry.com/temp-to-perm-conversion-ratio/.

Staffing Industry Analysts. (2019) 'SIA NATHO benchmarking survey provides insights into travel nurse trends', Healthcare Staffing Report. https://www2.staffingindustry.com/ eng/ Editorial/ Healthcare -Staffing -Report/ Archive -Healthcare -Staffing -Report/2019/July-18-2019/SIA-NATHO-Benchmarking-Survey-provides-insights -into-travel-nurse-trends#:~:text=The%2033%20companies%20participating%20in ,billion%20market%20size%20in%202018.

Sucher, S. J. and Gupta, S. (2018) 'Layoffs that don't break your company: Better approaches to workforce transitions', *Harvard Business Review.* Harvard Business School Publishing, 96(3), 122–129.

Thompson, P. (2020) The complete history of ERP: It's rise to a powerful solution. https://www.g2.com/articles/history-of-erp.

Todd, S. (2019) 'The short but destructive history of mass layoffs', *Quartz at Work*, p. 12.

Tushman, M. L. (1977) 'Special boundary roles in the innovation process', *Administrative Science Quarterly.* JSTOR, 587–605.

US Department of Labor, Employment and Training Administration, Unemployment Insurance Service. (1996) *Employee Leasing: Implications for State Unemployment Insurance Programs Final Report.* https://oui.doleta.gov/dmstree/op/op97/op_01-97.pdf.

US Department of Labor. (2021) 'H-1B Workers'. https://www.dol.gov/agencies/whd/workers/h1b.

Wallins, B. (2020) 'Gross Margin and bill rate trends. Staffing industry sssociates'. December.

Weber, L. (2017) In the $75 billion Videogame Industry, Hiring People is a Last Resort. *Wall Street Journal.* April 10.

Weil, D. (2014) 'The fissured workplace', in *The Fissured Workplace.* Harvard University Press.

Williamson, O.E. (1981) 'The economics of organization: The transaction cost approach', *American Journal of Sociology,* 87(3), 548–577.

Zelinsky, E. A. (2004) 'Defined Contribution Paradigm, The', *Yale LJ.* HeinOnline, 114, 451.

7 Networked-based strategic human resource management: managing people within and beyond the boundaries of organizations

Juani Swart, David Cross, Nicholas Kinnie and Scott Snell

Introduction

Contemporary work organization has emphasized the focus of SHRM from managing people only within the firm to include the management of people across organizational boundaries in networks (Manning, 2017; Moliterno and Mahony, 2011; Swart and Kinnie, 2014; Weil, 2014). The co-existence of traditional forms of working and networked working poses challenges to the taken-for-granted assumptions underlying contemporary SHRM which run the risk of becoming anachronisms impeding rather than enhancing performance. The core practices of recruiting, developing and rewarding individuals in organizations will be different in a more loosely structured way of managing people in networks. Indeed, these changes in work organization have profound implications for links between SHRM and performance because of the increased importance of social capital.

It is timely to appreciate and extend some of the original premises of SHRM, i.e., the managing of employees *within* the organization via a series of practices that are controlled by the organization as an isolated entity. It is also important to acknowledge that, as we take into account a networked system, rational individual choices continue to shape how people are managed. We focus on the implications of fluid boundaries within traditional organizations as well as networked working for SHRM by addressing the question: What are the key factors that impact upon SHRM in a networked context? To answer this question, we first discuss the *different of ways of working*, a typology, along a continuum from the organizational, to that of inter-organizational and ultimately the network level. Second, we refer to the characteristics of networked working within this typology, such as *collaboration, access to knowledge and skills, and tempo of working* in organizations and their networks. Third, drawing together these two points, we reflect on the aspects of (i) knowledge and skill, (ii) knowledge flow and (iii) attitudes, such as commitment, that need to be (re) considered in the context of network SHRM. Fourth, we put forward a future research agenda, building upon the principles put forward as well as the central focus on social capital. Finally, we draw on our reflections on contemporary work and consider the practical implications of networked SHRM.

Contemporary work organization

Contemporary work organization requires a shift in how we think about and understand organizational boundaries and relationships, as well as the employment status of workers (Weil, 2014). Increasingly, work takes place both fluidly within organizations as well as across organizational boundaries. Whereas previously the ability to compete in the market was critical to organizational performance, we now find greater need for the reliance on relationships and collaboration with other organizations and self-employed individuals to achieve networked level outcomes. This can be linked to the greater complexity in market dynamics, which may also be associated with environmental and social complexities (Snell and Morris, 2021). That is to say, social capital becomes a focal point of SHRM practices. In other words, informal attachments and contractual relationships may take the place of formal employment contracts. Assumptions about the need to directly employ large groups of workers have been replaced by myriad tiers of organizations and individuals who combine to provide goods and services; the organization is but one actor within a network (Camuffo and de Stefano, 2019; Snell and Morris, 2021). In order to advance both theory and practice, we therefore need to consider the different types of work organization, both within and across organizational boundaries. This will enable us to understand the importance of social capital in the sustainability of SHRM practices.

Importantly, in the context of the discussion of the typology of work organization, and the increasing emphasis on social capital, we need to point to the fact that organizations and individuals may not only exist at one point of the continuum. Indeed, they may occupy all of the points at any one point in time (Weil, 2014; Kinnie and Swart, 2020). This presents a need to consider the practical implications of implementing the various SHRM practices which may be relevant at any point in the continuum.

At the first point along the typological continuum, the boundaries of the firm have become increasingly fluid even in traditional organizations. Here, even within the organization, there is increased reliance on social capital, i.e., relationships with collaborators and contractors. This means that the SHRM practices remain more traditional but allow for contractual relationships to have an impact on who may have control over people management. For example, professional services firms who employ much of their human capital directly rely on external contractors for services ranging from high-end legal advice and consultancy, to document preparation, to driving and catering. Moreover, traditional organizations are increasingly working closely with clients, suppliers and distributors to deliver market-driven and tailored complex products and services (Marchington et al., 2011; Weil, 2014). This has been driven by cost pressures, dynamic markets, and a wider desire for flexibility and agility.

The widespread use of outsourcing and subcontracting distinguishes between the part of the workforce which is core to business success and another which is peripheral (Bidwell, 2009; Fisher et al., 2008; Weil, 2014). This means that an organization is comprised of both an employed workforce and other individuals who work for the organization but are not directly employed by it; some of these will be physically on the organization's premises whereas others will be off site (Marchington at al., 2011; Coyle-Shapiro and Morrow, 2006). Many traditional organizations retain a substantial core with limited out-sourced services. These trends highlight a need to reframe the way in which we think about the interrelationship between human and social capital; i.e. the knowledge, skills and abilities of individuals and the knowledge embedded in and available through relation networks (Kang and Snell, 2009). In this context, SHRM is focused on permanent employees. The supply of talent, predominantly within the organization, and the interrelationship between employees and clients, will ultimately define the way in which networked HRM practices are implemented.

The second point on the typological continuum shifts to that of the project level. Here the SHRM practices straddle the boundaries between the firm and the project. We can observe this in the use of integrated project teams (IPTs) and alliances, where a whole series of firms collaborate intensively around a specific opportunity. These inter-organizational relations are now the standard way of working on large-scale projects such as aerospace, transportation, pharmaceuticals, and urban development. Hundreds of organizations, some major and some much smaller, work together over perhaps five to 10 years both physically or virtually on a shared site (Flyvbjerg, 2014). Professional and managerial talent are seconded from, but remain members of, their own organizations and bring together complementary knowledge and skills to focus on the project. Employees may work together on a shared physical site and will often work on the project for both defined as well as open-ended time periods even as long as a decade. Camuffo and de Stefano (2019) cite Novartis Oncology as a key example for this inter-organizational way of working with research institutions and universities to develop new technologies and make breakthroughs in critical healthcare. In these instances, the collaborative project rather than the firm becomes the focus of the SHRM practices. There are several reasons for engaging in these collaborative activities such as increasing revenue by winning more work or reducing costs through increased efficiency. Firms would want to maintain their network relationships because of several co-operative forces at play at the level of the firm, for example to provide market credibility and generate brand value. Finally, there are motivational reasons, i.e., to provide an exciting environment for development of knowledge and skills (Swart and Kinnie, 2014). Furthermore, the network comprises complementary skill sets wherein firms will hardly ever collaborate with firms that 'know similar things'.

The final point in the typological continuum is where we find individuals and firms who often collaborate to form project network organizations (PNOs) to produce network level outcomes (Manning, 2017; Moliterno and Mahony, 2011). Here there may be a very small core of individuals, which mainly serves a co-ordination purpose, and a loosely coupled wide network of members and individuals with the necessary skills to generate outcomes required for specific projects.

In this context there is a clear reliance on self-employed or individual workers with valuable talent but who may not need to be employed, or may not want to be employed, on a formal, contractual and permanent basis (McKeown and Pichault, 2020; Cross and Swart, 2020a; Spreitzer et al., 2017). This form of work organization is partly based on cost and flexibility pressures, but it is also a response to generational changes in how individuals want to work, for instance a preference to be self-employed, work independently or to have multiple careers.

These individuals, also known as solo self-employed, freelancers, and independent contractors, have relationships governed by contract rather than employment law. They do not employ others and they are neither subject to the mutual obligations of employment relationships nor bound by the directive control of an organization (Cappelli and Keller, 2013; Spreitzer et al., 2017). They span the full spectrum of skills, knowledge, and income and importantly the majority operate offline rather than via online platforms (Katz and Krueger, 2019). However, they are also the point at which the transaction cost economics of firms and organizational structures meet those of the market (Cross and Swart, 2020a) and this often dictates when the relationship is instigated and works well, and when it does not.

Independent workers occupy a curious position in organizations and have a simultaneous insider/outsider status – not quite in yet not quite out. In theory they are distanced from the coordination and politics of everyday organizational life, yet in reality they are not (Anderson and Bidwell, 2019). They may have uniforms, IT accounts, and work alongside regular employees and yet are still classed as visitors or outsiders. This presents clear challenges to SHRM practices as these individuals may also transition multiple times between employment and self-employment for financial reasons or for skills and relationship development.

While the benefits of working in the PNO context include instant access to knowledge and skills at a strategic level (Cross and Swart, 2020b; Flinchbaugh et al., 2020), there are multiple associated challenges. For SHRM this includes strategic control and the particular boundaries of people management practices (Cross and Swart, 2021). Control is a key legal issue yet one that is often overlooked. The result is that valuable skills and knowledge are now situated outside the legal boundaries of the firm (Weil, 2014; McKeown and Pichault, 2020). Importantly, in contemporary settings, knowledge and skill frequently move across organizational boundaries. Indeed, McKeown and Pichault (2020) show that this challenges our assumptions regarding talent management and 'talent' which becomes both an organizational and individual resource.

At this point in the typological continuum of work organization the network is held together by long standing, familiar relationships, as opposed to traditional employment law-driven relationships. However, once the network level outcomes have been achieved the PNO may become dormant before being re-energized and re-configured to meet the needs of the next project. This is where the notion of the pace or speed of working, and the underpinning social capital, becomes an important variable to consider in networked level SHRM practices. How would several organizations draw together in a short space of time to recruit, develop and reward individuals? For example, in humanitarian aid organizations, several member agencies and donors will work together at high speed to secure donations and address large scale disasters (Cross and Swart, 2020b). In the film and TV industry and research missions, specialists are brought together for a production and they then disband until they are brought together, perhaps in a different configuration for another production (Manning, 2017).

In the first part of this chapter, we have outlined three different ways of working along a typological continuum: (i) traditional organizations rely on permanently employed human capital and work closely with clients and suppliers; (ii) collaborative organizations often work in IPTs and rely on valuable human capital across organizations, which will work in a project for a period of time and then return to the organization, and (iii) within loosely coupled networks, such as PNOs, there is a reliance on a variety of skills from a very small coordinating group of individuals with an emphasis on social capital to co-ordinate skills to deliver projects which may be particularly time sensitive. In each of these, the relationships drawing on social capital between clients, contractors, suppliers and independent workers will be critical to the successful operation of SHRM practices.

The central role of social capital within networked SHRM

We now need to consider the key characteristics of the continuum of contemporary work organization in more detail to understand the nature of SHRM at the network level (Coff, 1997; Soltis et al., 2018; Hollenbeck and Jamieson, 2015). To do this we examine the consequences for human and especially social capital when work takes place across organizational boundaries (see Table 7.1). We focus on: (i) a demand for *collaboration*, emphasizing the reliance upon social/relational capital, (ii) which has an impact upon the *sustained availability of human capital*, i.e., relationships enable individuals within organizations and across networks to work together, and stay together, and (iii) *tempo of work*, i.e. there are specific times when SHRM enables organizational and networked working to create momentum to deliver products and services in a short period of time. In these contexts, and in order to maximize that value generated from human capital, the reliance on social capital becomes the focal point of SHRM.

First, we have seen the emergence of greater emphasis on collaboration, in particular the relational dimension of social capital within and across organizations (Nahapiet and Ghoshal, 1998). There is not a single organization that has complete strategic freedom over how value will be generated from human capital; they are, instead, much more reliant on the way network relationships influence individual attitudes and behaviours. This reliance on collaboration is intensified given that, in some cases, organizations and individuals may need

Table 7.1   Networked SHRM practices: impact on knowledge and skills

	Networked version
Resourcing	Social capital will influence network structure and density. Happens via network coordinator or project-based firm. Based on 'who do we know', 'who would be good' and 'who do we trust'.
Training and development/ learning	Relational approaches to 'training' within the network minimal. Often an individual responsibility. The assignment itself is the development opportunity, often through stretch work if it is a new industry/ method/approach. A tension here between developing HC of those who may not remain for long.
Reward	Often on a project or *per diem* basis for wider network members. Paid more than employees, but with greater risk and variability. The core is more likely to be employed. Network members are more likely to work for free to get the experience of work that will develop them, or as a favour to a trusted network partner.
Performance management	Although this happens through contracts officially, these do not always exist. The need for this is minimized due to shared codes and language that exist prior to the work taking place. Relational ties means that norms and obligations are already set so poor performance is less likely. When there is poor performance by an individual or trust is broken they are unlikely to be asked back for future work/projects.

to work together at a fast pace for a short period of time. The further aspect of collaborative intensity refers to the fact that there is intense pressure on the collaborative aspects to hold the network 'together'. This clearly has implications for SHRM given that individuals within and across organizations need to be able to engage with a variety of SHRM practices that encourage close relationships in a way that enables networked level performance.

This environment is also increasingly characterized by a mix of centrifugal and centripetal pressures (Kinnie and Swart, 2020). The centrifugal pressures pull organizations apart because work and individuals are often physically and attitudinally dispersed. Centripetal pressures, such as shared project deadlines, are those which pull the organizations involved together and encourage collaboration. Importantly, we can see the relationship here between the dimensions of social capital; there are strong attitudinal, cognitive and structural aspects that can pull individuals together across projects in a network, – that is to say, having strong and lasting relationships, a similar focus (for the projects) and structural organization (processes) that keep individuals together.

Individuals may need to interact frequently for extended periods of time, compared with previous arrangements where a supplier traded with a client on a purely transactional basis, which is the first point on our typological continuum. Hence, the emphasis is on continued collaboration during and across various projects. The growth of IPTs and PNOs are the best examples of this, and both are associated with large-scale, long-term projects. IPTs, common in defence, construction and transport infrastructure, work best when physically co-located teams from different organizations integrate their cross-functional knowledge in the pursuit of strategic, programme level activities (Roerich et al., 2019). The intense collaboration requires trust and quality relationships to integrate the various views, personalities and professional perspectives. In PNOs, Cross and Swart (2020b) show the importance of cultivating these network relationships, as well as stocks of specialist and generalist human capital, through regular structured contact in order to develop trust and routines. These stocks located throughout the network can be drawn on when disaster strikes. We also see this in consultancy when working with clients, such as the National Health Service, which over a long period of time leads to the development of client-specific knowledge and relationships that can be drawn on repeatedly through the assignment as well as in future bids for work in this area. Collaborative intensity elevates the notion of human capital as a co-constructed asset which is shared among the parties to the network rather than retained within a single firm. This requires that future research and SHRM practices address the importance of social capital from a relational as well as cognitive perspective.

Within this relational approach we see the element of trust as vital. Trust helps to lubricate cooperation, yet repeated cooperation leads to more trust (Nahapiet and Goshal, 1998); however, crucial aspects of trust are obligations and expectations within networks. Bechky (2006) shows that the expectation of future work relationships can help to build this trust and support alternative forms of contracts. This is not only the promise of future income but the prospect of future working together and therefore the possibility of repeated reciprocity. Yet within networks and PNOs in particular, the obligation of future work or reciprocation is by no means guaranteed. The 'credit slip' that exists between individuals is not necessarily redeemed. Nevertheless, within these networks, trust is what gets the work with clients – because clients have to have confidence in the competence, capability and reliability of those providing the service. Trust also ensures that teams stay together and are comfortable to work together in the future, and that individuals can work with new individuals – again, often at speed with so-called 'swift trust' (Bakker et al., 2013). This latter happens via shared norms within the wider network; this may be through ethical norms in collegial professions or through specific methodologies and tools in consulting, coaching, and project management. Our own research in this area shows that frameworks such as PRINCE2, 'Scrums', and the philosophy of W.E. Deming act as a way for individuals to have a shared language and belief system. These lead to identification with a community and act as a kind of 'glue' that not only holds the network together but also facilitates further trust and collaboration. This all takes on a different intonation when we look at the network rather than organizational level. The lack of formal ties, especially regarding employment and identification with a single organization, means that individuals are not bound by the same web of rules.

Second, we need to consider the impact of relationships in the network on the *sustained availability of human capital* and whether firms have strategic control over human capital within a network. Shrinking the size of the directly employed staff to reduce costs and provide access to human capital that could not otherwise be reached has consequences for the availability of those workers (Weil, 2014). Long-term relationships become increasingly important; there is a loss of control because organizations cannot simply call on these workers almost instantly in the way they did when they were directly employed. Indeed, there are circumstances where the bargaining power over employment shifts from the organization to the individual. Hence, the centrality of social capital becomes the bedrock for SHRM. Take, for example, the 'Gurus' of Barley and Kunda (2006) who prefer to develop a portfolio career, where their human capital is no longer specific to the organization and they can trade their skills across organizations, staying fluid and flexible and matching their work to the market of clients (Cross and Swart, 2020a). This has direct implications for SHRM practices and in particular on knowledge creation and skill development.

In networks, the sustained availability of human capital becomes a lot less certain. For the network coordinator, especially in PNOs, long-term relationships can help to develop firm-specific human capital and relational social capital. Yet too much permanence risks accusations of 'sham contracting' whereby organizations try to disguise employment as a contractor relationship and thereby avoid responsibilities, entitlement and taxes. Permanence also promotes dependability on both the client and the network which undermines the perceived benefits of autonomy that working in networks enables. Similarly, network coordinators will also want human capital that is available and visible – both for the project itself and for future work. Yet those who are seen as 'gurus' or valuable will be in demand elsewhere. Clients also want someone who is in demand yet not too much so. As such we see a fine line between permanence and availability. Too much permanence can lead to negative effects; too much availability denotes someone not in demand by the market.

This speaks to the focus of SHRM and how the networked-level practices impact on individuals and organizations that operate within the network. Specifically, the way in which the SHRM practices can generate a strategic advantage beyond the boundaries of the firm. Specifically, here it is the idea of developing relationships such that individuals will 'want to come back' to work on a project/client/collaboration again. This is akin to turnover and retention for employees but could be operationalized as the 'return-rate'. This means a shift away from compliance – or control – based HRM and a move towards relational approaches that promote a blend of independence and interdependence (Manning, 2017; McKeown and Cochrane, 2017). Furthermore, this points to the importance of a focus on both human and social capital within the future of SHRM practices.

Third, traditional SHRM practices which are solely organization-focused may lead to people management practices that lag behind market demands and response speed. The networked ways of working that we have outlined above call for SHRM to respond to the *tempo and/or dynamics* that are present in the market. In some cases, slower, long-term ways of working are needed whereas in others a high-speed response across a network is essential for both innovation and societal benefit. Their ability to do this is and respond to changing demands is at the very heart of why networks become the organizational design of choice. These demands may be because consumers' preferences are unstable, because a start-up has spotted a gap in the market and wants first mover advantage, or because a competitive tender has been issued which needs a quick response. Consequently, there is an increased reliance on a smaller centre (which could be just one person) that scans for opportunities and maintains the core competence of the outfit, and external pools of flexible human capital of various kinds. This core has a high degree of 'know what' but also has the 'know who' to fill in the gaps required by the demand. In this context, social capital becomes a core resource which enables flexible work organization and faster ways of responding to demands. Importantly, the more dispersed the network, the more it relies on centripetal forces, drawing on social capital, to enable the management of talent across dispersed organizations. Even the more temporary relationships need to be managed in a relational manner to respond to fast-changing market demands; such is the nature of these ways of work which are able to provide flexibility and agility and meet demand surges (Spreitzer et al., 2017) with 'just-in-time' labour.

Nevertheless, we see that the tempo and dynamics can vary significantly. For complex products and systems such as ships or simulators (Manning, 2017), the network may be slow to form and the project may last for decades. Yet for others, such as disaster relief (Cross and Swart, 2020b), the network and relationships are built over a long period of months and years but the work happens fast – measured in minutes and hours with the intensity lasting for weeks. In these two opposing examples, the time and tempo constraints (or luxury) are the difference between when the network needs HC available instantaneously with relational pathways and reliable trust already formed before activation (disaster relief), and those situations where these can be developed after activation (complex products and systems).

These factors (collaboration, sustained availability of human capital, and tempo of working), when considered together, indicate that social capital becomes a central focus in networked SHRM. In particular, given the reliance of distributed valuable human capital across the network we need to understand the impact of social capital-driven practices on knowledge and skills as well as attitudes when considering networked SHRM.

In this context, we consider the following key themes: (i) the nature of knowledge and skills, (ii) knowledge flows, and (iii) the management of attitudes, specifically commitment within the network. Together, these themes require us to consider the nature of SHRM within a collaborative network. This requires a paradigm shift from within a firm control model to a way of managing valuable human capital through a focus on social capital.

Knowledge and skills within networks and the implications for SHRM

The increasing reliance on social capital presents challenges to existing SHRM practices which have developed during earlier work arrangements and are difficult to modify. Perhaps the biggest single change needed is the realization that SHRM becomes the property of the networks within and across organizations. This requires the identification of SHRM practices that can leverage knowledge and skills which will benefit individuals, organizations and networks.

More subtly, existing SHRM practices need to operate alongside new practices across boundaries, because as we know, organizations do not simply replace one old set of knowledge and skills with a completely new set of knowledge and skills. This integration of 'old' and 'new' relies on social capital for both design of SHRM practices, as well as their adoption and implementation. The new exists alongside the old and the resulting SHRM practices are layered, with one set placed on top of another (Kinnie and Swart, 2020; Grimshaw and Rubery, 2005).

The central focus on the links between social capital and human capital in networks is that of collaboration, which we discussed earlier. In particular, it is important to consider the key SHRM practices that may enhance collaboration; for example, enabling T-shaped professionals where there is a clear link between subject profession as well as a general understanding of knowledge within the organization and the network. This clearly relates to component (professional) and architectural (generalist) knowledge which enables the knitting together of skills that makes the network function (Kang et al., 2007). Furthermore, prior research (Bechky, 2006) indicates that trust between individuals in the network is critical to knowledge sharing and timely delivery of products and services. It is also clear that a shared language and common goals will enable collaboration both within and across organizations. These are clearly important aspects to take into account in the design of future SHRM practices.

A raison d'être of future SHRM practices centres on the links between social capital and the fostering of knowledge and skills which are shared across the network to generate advantage beyond individual organizations. The way in which social capital influences the structure and content of knowledge and skills in the network becomes significant. Perhaps the most important issue here is to recognize that the changes in the structure of work moves the focus from 'jobs' to that of multiple careers within and across organizations. Human capital pools are becoming increasingly fluid (drawing on skills across boundaries) and contemporary organizations often take an 'assignment'-based perspective to generating strategic value – that is to say, shaping the generation of the link between SHRM and human capital in a way that achieves cross-boundary project objectives.

The contemporary work context also raises the issue of how network-, rather than just firm-, specific knowledge might generate strategic advantage (Lepak et al., 2003). In this context it is important to note that the management of knowledge and skills, driven by social capital, would still need to be implemented, albeit at the network level. However, the nature of these practices may be very different from what we may see in traditional organizations (see Table 7.1). Value-generating SHRM practices are needed across organizational boundaries where, for example, recruitment and selection takes place in a co-operative manner among multiple organizations, by a network co-ordinator, or a project-based firm.

Importantly, we note that in a networked environment, SHRM shifts from a hierarchical/bureaucratic model to one that is more informal and driven by social capital rather than bureaucracy. In recruitment and selection, we see changes to 'resourcing' based on who we know, who would be good, and who we trust. It is often at the individual level and the assignment itself is the training opportunity or 'stretch-work' (Cross and Swart, 2020a). However, while value may be generated for the project there is some tension in developing the human capital of those who may not remain for long. Reward is determined by the achievement of network level objectives and often on a project or *per diem* basis. We also see here that many network members may work for free in order to get the aforementioned development or as a favour for future exchange with desired or trusted network partners. Finally, performance management is officially done via contracts but, in reality, these contracts do not always exist. Shared languages, codes, norms and 'gentlemen's agreements' are more common and likely to be in place as work starts. When there is poor performance, this can be a breach of trust and rather than 'employee turnover', they are unlikely to be invited back to work again with those partners. The central premise is therefore that core forms of traditional SHRM will continue to exist, i.e., recruitment, development, reward and performance management (Cross and Swart, 2021). However, these practices will be driven by social capital and enacted by various stakeholders across the network. These stakeholders may vary from project managers, to contract agencies and clients.

Encouraging knowledge flows across the network

Developing knowledge and skills appropriate for working between organizations is, on its own, of limited value in the network environment. It is not simply the stocks of human capital which are important but, critically, the flows of knowledge and skills across organizational boundaries (Kang and Snell, 2009). The way in which knowledge would be exchanged in the network, i.e., the flow of human capital, is clearly facilitated by social capital. It is only by relating to individuals and network partners that the willingness to share knowledge would be facilitated. Hence, the interconnection between social capital, human capital and SHRM practices becomes a focal point at the level of the network.

Network members may possess relevant knowledge and skills but are they willing to share them? How can SHRM practices create the necessary conditions to maximize the gains from combining and sharing knowledge across boundaries? The main problem is that stakeholders in the network have much less control over individual attitudes and behaviours than in traditional organizations. There is no contract of employment, shared working space opportunities, or peer pressure to share knowledge. This indicates that the focal point of interaction and the way in which SHRM practices address this within and across organizations will influence knowledge sharing (Swart et al., 2014). Consequently, there is much more emphasis on SHRM actions which influence knowledge-sharing attitudes and behaviours.

Nahapiet and Ghoshal (1998) argue that this flow of knowledge across organizational boundaries can be encouraged by the development of shared language, codes and narratives. This suggests that the role of SHRM in integrating the knowledge and skills across the network is especially important. For example, we may ask: How might the SHRM create shared language and the narratives needed to allow multiple groups to work together effectively across organizational boundaries in a network? As we consider that networks would exist across time, the notion of transactive memory (Wegner, 1987), i.e., how we draw on shared language across networks, becomes important, hence the emphasis remains on social capital. Swart and Kinnie (2014) provide some insights from a retail organization into possible HR practices including direct actions such as creating shared work teams across organizational boundaries and more indirect approaches such as encouraging movement, both temporary and permanent, of staff between collaborating organizations. Further research into the barriers to sharing knowledge which has accumulated in silos would be particularly valuable.

Knowledge sharing within a network is closely linked to attitudes and behaviours, most notably that of commitment. That is to say, a strong bond with a team, client, or project will strongly influence knowledge-sharing behaviours (Swart et al., 2014). Given that the effectiveness and sustainability of the network is closely linked to knowledge sharing, it would mean by implication that SHRM practices therefore need to embrace how social capital influences these attitudes, such as commitment. In particular, our focus is on the network, and we therefore need to understand the nature of multiple targets of commitment and how networked SHRM practices can create synergies between these.

Managing commitment across the network

We see that the network-based approach raises many aspects for SHRM and the management of commitment, which will have a direct impact on behaviours that impact on the performance of the network. Organizational commitment is an established part of traditional SHRM practice design. Yet 'the firm' can no longer been seen as central, or even relevant, when we look at networks (van Rossenberg et al., 2018). From an individual perspective, there may be multiple jobs, multiple networks and multiple organizations. They may be directly employed by one organization and work part-time with another on a temporary contract or on self-employed basis (Katz and Krueger, 2019). Alternatively, they may be legally employed by one firm but be physically working on the site of a client or at the location of a project involving multiple contractors. Here, other targets may come to the fore such as clients, professions and collaborators (Cross and Swart, 2020a). These are often based not on what 'the organization' dictates but more on an instrumental and rational choice based on an individual's own perceptions of best interests and benefits. As such, the picture becomes increasingly fluid and complex (Kinnie and Swart, 2012; Manning, 2017) and this has a direct impact on the design of network level SHRM practices. The consideration of future SHRM practices would therefore need to consider the interrelationship between social capital and what has recently been labelled as commitment systems or constellations (Klein et al., 2020). This enables a more dynamic picture to be examined and brings into focus a greater role for context in the interaction and relationships between commitment targets. We see that understanding commitment and work across different sub-systems may be of particular use for networked working.

Important in understanding the nature of networked SHRM practices is that there is evidence that suggests approaches to managing the commitment in a network with few if any 'employees' are not too dissimilar from those required from employers (McKeown and Cochrane, 2017). SHRM practices therefore need to consider how a sense of belonging to a client, team or other individuals in the network will drive behaviour. That is to say, I will stay loyal and continue to work with an entity that I am committed to (Swart et al., 2014; Yalabik et al., 2015, 2017). Clients, for example, still want individuals who want to work there, feel a sense of dedication and responsibility for the success of the project – and it is they who will now be able to drive the behaviour of individuals. We therefore do not see a change in the need for commitment but instead see the organization as 'an employer' released from this responsibility. As such these individuals are operating in a network with increased autonomy and individual choice over who one commits to with no organization to dictate it. An individual chooses who they collaborate with repeatedly, and in collaborative networks they can collectively decide on their clients and the services that they offer. Strategic control by the organization is therefore not assumed. That is to say, organizationally focused SHRM cannot dictate commitment in this context but its facilitation is crucial to generating strategic value within the network. This is, we believe, due to the complex interaction of human capital, social capital and commitment.

This interaction mainly stems from the fact that trust and shared values are vital to social capital, yet values are an antecedent of commitment and trust is part of the cognitive and affective processes that contribute to commitment (Klein et al., 2012). As such, those SHRM practices that build trust and targets that are aligned with shared values are more likely to develop bonds of commitment and therefore deliver value. As such, these practices may be relational rather than treating the individual in a transactional way.

We can see the importance of values clearly in our previous work where commitment to a shared set of values and morality within a field such as humanitarian relief acts as a kind of 'glue' that holds a network together (Cross and Swart, 2020b). This supersedes commitment to any given organization within the network and often means that individuals will go above and beyond to shape actions to bring about change. Once again, this relies on the foundation of social capital as a facilitator of future networked practices.

Implications for further research and for practice

This chapter aimed to position SHRM within a network context, first, by examining the various developments in contemporary work organization, portrayed here as a typology of ways of working along a continuum, from the organizational, to the inter-organizational level, and ultimately the network level. We focused on the key characteristics of networked working, i.e., collaboration, access to skills and the need to work at a faster tempo within and across networks. We reflected on the impact that these aspects would have on SHRM, particularly on the networked management of knowledge and skills, knowledge flow and attitudes, such as commitment. We now develop a future research agenda based on the above-mentioned dimensions and reflect on the practical implications of SHRM at the network level.

There are four major implications for future research. First, given the complexity of contemporary organizations and the nature of the performance-generating potential that it holds, there is the need to recognize that the *level of analysis* should not be restricted to the firm or enterprise. This is because most organizations are not independent and are typically part of a complex set of stakeholders such as clients, suppliers and partners. The change in the level of analysis could be explored in several ways. The network perspective calls for insight into an understanding of how multiple firms could engage with different groups of individuals and organizations to enable the generation of strategic value at the level of the network. Furthermore, there is a need for the exploration of the simultaneity of the existence of multiplicity of SHRM practices at the level of the network, that is to say, how the network would coordinate the leveraging of different sets of knowledge and skills at the same time.

Second, prior research (Lepak et al., 2003) distinguished principally between firm and industry-specific human capital. The changes referred to above mean that we must look at human and social capital in terms of the network as well as the firm level of analysis. The concept of human capital specific to a particular network is needed to reflect the reality of many contemporary ways of working. Human capital at this level is likely to become critical to achieving the strategic goals of particular types of networks. In some ways the importance of individual human capital has long been recognized (Barley and Kunda, 2006).

Third, what is really novel in contemporary working is the *dynamism* of these networks which operate at the speed of light compared with the speed of sound in the past. Various online platforms developed over the last 20 years have revolutionized the way business is done and work is organized. Technical advances and globalization have gone hand-in-hand to decouple time and space and allow business and individuals to work across several projects in real time. This generates an assignment-based approach to developing skills and knowledge. Given the pace of change, disruption and innovation, we need to develop appropriately dynamic SHRM models. Static approaches to human capital can be extended to focus on new, fast-paced learning, transfer of knowledge, and the recombination of human capital which is essential for competitiveness. Future developments of the model will need to capture how knowledge flows within networks, especially what enhances and inhibits this flow (Kang et al., 2007).

Fourth, the emphasis on the value generated from human capital in a networked world calls for future SHRM models to focus on *co-ordination, collaboration and a shared purpose to achieving the desired outcomes*. The notion of heedful interrelation (Stephens, 2020; Weick and Roberts, 1993) therefore becomes important as a variable in the SHRM agenda. That is to say, how does a network, rather than a single organization, co-ordinate, read from one another and share action and knowledge in a sustainable manner? This means that all the associated assumptions about the links between HR practices, employee attitudes and behaviour and organizational performance could be considered afresh. These developments have profound and pervasive implications for HR practices.

We identify the importance of the firm and network levels of analysis, specifically the role that social capital will bring to the knitting together of SHRM practices at the network level. This fulfils one of the basic aims of any set of SHRM practices, i.e., to identify and establish the connections between the strategic objectives and their implications for generating positive and sustained performance at every level of the network.

Our conception of SHRM practices within a networked world emphasizes flexibility and the acknowledgement of shared strategic control. Instead of concentrating on tools and rules to regulate organizational behaviour we increasingly have to think about the processes needed to develop the skills and knowledge people need to flourish in contemporary organizations. We need to focus on the more intangible elements such as developing relationships, co-operation and commitment to both organizational and network-level objectives. For example, we might think in a creative and appropriate way of the processes needed at both the organizational and network levels to develop attachment, learn relevant skills, share knowledge and manage performance in an inter-organizational project.

In particular, the arguments that we put forward in this chapter emphasize the need to rely on social capital, which has clear practical implications. Consideration of the practical implications of our discussion requires adopting the network, rather than the organizational, level perspective. In particular, we need to think about: who are the parties involved; whose managerial practices are important; and what issues are on the SHRM agenda.

First, the network perspective identifies the multiple parties involved including those at the individual, organizational, project and network levels. This presents a possible tension as these parties need to share control over SHRM design across organizational boundaries in ways which are unfamiliar to them, e.g., agreeing common performance standards or reward mechanisms across the network. Furthermore, network parties need to collaborate when setting SHRM practices. This might involve encouraging talented people to move across the network; investing in the skill development at the project level;

sharing best practice through common training and development initiatives; and exchanging information on performance against standards. In short, network-based SHRM requires a multi-level way of collaborating to enhance network-level talent. The tension here, though, is between co-operating with parties outside the organization and the legacy of competition or transactional relationships with these parties (Swart and Kinnie, 2014).

Second, we need to consider whose managerial practices are part of SHRM implementation at the network level. HR specialists will have some role to play but their influence typically is limited to their organizational boundaries. Other senior managers will exercise pervasive influence over SHRM issues throughout projects and networks. Project managers at the organizational and network level have a strategic influence by, for example, estimating knowledge and skills requirements at different project stages. These requirements will be passed to managers responsible for allocating people to different parts of the project through sub-contractors or various labour market intermediaries. All these parties seek to balance the conflicting pulls between achieving their own performance targets and hitting wider project and network level objectives. Decisions made by self-employed workers about their level and type of involvement are also part of this complex mix. Often, they will weigh the benefits of interesting, challenging work which develops their skills and improves their CVs against shorter-term consideration for financial security. Just in the same way that the design of practices is diffuse, the people involved in implementing them are dispersed across the project or network.

Finally, we have to consider the key SHRM issues that need to be managed in a network environment. Research suggests that people working in networks have very much the same concerns as those working within organizational boundaries (McKeown and Cochrane, 2017; Cross and Swart, 2021). They are looking for career opportunities, a chance to learn and develop their skills, to receive feedback on their performance and to be rewarded fairly for the work their work. The SHRM agenda remains much the same even though the parties and practices involved differ considerably from those confined to the organization. This reinforces the notion that SHRM in a networked world is based on informal and relational exchanges rather than transactional agreements.

Our discussion of the practical implications of network-level SHRM reveals the relevant parties, practices and issues which have to be examined. This combination brings with it a new set of tensions to be managed. We argue that these are managed most effectively when consideration of social capital is at the heart of SHRM at the network level. This enables both scholars and practitioners alike to understand the contemporary forms of working and the associated employment and non-employment modes inside, outside and critically between and among organizations. This provides fresh insight into the importance of human and social capital, inside and across the boundaries of organizations.

References

Anderson, T. and Bidwell, M. (2019). Outside insiders: Understanding the role of contracting in the careers of managerial workers. *Organization Science*, 30(5), 1000–1029.

Bakker, R. M., Boroş, S., Kenis, P. and Oerlemans, L. A. (2013). It's only temporary: time frame and the dynamics of creative project teams. *British Journal of Management*, 24(3), 383–397.

Barley, S. R. and Kunda, G. (2006). *Gurus, hired guns, and warm bodies*. Princeton University Press.

Bechky, B. A. (2006). Gaffers, gofers, and grips: Role-based coordination in temporary organizations. *Organization Science*, 17(1), 3–21.

Bidwell, M. (2009). Do peripheral workers do peripheral work? Comparing the use of highly skilled contractors and regular employees. *ILR Review*, 62(2), 200–225.

Camuffo, A. and De Stefano, F. (2019). Getting access to strategic human capital resources: a multiple strategic factor market approach. In A. J. Nyberg and T. P. Moliterno (Eds.), *Handbook of Research on Strategic Human Capital Resources*. Edward Elgar Publishing.

Cappelli, P. and Keller, J. R. (2013). Classifying work in the new economy. *Academy of Management Review*, 38(4), 575–596.

Coff, R. W. (1997). Human assets and management dilemmas: Coping with hazards on the road to resource-based theory. *Academy of Management Review*, 22, 374–402.

Coyle-Shapiro, J. A.-M. and Morrow, P. C. (2006). Organizational and client commitment among contracted employees. *Journal of Vocational Behavior*, 68, 416–431.

Cross, D. and Swart, J. (2020a). Professional fluidity: Reconceptualising the professional status of self-employed neo-professionals. *Organization Studies*. https:// doi .org/10.1177/0170840620964985.

Cross, D. and Swart, J. (2020b). In a flash of time: knowledge resources that enable professional cross-boundary work. *Journal of Professions and Organization*. https:// doi.org/10.1093/jpo/joaa025.

Cross, D. and Swart, J. (2021). The (ir)relevance of human resource management in independent work: Challenging assumptions. *Human Resource Management Journal*. https://doi.org/10.1111/1748-8583.12389.

Fisher, S. L., Wasserman, M. E., Wolf, P. P. and Hannan Wears, K. (2008). Human resource issues in outsourcing: Integrating research and practice. *Human Resource Management*, 47, 501–523.

Flinchbaugh, C., Zare, M., Chadwick, C., Li, P. and Essman, S. (2020). The influence of independent contractors on organizational effectiveness: A review. *Human Resource Management Review*, 30(2), 100681.

Flyvbjerg, B. (2014). What you should know about megaprojects and why: An overview. *Project Management Journal*, 45, 6–19.

Grimshaw, D. and Rubery, J. (2005). Inter-capital relations and the network organisation: redefining the work and employment nexus. *Cambridge Journal of Economics*, 29(6), 1027–1051.

Hollenbeck, J. R. and Jamieson, B. B. (2015). Human capital, social capital, and social network analysis: Implications for strategic human resource management. *Academy of Management Perspectives*, 29(3), 370–385.

Kang, S. C. and Snell, S. A. (2009). Intellectual capital architectures and ambidextrous learning: a framework for human resource management. *Journal of Management Studies*, 46(1), 65–92.

Kang, S.-K., Morris, S. and Snell, S. (2007). Relational archetypes, organizational learning and value creation: extending the Human Resource Architecture. *Academy of Management Review*, 32, 236–256.

Katz, L. F. and Krueger, A. B. (2019). The rise and nature of alternative work arrangements in the United States, 1995–2015. *ILR Review*, 72(2), 382–416.

Kinnie, N. and Swart, J. (2012). Committed to whom? Professional knowledge worker commitment in cross-boundary organisations. *Human Resource Management Journal*, 22(1), 21–38.

Kinnie N. and Swart J. (2020). Cross-boundary working: Implications for HRM theory, methods, and practice. *Human Resource Management Journal*, 30(1), 86–99.

Klein, H. J., Molloy, J. C. and Brinsfield, C. T. (2012). Reconceptualizing workplace commitment to redress a stretched construct: Revisiting assumptions and removing confounds. *Academy of Management Review*, 37(1), 130–151.

Klein, H. J., Solinger, O. N. and Duflot, V. (2020). Commitment system theory: The evolving structure of commitments to multiple targets. *Academy of Management Review*, DOI: https://doi.org/10.5465/amr.2018.0031.

Lepak, D. P., Takeuchi, R. and Snell, S. A. (2003). Employment flexibility and firm performance: Examining the interaction effects of employment mode, environmental dynamism, and technological intensity. *Journal of Management*, 29(5), 681–703.

Manning, S. (2017). The rise of project network organizations: Building core teams and flexible partner pools for interorganizational projects. *Research Policy*, 46, 1399–1415.

Marchington, M., Rubery, J. and Grimshaw, D. (2011). Alignment integration and consistency in HRM across multi-employer networks. *Human Resource Management*, 50, 313–333.

McKeown, T. and Cochrane, R. (2017). Independent professionals and the potential for HRM innovation. *Personnel Review*, 46(7), 1414–1433.

McKeown, T. and Pichault, F. (2020). Independent professionals as talent: Evidence from individual views of working as a contractor. *Human Resource Management*, 60(2), 313–328.

Moliterno, T. P. and Mahony, D. M. (2011). Network theory of organization: A multi-level approach. *Journal of Management*, 37, 443–467.

Nahapiet, J. and Ghoshal, S. (1998). Social capital, intellectual capital and organizational advantage. *Academy of Management Review*, 23, 242–266.

Paauwe, J. (2009). HRM and performance: achievements, methodological issues and prospects. *Journal of Management Studies*, 46, 129–142.

Paauwe, J., Boon, C., Boselie, P. and den Hartog, D. (2013) in Paauwe, J., Guest, D. and Wright, P. (2013) *HRM and Performance: Achievements and Challenges*, Wiley, Chichester.

Pfeffer, J. (1998). *The Human Equation: Building Profits by Putting People First*, Boston, MA: Harvard Business School Press.

Roehrich, J. K., Davies, A., Frederiksen, L. and Sergeeeva, N. (2019). Management innovation in complex products and systems: The case of integrated project teams. *Industrial Marketing Management*, 79, 84–93.

Snell, S. A. and Morris, S. S. (2021). Time for realignment: The HR ecosystem. *Academy of Management Perspectives*, 35(2), 219–236.

Soltis, S. M., Brass, D. J. and Lepak, D. P. (2018). Social resource management: Integrating social network theory and human resource management. *Academy of Management Annals*, 12(2), 537–573.

Spreitzer, G. M., Cameron, L. and Garrett, L. (2017). Alternative work arrangements: Two images of the new world of work. *Annual Review of Organizational Psychology and Organizational Behavior*, 4, 473–499.

Stephens, J. P. (2020). How the Show Goes On: Using the Aesthetic Experience of Collective Performance to Adapt while Coordinating. ASQ: DOI: 10.1177/0001839220911056.

Swart, J. (2007). HRM and knowledge workers. In P. Boxall, J. Purcell and P. Wright (Eds.), *The Oxford Handbook of Human Resource Management*, Oxford: Oxford University Press.

Swart, J. and Kinnie, N. (2013). Managing multi-dimensional knowledge assets: HR configurations in professional service firms. *Human Resource Management Journal*, 23, 160–179.

Swart, J. and Kinnie, N. (2014). Re-considering boundaries: Human Resource Management in a networked world. *Human Resource Management*, 53, 291–310.

Swart, J., Kinnie, N., van Rossenberg, Y. and Yalabik, Z. (2014) Why should I share my knowledge? A multiple foci of commitment perspective. *Human Resource Management Journal*, 24(3), 269–289.

van Rossenberg, Y. G. T., Klein, H. J., Asplund, K., Bentein, K., Breitsohl, H., Cohen, A., and Yalabik, Z. Y. (2018). The future of workplace commitment: key questions and directions. *European Journal of Work and Organizational Psychology*, 27(2), 153–167.

Wegner, D. M. (1987). Transactive memory: A contemporary analysis of the group mind. In *Theories of Group Behavior*, Springer, New York, NY.

Weick, K. E. and Roberts, K. H. (1993). Collective mind in organizations: Heedful inter-relating on flight decks. *Administrative Science Quarterly*, 38(3), 357–381.

Weil, D. (2014). *The Fissured Workplace: Why Work Became So Bad for So Many and What Can Be Done to Improve It*, Boston, Harvard University Press.

Wright, P. and Snell, S. (1998). Toward a unifying framework for exploring fit and flexibility in strategic human resource management. *Academy of Management Review*, 23, 756–772.

Yalabik, Z. Y., Van Rossenberg, Y., Kinnie, N. and Swart, J. (2015). Engaged and committed? The relationship between work engagement and commitment in professional service firms. *The International Journal of Human Resource Management*, 26(12), 1602–1621.

Yalabik, Z. Y., Swart, J., Kinnie, N. and Van Rossenberg, Y. (2017). Multiple foci of commitment and intention to quit in knowledge-intensive organizations (KIOs): what makes professionals leave? *The International Journal of Human Resource Management*, 28(2), 417–447.

Youndt, M., Snell, S., Dean, J. and Lepak, D. (1996). Human resource management, manufacturing strategy, and firm performance. *Academy of Management Journal*, 39, 836–866.

8 HRM practices for value creation and value capture in online labour platform ecosystems: towards an integrative perspective

Anne Keegan and Jeroen Meijerink

Introduction

Studies of HRM in online labour platforms identify contradictions (Kuhn and Maleki, 2017; Meijerink and Keegan, 2019; Duggan et al., 2020; Waldkirch et al., 2021) compared to extant models in HRM scholarship (Lepak and Snell, 1999). Researchers describe how platform firms both disavow employment relationships with workers, while also controlling worker behaviour (Meijerink and Keegan, 2019) in ways that contradict traditional freelancing (Kuhn and Maleki, 2017) and are far-reaching (Gawer, 2021; Kellogg, Valentine, and Christin, 2020). Others discuss how platform firms control workers in unprecedented ways, while simultaneously offering far-reaching autonomy inconsistent with typical models of control oriented HRM (Wood et al., 2019). These contradictory HRM patterns have been observed in numerous settings including app work and crowdwork platforms.

According to Howcroft and Bergvall-Kåreborn (2019), app work refers to the organization of labour to deliver services on demand *in person* using mobile phone applications or apps (De Stefano, 2016; Rosenblat, 2018; Duggan et al., 2020). Crowdwork refers to organizing labour to deliver services *remotely* using digital platforms (De Stefano, 2016). There are two broad categories of crowdwork: If the tasks performed by crowdworkers are sub-divided and disaggregated, and require little prior knowledge (Gegenhuber et al., 2021) as is the case with so-called HITs (human intelligence tasks) hosted by platforms like Amazon's Mechanical Turk, we refer to microtasks or microworking (Irani and Silberman, 2013; Gray and Suri, 2019). If tasks hosted are performed holistically, are knowledge-intensive, or are creative tasks that require specialized knowledge, we can refer to macrotasks or macroworking (Gegenhuber et al., 2021; Boons, Stam and Barkema, 2015).

One empirical study suggests that 'platforms employ a "hybrid HRM approach", i.e., an approach that blends philosophies and practices from a control-based approach and a high-performance approach to HRM systems' (Waldkirch et al., 2021: 2665). While providing examples from their data showing that hybrid philosophies go against core tenets of HRM theorizing, the authors fall short of explaining why this hybridity is manifest in platform ecosystems. Following Meijerink and Keegan (2019: 219), by ecosystem we mean "a group of inter-acting, yet semi-autonomous entities that depend on each other's activities and therefore are somewhat hierarchically controlled" (Wareham et al., 2014; Jacobides et al., 2018). The core entities (or core actors) in an online labour platform ecosystem interact by supplying labour (i.e., gig workers), demanding labour (i.e. requesters), or matching labour supply and demand (i.e., interme-diary platform firm). Each can opt out due to limited legal requirements that bind them to each other (Stanford, 2017). The exchanges among the actors are both interdependent *and* multilateral as each ecosystem actor can only continue transacting with others as long as all continue to transact (Adner, 2017). In other words, the ecosystem cannot be seen as independent bilateral exchanges and the ecosystem fails when one actor stops transacting with the others. If workers stop working, neither platform firm nor requestors can continue alone.

Some scholars draw on institutional complexity to explain contradictory tendencies in HRM practices in platform ecosystems. Meijerink, Keegan and Bondarouk (2021a) argue that they arise dynamically from platform firms con-trolling workers in order to grow, while avoiding the appearance that workers are employees. This explains the observed dynamism in HRM practices in online labour platform ecosystems. However, it is not clear why platforms risk complexity and the legitimacy problems that go along with it (Frenken et al., 2020).

We build on this prior work to offer a complementary explanation for the contradictory approaches taken by corporate platform firms to HRM. The main argument we make is that HRM practices in all online labour platform ecosystems are used for two independent though inter-related reasons which are (1) to create (use) value and (2) to capture (exchange) value. All parties to the ecosystem benefit from the role of HRM practices in value creation (Meijerink, Bondarouk and Lepak, 2016), while corporate platform firms use HRM practices to try and capture value created within the ecosystem, and also by workers, whom they treat as competitors, and to whom they try and prevent value slippage (Lepak, Smith and Taylor, 2007). We also contend that the dynamism often seen in HRM practices in corporate platform ecosystems can be explained, at least partly, by pressures from above (institutional actors, courts) and below (grassroots unions, workers' direct actions) to change how value is captured in such ecosystems. Value creation and value capture therefore provide a valuable lens for understanding HRM practices in platform ecosystems.

The chapter is structured as follows. First, we introduce the context of online labour platform ecosystems (OLPEs). We then introduce the concept of value creation and discuss how HRM value creation and employment relationships are currently theorized in HRM scholarship. Next, we analyze how HRM practices are deployed to create value in OLPEs without employment relationships. We introduce the concept of value capture and discuss how HRM practices are used for value capture in OLPEs without employment relationships. Throughout, we foreground differences between types of platform activities (e.g., app work, crowdwork) orchestrated by corporate platform ecosystems. Our discussion then focuses on the interlocking nature of HRM practices in value creation and value capture. We conclude the chapter with final remarks on the role HRM activities play in platform ecosystems by favoring platform firms to capture more value than workers, and the implications this has for fair platform enabled gig work, as well as for HRM in more traditional contexts.

Online labour platform ecosystems

The gig economy has recently gained attention as an important but nascent topic in HRM studies (Kuhn, Meijerink and Keegan, 2021; Kuhn and Maleki, 2017; Meijerink and Keegan, 2019; Duggan et al., 2020). HRM practices that might be seen as particular to this context include algorithmic management. Following Meijerink et al., (2021b), most definitions of algorithmic management highlight the generation and utilization of digital data, the deployment of software algorithms to process that data, and the subsequent partial or full automation of management- (and human resource management-) related decision-making (Duggan et al., 2020; Waldkirch et al., 2021; Kellogg et al., 2020; Lee et al., 2015; Leicht-Deobald et al., 2019; Newlands, 2021; Veen et al., 2019). Another HRM practice particular to this context is the distribution of HRM practices to customers (Meijerink and Keegan, 2019). Platforms now "support millions of transactions a day across disaggregated workforces" (Jarrahi et al., 2021: 1). A novel feature from a HRM perspective is that firms like Uber, Fiverr, Upwork, Handy, Ola, Didi, Deliveroo, Meituan and

Crowdflower, or the countless other platforms hosting millions of workers worldwide (Kässi and Lehdonvirta, 2018), do not employ their workforce. The dominant model is to rely on freelancers or independent contractors in platform ecosystems where "resources can be controlled without formal ownership or employment" (Gawer, 2021: 2).

Good gig, bad gig?

Controversy has emerged over whether platforms represent a positive development for workers (Wood, et al., 2019; Van Doorn and Badger, 2021). While some see platforms as enabling entrepreneurial individuals to reap the benefits of autonomy (Sundararajan, 2016), others see platforms as exploiting vulnerable workers (De Stefano, 2016; Aloisi, 2016) while exercising unprecedented power over human labour (Gawer, 2021). Schor and Vallas (2021) highlight tensions linked with questions of autonomy/control, while Wood et al. (2019) discuss how platform work offers both autonomy in unusual ways especially in low-wage work while at the same time controlling workers to an unprecedented degree using novel algorithmic and data-driven management techniques. Close surveillance of gig workers and use of algorithms to shape work processes (Kellogg et al., 2020), combined with claims that workers are independent contractors, are all seen as controversial.

Platform heterogeneity

The preceding discussion highlights the heterogeneity of platforms and difficulty drawing general conclusions because of that (Schor and Vallas, 2021). Platform firms act as intermediaries between clients and highly qualified workers with scarce skills (Boons, Stam and Barkema, 2015) as well as between clients and largely undifferentiated labour forces of in-person app workers (Aloisi, 2016) and online, micro-tasking crowdworkers (Gray and Suri, 2019). Reflecting the sheer heterogeneity of platform-enabled gig work, Kittur et al. (2013: 1301) argue that:

> anyone with access to the internet can perform micro-tasks on the order of seconds using platforms such as Amazon's Mechanical Turk, while more skilled workers can complete multi-hour tasks on professional online marketplaces such as oDesk or work for months to solve R&D challenges on open innovation platforms (e.g., Innocentive). Incentives and work structures also vary tremendously, ranging from crowdsourcing contests awarding prizes to winners (e.g., programming tasks on Topcoder) to micro-labor platforms that pay workers per task.

The behavior of highly leveraged corporate platforms in the latter context is closely scrutinized for bad gigs (Prassl, 2018). Research on how platform firms use HRM practices can shed light on debates in the literature on who benefits, and who pays the costs, in platform work.

Value creation or value capture?

It is difficult to comment generally on whether or not platforms are good for workers, not only because of platform heterogeneity, but also due to the conflation of value creation and value capture in much writing on gig work. While the opportunities for workers that arise from engaging in platform ecosystems has been broadly extolled (Kittur et al., 2013), this does not automatically mean that workers *must* benefit from participation. While this may be the case, it is difficult to evaluate whether platforms are positive for workers (or others) without paying explicit attention to value capture (Lepak et al., 2007; Bowman and Ambrosini, 2000). Do workers who create value also capture it? Or do they simply create value for others to capture? For our analysis, we distinguish between types of platforms in terms of the interactions they facilitate (Kuhn and Maleki, 2017; Duggan et al., 2020).

HRM value creation and employment relationships

Studies that analyze links between human resource management (hereafter HRM) and value creation (Ruël and van der Kaap, 2012; Malik, Pereira and Budhwar, 2017) are increasing in recent years. Value creation occurs when organizations are developing new ways of doing things and using new methods (Porter, 1985) to serve their customers, internal and external. For example, Ruël and van der Kaap (2012) argue that eHRM (i.e., the use of information technology for executing HRM activities: Bondarouk and Ruël, 2009) can lead to value creation at the organizational level through improved HR service delivery. Value creation through HRM has also been linked with technology enabling transactions (Amit and Zott, 2001) and increased service quality (Wahyudi and Park, 2014). Dovetailing with the enormous interest in the links between HRM and organizational performance, studies of value creation draw mainly on RBV (resource based view) theorizing where HRM practices are seen as contributing to sustained competitive advantage by allowing organizations to leverage superior human capital resources to create innovative and novel solutions for customers (Lepak et al., 2007; Amabile, 1996). RBV-based approaches highlight how HRM practices attract valuable and rare human capital and motivate inventive individuals and teams to create new products and services. In this respect, value creation equates with the creation of use value (i.e., the qualities of a product or service that customers perceive as meeting their needs) which in turn is translated into exchange value which amounts to the price that customers pay in return for the use value of a product or service (Bowman and Ambrosini, 2000). Where value capture is the focus, it is thus mainly about capturing exchange value from customers and preventing competitors from offering similar use value which would lead customers to pay exchange value to competitors.

This leads to HRM theorists focusing on employees as sources of human capital capable of enhancing offerings to customers which they value and are willing to pay for in preference to competitors' offerings. Sustained competitive advantage is linked with *employees* acting as core, internal, firm specific resources (Lepak and Snell, 1999) which can be combined in socially complex and ambiguous ways (Wright and McMahan, 1992) to create use value through HRM practices (Lepak et al., 2007) and in turn through novel approaches to customers' needs (Amabile, 1996). Social complexity, derived from teamwork and superior leadership, erects barriers to imitation to prevent competitors from eroding an organization's competitive advantage (Wright and McMahan, 1992). A focus on employees, and employment relationships (Meijerink et al., 2021a) is central to theorizing on how HRM practices contribute to organizational performance, and to value creation in HRM. This is evident from how HRM systems, processes and practices are seen in terms of employees and the employment relationship (Chen et al., 2007; Delmotte, de Winne and Sels, 2012; Bowen and Ostroff, 2004).

Workers who are not considered core human resources, capable of delivering value and rarity, are viewed as best managed through outsourcing or arm's-length partnering (Lepak and Snell, 1999). These contractors are externalized from the HRM system (Lepak and Snell, 1999) in ways that are highly questionable today bearing in mind the rise of non-standard forms of employment and core roles played by independent contractors and freelancers in many settings (Leighton and McKeown, 2015). Despite this, the aim of the HRM system is still seen as optimally managing core employees and their links with internal or external partners, but not their links with contractors (Kang, Morris and Snell, 2007) as the route to value creation and organizational performance (Wright and McMahan, 1992). In other words, contractors are still generally viewed as offering noncore and low-level knowledge and skills and as not creating value (Kang, Morris and Snell, 2007), a position that Keegan and Meijerink (2022) argue is increasingly untenable.

HRM value creation in OLPEs without employment relationships

In online labour platforms, HRM does not entail the management of employment relationships (Meijerink and Keegan, 2019; Meijerink et al., 2021a). Rather, HRM practices are deployed specifically to manage workers as independent contractors delivering services to customers while also (semi) controlled by platform firms through digital technologies and algorithms (Meijerink and Keegan, 2019; Wood et al., 2019; Waldkirch et al., 2021). How do HRM practices create value in this context? Following Lepak et al. (2007), we identify both sources and targets of value creation in online labour platform ecosystems, and we distinguish between use value and exchange value.

The *platform firm* is one key source of value creation in online labour platform ecosystems. It creates use value for at least two distinct targets, workers and customers, by facilitating and coordinating a market for their transactions at a scale and with speed which is unprecedented and novel (Lepak et al., 2007; Amabile, 1996). *Workers* are another source of value creation, and their targets include customers who benefit from their services (use value) in return for a monetary fee (exchange value). Put differently, *customers* are a source of value creation to workers, and they also create use value for workers by offering them opportunities to work, and exchange value by facilitating them to earn an income. Customers also create exchange value for platform firms by paying commissions/fees to find workers through the platform's technology or by hiring workers who pay commissions/fees to the platform for access to customers. Accordingly, both customers and workers offer use value to the platform firm: by joining a platform and transacting in online marketplaces, they offer platform firms the possibility to offer their intermediation services.

Before moving on to discuss HRM practices in detail, we note that another target for value creation by platforms firms, workers and customers is the platform firms' investors or shareholders. Many online labour platforms are technology startups that benefit from investor capital to grow the platform to a scale where they can outcompete others in the same segment (Birch and Cochrane, 2021; Prassl, 2018). Investors capture exchange value from platform ecosystems when platforms exit to IPO and are valued higher than the investor's stake, and/or when platforms pay dividends to shareholders, or repay loans at interest (Birch and Cochrane, 2021; Prassl, 2018; Van Doorn and Badger, 2021). We now discuss HRM practices deployed in platform ecosystems.

Attraction and platform branding

To attract workers who are a key source of value creation, platforms firms use platform specific branding as well as branding of platform-based gig work as an attractive and aspirational idea. For example, online labour platforms Fiverr and Doordash both recently launched high-profile advertising campaigns during the 2021 US Superbowl,[1] and Uber and Deliveroo have advertising and social media campaigns, all extolling the virtues of freelance platform work for both workers and for customers. The marketing of specific platforms using advertising to promote their own platform brand is reinforced by branding of a culture that claims platform work is transformative and liberating for workers (Prassl, 2018). Lyft's Ridesharing Marketplace involves current drivers in recruitment and platform branding, offering incentives to existing drivers to refer new drivers.[2] For app workers who must invest in expensive equipment such as cars, aspirational platform branding is a key HRM practice to attract new workers (Rosenblat, 2018). This has overlapping implications for value capture because incentivizing the purchase of expensive equipment using aspirational language about autonomy and high earnings can encourage significant investment, which later presents a switching cost for workers who find they cannot simply leave the platform as they are required to finance considerable debt (Rosenblat and Stark, 2016; Rosenblat, 2018).

Selection

Platform firms offer use value using familiar selection practices such as testing, interviews and background checks to create institutional trust in the platform among customers and sometimes, also, workers. Platforms advertise their use of selection practices to screen workers to attract new customers who may be sensitive to the rigour of platform-selection practices due to privacy or safety concerns (e.g. home-cleaning) or the need for highly skilled labour to complete tasks for clients. Wonolo[3] advertises a "pre-screened worker pool"; Handy[4] provides a "booking system for pre-screened cleaning and DIY staff"; and Toptal[5] claim their selection process is based on rigorous testing and vetting of talent allowed on the platform. Noteworthy is that although rigorous selection creates use value for customers (e.g. high-quality service provision

---

[1]   https://www.cnbc.com/2021/02/04/super-bowl-will-welcome-some-new-advertisers-that-had-great-year-during-pandemic.html.

[2]   https://www.lyft.com/terms/referrals (updated at source January 2021).

[3]   https://www.wonolo.com.

[4]   *Irish Times*, 25 February 2021.

[5]   https://www.toptal.com.

by the worker), and encourages them in their decision about joining platform ecosystems, selection practices used by platform firms are often algorithmically managed and constitute part of a double layer of selection that workers must encounter before they can access work on the platform (Waldkirch et al., 2021). Navigating selection by algorithm can be a costly and frustrating exercise for workers (Gray and Suri, 2019), who are frequently unable to evaluate how algorithms judge them or what they should do to succeed (Bucher et al., 2021). Once past the algorithm, the client also selects workers, which represents HRM activity devolved by platform firms to customers.

Compensation

Platform firms design compensation or reward practices that create value for workers and customers by allowing each side to have confidence in transactions and that they will get paid and/or receive the services offered. In some cases, platform firms set up bank accounts and debit card services for workers. For example, Lyft's Ridesharing Marketplace offers an online bank account and debit card service to ensure drivers can earn.[6] Platform firms also offer escrow services where money/work is held in abeyance by the platform until each side is satisfied the work has been completed and/or payment has been made (Prassl, 2018). These services can be complemented by paid mediation services which are arranged by the platform. For example, Upwork arranges mediation by third parties to the ecosystem in cases where payment disputes arise, and also offers customers and workers payment protection and performance monitoring services linked with payment security for workers as the target of value creation, and surety that workers are performing as agreed for customers as a target.[7] Examples of monitoring services include keyboard monitoring, screen sharing, etc. (Waldkirch et al., 2021). These surveillance-based practices are also linked with value capture, as we see later, and have other far-reaching ethical consequences in terms of workers' rights to privacy, home-work boundaries, etc. (Gawer, 2021; Schor and Vallas, 2021).

Algorithmic management, and workforce planning

As well as somewhat traditional practices in areas such as selection and compensation, platform firms create value by using software algorithms to analyse data from apps and websites to automate HR-related decision making

---

[6]   https://www.lyft.com/driver/direct-debit-card.
[7]   https://support.upwork.com/hc/en-us/articles/211062568-Upwork-Payment
-Protection.

(Meijerink et al., 2021b; Duggan et al., 2020; Veen et al., 2019). Algorithmic management is used to achieve network effects (Frenken et al., 2020), which, following Van Alstyne, Parker and Choudary (2016: 58), are realized by "firms that achieve higher 'volume' than competitors (that is, attract more platform participants) and as a result offer a higher average value per transaction. The positive feedback loop and iterative effects of platform firms rapid and smooth scaling of a two-sided market, where customers benefit from superior matching with an available workforce, produces monopolies and market dominance". Customers gain use value from participation in platform ecosystems by having access to workers to augment or replace in-house labour in all kinds of markets from software development (e.g., Toptal) to language translation (e.g. Fiverr), bartending (e.g. Temper), housecleaning (e.g. Handy), warehousing (e.g., Wonolo), babysitting (e.g. care.com), ride-hailing (e.g., Ola, Didi, Lyft and Uber), food delivery (Meituan, Deliveroo, Doordash) and rapid grocery delivery (e.g., Flink, Getir and Zapp). In these examples, platform firms create use value for customers as well as for workers in an ever-expanding range of industries and sectors. Some advocates see platforms as particularly transformative for those who have traditionally had trouble participating in the labour force (Schor and Vallas, 2021) suggesting platforms create use value for workers in a novel manner by reducing barriers both physical and bureaucratic for labour force participation (Sundararajan, 2016). Through algorithmic workforce planning, platforms create novel forms of use value for workers and customers in the form of rapid (app work) and/or global (crowdwork) matching of customers with a vast and growing pool of instant labour.

Customer-led performance management

Another way that platforms create use value for customers is through designing and deploying performance management through customer-led rating and reputation systems. Although there is nothing new about performance management, or even customers giving feedback as part of a 360-degree processes, the complete devolving of worker ratings to customers is a particularly novel feature of online labour platform ecosystems (Rosenblat, 2018). Customers gain use value from belonging to a platform ecosystem where workers are evaluated by other customers across vast numbers of transactions. Platform firms use data collection, aggregation and analytics to rate or rank workers, often building a dynamic aspect in by linking ratings with rolling periods or windows. In the case of Upwork's JSS (job satisfaction score) (Waldkirch et al., 2021), workers JSS or ratings are calculated as an average of ratings received from clients over the previous month. This incentivizes workers to keep meeting (increasing) performance targets.

Rating overviews are made visible on apps or the website for customer ease in matching with a worker. Customers can select workers based on their ratings and view supporting metrics including number of gigs performed, tenure on platforms, and average ratings from customers. This may also offer (exchange) value to workers since research has shown that workers' numbers of gigs performed and average ratings are positively correlated with the hourly pay charged (by a worker) to customers (Lehdonvirta et al., 2019). Platform firms also capture value from customer involvement in performance management of the workers they hire through platforms since it reduces the costs for platform firms of deploying their own managers to evaluate workers and report on their performance.

Platform firms use ratings to algorithmically allocate gigs to workers as well as to deactivate or suspend workers who drop below certain ratings' thresholds. An associated trend in recent years is for platform firms to offer increased use value to customers based on customer-led performance ratings by differentiating workers in finer detail. For example, Amazon's Mechanical Turk has introduced a "Master Worker" category, using its marketplace design to provide more differentiated information on worker performance for customers: "A Master Worker is a top Worker of the MTurk marketplace that has been granted the Mechanical Turk Masters Qualification. These Workers have consistently demonstrated a high degree of success in performing a wide range of HITs across a large number of Requesters. We leverage statistical models that analyze all Workers based on several Requester-provided and marketplace data points to make that determination".[8]

To the extent that a worker can gain the necessary ratings, they have access to better and often higher paid gigs. Aspiring to "Master Worker", which provides access to better paying gigs, also serves as a form of additional platform control over workers who need to reach more consistently higher levels of performance to qualify for access to better gigs, but in terms of analysis performed by the platform in a way that is not fully transparent for workers. This means use value for customers may need to be traded off in terms of the effort workers must exert in anticipating the algorithm to qualify, when it is clear that many will not (Bucher et al., 2021).

Finally, some platforms, though by no means all, also create use value for workers by deploying systems for workers to rate customers. Uber is an example of this use value creation for workers, who gain from customer

---

[8]   https://www.mturk.com/worker/help.

ratings by having access to information on aggregate customer scores across many workers. In theory, this allows workers to have more confidence in working with a particular customer. To date, empirical research indicates that Amazon has been more lenient on customers' performance evaluations than on workers' performance evaluations, meaning use value for workers tends to be less a priority in platform design than use value for customers (Dube et al., 2020). Empirical research also indicates that Uber does not deactivate customers for low ratings quite as stringently as it deactivates workers for falling below consistently high-performance ratings (Rosenblat, 2018; Rosenblat and Stark, 2016).

Devolved coaching to workers and informal communities

We discussed earlier that algorithmic selection can be a challenging and frustrating experience for platform workers. Workers create value for several targets in the ecosystem by training and coaching workers, on a voluntary basis, in informal and formal communities. To gain insight on algorithms and how to anticipate their requirements to be (re)selected for access to gigs (Bucher et al., 2021), informal or grassroots worker communities such as Turkopticon (Irani and Silberman, 2013) and reddit forum r/Upwork (Waldkirch et al., 2021) have emerged to self-organize and offer support, coaching and training to new and existing workers. These communities also offer intelligence on clients to assist workers in deciding what gigs to bid for and/or accept, as well as advice on their profiles and other ways they seek to enhance the exchange value offered for their services (Lepak et al., 2007). Formal communities are hosted and sanctioned by platforms like Upwork, and other creative macrowork platforms (Gegenhuber et al., 2021). Subject to strict rules from the platform about what advice can and cannot be shared, this sharing of tacit knowledge by platform workers with no employment contracts, to create value in the platform ecosystem, can be assetized by platforms through data aggregation and analytics (Van Doorn and Badger, 2021).

Workers coaching and training each other creates value for the platform firm, but this also means that workers themselves cannot then use this knowledge to create a central network position to benefit in terms of higher exchange value for their own services. Voluntary coaching and supporting workers in formal or informal communities reduces the exchange value that workers might achieve if they retained and bargained based on their tacit knowledge on how to meet customers' or clients' needs. HRM practices being devolved by platform firms to other actors, like workers and customers, is a common pattern in platform ecosystem HRM-based value creation. Table 8.1 summarizes the HRM practices discussed in this section.

Table 8.1   HRM practices in platform ecosystems

HRM Practices	Examples
Attraction and Platform Branding	Ride-hailing platforms offer incentives for referring new drivers, e.g. Lyft Crowdword and app work platforms use high profile traditional advertising campaigns on primetime television, e.g. Fiverr, Doordash Aspirational platform branding of worker's autonomous and entrepreneurial lifestyle is a key HRM practice to attract new crowdworkers and app workers
Selection	Pre-screening of worker pools offered to clients Selection tests to vet talent who are given access to the platform Workers face double-layer selection – first selection by algorithm and then selection by clients
Compensation	Platform bank accounts and debit card services Escrow services Paid, third party mediation services in case of disputes Payment guarantees offered where crowdworkers agree to electronic workspace surveillance Surge pricing Dynamic pricing
Algorithmic Management and Workforce Planning	Algorithmic management automates decision making according to platform decision rules about gig allocation preferences – channeling gigs towards and away from app workers and crowdworkers To achieve network effects
Customer-led Performance Management	Customer-led rating and reputation systems Data collection, aggregation and analytics to rate or rank workers based on customer evaluations Dynamic performance management by linking customer ratings with rolling periods or time windows
Devolved coaching to workers and informal communities	Grassroots communities emerge to self-organize and offer support to crowdworkers and app workers Formal communities hosted by platforms using freelancers to offer advice and mentoring but content sanctioned by platform who can remove/block advice

HRM value capture in OLPEs without employment relationships

The question of whether "intermediary platform firms serve the creation of value for all actors versus the creation of value primarily for the intermediary firm" (Meijerink and Keegan, 2019: 25) is an important one, and as Jacobides, Cennamo and Gawer (2018: 2274, emphasis added) argue, "ecosystem research would benefit if it employed specific methodologies that have been developed to study joint value creation *and distribution* – as opposed to merely alluding to them". However, while interest in value creation in HRM scholarship has increased in recent years, the topic of value capture has not, with some notable exceptions (Lepak et al., 2007; Malik et al., 2017), received the same level of attention. This may be linked with the dominance of RBV theorizing, which Coff (1999: 119) argues "was formulated to explain when firms will generate rent – not who will appropriate it". Bowman and Ambrosini (2000) also see RBV theorizing as inspiring scholars to identify imitability of *already* valuable resources, rather than value generation by labour, and issues related to value capture. They highlight that "power relationships between economic actors" (2000: 1) are crucial in explaining value capture. Concerns about who benefits from HRM practices in platform-enabled gig work certainly resonate with those raised in critical HRM research on financialization in non-financial corporations (Cushen and Thompson, 2016) as well as doubts raised that high performance work systems deliver mutual gains rather than, as some argue, conflicting (Boxall and Macky, 2009) or ambiguous (Geary and Trif, 2011) outcomes.

In mainstream HRM writing, Lepak et al. (2007: 187) discuss value capture explicitly. They define value capture in terms of how sources of value creation (e.g. a platform firm, or worker) can prevent value slippage: "Value slippage – that is, when the party creating the value does not retain all the new value that is created – occurs when use value is high while exchange value is low". Value capture and the prevention of value slippage, whether by individuals or organizations, are linked with mechanisms including competition and isolating mechanisms (Lepak et al., 2007). A core assumption is that "monetary amount exchanged must exceed the producer's costs (money, time, effort, joy, and the like) of creating the value in question, at least for the single point in time when the exchange occurs" (Lepak et al., 2007: 182).

Studies of online labour platforms refer to power asymmetries between platform firms and workers which may be relevant to understanding value capture (Dube et al., 2020) and the use of algorithmic HRM by platforms (Kellogg et al., 2020; Bucher et al., 2021; Veen et al., 2019). An explicit focus on value capture is thus important for a comprehensive understanding of HRM practices in platform ecosystems. We now discuss HRM practices in online labour platform ecosystems that we see as related to value capture and ask if Lepak et al. (2007) are correct in assuming that the exchange value offered to platform workers, or that they can command in platform ecosystems, generally exceeds the costs (money, time, effort, joy, and the like) (Lepak et al., 2007: 182) they incur in co-creating value (with customers and the platform firm).

Platform work as independent contracting and value capture

Organizations have choices about how to arrange relationships with potential workers (Lepak and Snell, 1999). Most corporate platform firms in microwork, macrowork and appwork institute a freelance model treating workers as independent contractors (Kuhn and Maleki, 2017; Frenken et al., 2020; Veen et al., 2019). The use value created by platform firms by allowing workers to use their technology to find customers converts to a higher level of exchange value when platform firms adopt freelance models and bear few costs compared to traditional employers who pay benefits to workers (De Stefano, 2016; Aloisi, 2016). Making others pay for worker-related protection and rights, including workers themselves but also governments and institutions of social protection, increases value capture for platform firms in ways that deserve critical attention.

Platform work, definitions of labouring time and value capture

The independent contracting model of most platforms means workers struggle to capture value because they solely bear the costs of time spent labouring while waiting on gigs through apps (e.g. Uber), and equally time spent searching for gigs on microtask sites (e.g. Amazon's Mechanical Turk, Microsoft's UHRS), or crowdwork platforms (Upwork, Fiverr, Toptal, Crowdflower). App workers are only paid while logged onto the app *and* carrying out a gig, for example a food delivery on China's Meituan app or driving a passenger using India's Ola app. Their availability creates use value for customers who have rapid access to workers when needed but lowers workers' abilities to capture exchange value from participation. Their availability is not translated into exchange value, particularly when platforms over-recruit and favour the client side of the market over the worker side (Dube et al., 2020).

Platform compensation practices and value capture

Platform firms use dynamic pricing models which undermine workers' abilities to decide if gigs are worthwhile, ex ante, before they accept them (Rosenblat, 2018). According to Prassl and Risak (2015: 641), dynamic pricing is based on algorithms which determine "remuneration for distance and time on the basis of factors such as individual city pricing levels, or even demand specific to a particular location and time through so-called surge pricing". Algorithmic workforce planning means apps are often designed to insist on rapid responses by gig workers of sometimes only seconds before the offer of a gig disappears and is reallocated to another gig worker. Platforms like Uber rely on surge pricing algorithms that nudge taxi drivers to selected geographical areas, often with surges disappearing once drivers reach those areas (Rosenblat, 2018). Anticipated level of value capture is thus difficult for both app workers and crowdworkers to discern with algorithmic factors determining pricing levels not fully transparent, stable or consistent from the perspective of workers. According to Dube et al (2020: 45) "the source of the monopsony power on MTurk likely lies in the information and market environment presented to workers and requesters, together with the absence of bargaining or many margins of wage discrimination. In particular, the tastes different workers have for a given task may be quite dispersed and not easily discerned by requesters, which induces requesters posting a wage to trade-off the probability of acceptance against a lower wage". This benefits the platform firm because keeping customers happy is usually more important for value capture by the platform firm (Prassl, 2018)".

Moreover, algorithmic pricing systems offer platform firms the chance to automatically capture surplus value when increases in exchange value paid by customers (e.g. when labour demand outstrips supply) are not transferred to workers in full. On top of this, corporate platform workers do not have access to legislation on minimum pay to balance the power of platforms, and also lack the ability to mobilize for collective action, which is difficult for disaggregated workforces and sometimes prohibited by competition law (De Stefano, 2016; Aloisi, 2016). Despite a recent UK Supreme Court ruling that Uber must implement a minimum wage for drivers, Uber's recent agreement with Britain's GMB union explicitly excludes collective bargaining on earnings as well as the implementation of a minimum wage.[9] To date, Uber maintains that any minimum wage will only apply to time logged onto the app, which is a source of contention with unions and workers who claim that all time spent labouring must be compensated at minimum wage levels. Even when the courts have found that workers should have additional rights, including to minimum wages, platform firms have thus far succeeded in avoiding having to pay minimum wages by appealing decisions, refusing to change their model, or lobbying for exemptions and controversial carve-outs like Prop22 in California[10] to avoid giving workers more rights that would undermine the platform firm's power to capture value. The question of what constitutes working time in platform ecosystems greatly influences how workers who create value can capture a fair share of that value.

---

[9]   https://www.ft.com/content/f44e60c0-ce61-4d98-a31f-5e4af8da3562.
[10]   https://www.latimes.com/business/story/2021-08-20/prop-22-unconstitutional.

Algorithmic management, network effects and value capture

We have previously discussed how algorithmic management is used to achieve network effects (Frenken et al., 2020) and monopolies and market dominance (Van Alstyne et al., 2016). Birch and Cochrane (2021: 7), for example, describe Uber and Lyft as pursuing "expected monopoly rents", which entails winning investment on the basis that "their expected control over existing and developing assets [which] provides the rationale for investors to expect future returns, which translates into higher capitalization". The advantages of network effects that create value for platform workers in allowing them to access and engage with customers in unprecedented ways can also prevent workers from capturing value. When platforms reach network effects and are so dominant that they have eliminated most competition for workers from other platform rivals, they can increase both the fees and commissions they charge workers (or customers) for accessing work (or workers) through the platform. Platform firms capturing value through higher fees/commissions having dominated competitors has been widely observed in studies of online labour platforms (Schor and Vallas, 2021; Prassl, 2018; De Stefano, 2016; Aloisi, 2016; Van Doorn and Badger, 2021; Rosenblat, 2018). This has the effect of depressing wages (Dube et al., 2020). Without employment relationships, which is the HRM model pursued by most platforms, workers have little recourse to either minimum wage legislation or collective bargaining rights. Platforms firms currently have power over workers in setting price levels and capturing value which is very difficult for workers to counter under current legislative conditions in most countries.

This may be changing, however, as court cases around the world, in Spain, the US, the Netherlands, the UK and elsewhere, currently attest. Additionally, research suggests that both app workers and crowdworkers exercise agency and resistance in numerous ways. Veen et al. (2019: 399) studied food delivery app work in Australia and found "most expressions of agency in the form of individual resilience and reworking (Katz, 2004). Nonetheless, some collective agency was expressed, including the sharing of resources and information as well as assisting others in case of accident or breakdown". Others have researched how delivery couriers and taxi drivers form communities for mutual support and collective action (Tassinari and Maccarrone, 2020), while crowdworkers form online support groups to inform and train each other in recognizing exploitative or abusive clients (Irani and Silberman, 2013; Gray and Suri, 2019; Anwar and Graham, 2020). Therefore, while voice in the gig economy is often curtailed (Gegenhuber et al., 2021), platform workers are not merely passive but also act individually and collectively to counter platform power and control and to exercise agency. Changes in the broader institutional context may bolster platform workers' efforts to gain more rights and a fairer distribution of rewards from platform work.

Work design, tacit knowledge and value capture

Platform firms also use work design, a typical HRM practice area, to shape how value is captured within platform ecosystems. By capturing data from workers' activities while they complete tasks (Gawer, 2021; Van Doorn and Badger, 2021), platforms gain insights into the inventive ways that workers manage their work. These value-generating insights are captured and used to optimize the algorithms that, for example, dispatch riders or drivers, thus sharing the worker's inventive ways of working with other platform workers (Van Doorn and Badger, 2021). Coff (1997: 374) argues that one reason scholars overlook value capture is because of reliance on RBV theorizing, and RBV theorizing in turn assumes that "human assets are often hard to imitate due to scarcity, specialization, and tacit knowledge". However, platform designs that convert tacit knowledge into data assets, to be exploited by the platform, prevent individual workers from capturing value using their own tacit knowledge as an isolating mechanism from which they can capture higher exchange value (Lepak et al., 2007). Platforms like Microsoft's UHRS and Amazon's Mechanical Turk disaggregate and codify tasks to make them available for a large and undifferentiated labour pool (Gray and Suri, 2019). This gives clients (or requestors) (Dube et al., 2020) considerable power to set low pay rates while leveraging a global supply of labour. These platform work design features drive down workers' wages. By reducing workers' potential for developing and exploiting tacit knowledge, platform firms remove a central mechanism for workers to achieve a strong position from which to capture value (Lepak et al., 2007).

Platform HRM, workers' perception of bargaining power and value capture

Platform firms can influence the perceptions of worker bargaining power, which in turn can influence the prices they accept or offer for their labour (Bowman and Ambrosini, 2000), respectively, depending on whether they set prices themselves by bidding for work (e.g. Upwork), or respond to prices offered by customers (e.g. Amazon's Mechanical Turk) or set by platform firms as fees per gig (e.g. Deliveroo, Meituan, Doordash). If workers perceive they have a strong bargaining power, they can capture more of the value they create (Bowman and Ambrosini, 2000). However, if platform ecosystems are designed to stimulate perceptions of low worker bargaining power, then this will be linked with fewer opportunities for workers to capture part of the value they create with others in the ecosystem. We discuss two main HRM practices which are linked with this – work design, and algorithmic work allocation and workforce planning.

Work design

Workers who respond to highly atomized tasks for which there is huge competition may be disposed to perceiving their bargaining power as low and accepting low pay for tasks. This scenario is borne out by empirical research on wage rates on Amazon's Mechanical Turk by Dube et al. (2020) where platform work design leads to atomization of tasks, maximizing worker substitutability, and creating high levels of competition between workers. These are all factors undermining workers' bargaining power with clients. Value capture is difficult for workers who cannot use competition as an isolating mechanism to protect value they create in platform ecosystems from slipping to others, e.g. customers or platform firms (Lepak et al., 2007).

Algorithmic work allocation and workforce planning

On platforms where workers perform creative tasks, and need qualifications to join, like Upwork, competition for tasks is also significant (Waldkirch et al., 2021) and workers spend a lot of time trying to find decent work. The use of algorithms to allocate tasks generates what Bucher et al. (2021) refer to as anticipatory compliance, which Waldkirch et al. (2021) observe can lead to workers setting their low fee rates. Anticipatory compliance can be understood as how "digital workers 'preemptively' adjust their behavior (anticipatory compliance practices) in light of algorithmic management" (Bucher et al., 2021: 49) and includes undervaluing their own work, staying under the radar, curtailing their outreach to clients and keeping emotions in check. Even though they have the autonomy to set rates as they wish, algorithmic management and low or no transparency regarding the criteria used by algorithms to make gigs visible to workers (and/or workers visible to clients) engenders insecurity. This can undermine workers' perceptions of their bargaining power, feeding insecurities about who they are competing with or that the algorithm will favour others based on factors not quite understood, but likely to include the rates they offer clients to complete tasks. Research suggesting that platform firms favour clients in disputes is gaining traction (Bucher et al., 2021; Waldkirch et al., 2021; Rosenblat and Stark, 2016; Van Doorn and Badger, 2021). Algorithmic work allocation and workforce planning means apps for on-demand in person services (Aloisi, 2016) are often designed to insist on rapid responses by gig workers, of sometimes only seconds before the offer of a gig disappears and is reallocated to another gig worker. Under pressure from this type of allocation, workers may accept gigs which are simply not worth the value of the time they cost a worker to complete (Rosenblat, 2018) or the damage they cost a gig worker in terms of declining performance ratings if they do not accept (Waldkirch et al., 2021).

Platform firms do not give workers a real voice to improve how they interact with clients (Gegenhuber et al., 2021) which lowers the power of workers. This reinforces what Bowman and Ambrosini (2000: 13) state: "although labour is the source of value, bargaining relationships determine the capture of value". App workers also complain about lack of work, and excessive time spent waiting for gigs, which drives down their value capture from time spent labouring (Rosenblat, 2018; Van Doorn and Badger, 2021). While platform firms in theory have power to restrict access to the platform in order to reduce competition among workers, empirical research on microtask platforms indicates that platforms prefer to satisfy clients' (requestors') desire for supply over workers' desire for less supply, as clients are the more sensitive side of the market and favouring them benefits platforms in terms of their value capture from transactions (Dube et al., 2020). The difficulty for crowdworkers in estimating the nature of a HIT which is a task posted on a site like AMT, or the nature of a task offered on sites like Fiverr, combined with pressure from algorithms to accept tasks or risk lowering ratings which are often linked with acceptance rates (Bucher et al., 2021; Waldkirch et al., 2021) explains the observed tendency for workers to accept tasks even if they ultimately do not pay well for the effort made by workers (Dube et al., 2020).

Discussion: interlocking value creation and value capture HRM practices

Scholars have noted already that value creation, and use value in particular (Ruël and van der Kaap, 2012), gains more attention than exchange value, and value capture, in HRM theorizing. Analyzing value creation and value capture separately, and as independent factors, is therefore important. However, the way they interact dynamically over time is also important for understanding workers' experiences of value capture in online labour platform ecosystems.

Everything workers do in algorithmically managed HRM systems (Meijerink et al., 2021b) has implications for the immediate term (as expressed in exchange value that workers can command) but also, in the longer term, as decisions that workers make about what gigs to accept, or not, interact recursively with their opportunities to gain access to work. Kellogg et al. (2020) have noted how algorithms are used to manage workers in many different ways, and these all interact with each other to tell the whole story about the value that workers capture from their participation in ecosystems. Payment for gigs (exchange value for workers, possible value capture) is linked with access to gigs, and access to many corporate platform ecosystems is determined by workers meeting performance targets that often include (recursively) gig acceptance rates (Waldkirch et al., 2021). Workers are not wholly autonomous in deciding to accept gigs, even though gigs may not pay well at the point of exchange. The interlocking effects of algorithms recommending, rating, and restricting and rewarding workers (Kellogg et al., 2020: 366) can lead to worker anxiety about rejecting gigs, or complaining about pay rates, as has been reported in the literature (Bucher et al., 2021; Waldkirch et al., 2021; Rosenblat, 2018). For workers to gain access to the platform (chance to create and capture value) and avoid deactivation (being blocked from value creation), they may accept gigs which yield less exchange value than it costs them in terms, as Lepak et al. (2007: 182) richly state, of "money, time, effort, joy, and the like".

Workers' exchange value is frequently lowered when they must spend a long time searching for work on microtask platforms, or waiting for app work (Dube et al., 2020). Workers also encounter high switching costs due to lock-in mechanisms of having invested time building online ratings and a strong reputation, an issue of general concern in the platform economy where client ratings play a key role (Lehdonvirta et al., 2019; Meijerink and Schoenmakers, 2020). Fear of losing ratings may prevents workers responding to unfavourable changes in how platforms set prices for workers (Dube et al., 2020), and shows how HRM practices interact in value creation and capture dynamics on platforms. If workers have few alternatives because a platform has a (near) monopoly, workers may be unable to quit an ecosystem, or they may have to switch to another ecosystem with similarly disadvantageous value capture policies (Rosenblat, 2018) or resort to informal work that offers fewer and more precarious opportunities for value capture (Van Doorn, Ferrari and Graham, 2020). Prevailing assumptions in HRM scholarship in terms of value creation and value capture do not account for these interlocking mechanisms and power imbalances between workers and corporate platform firms. Even when microwork sites allow workers to set prices and bid for work, workers may set prices at low levels to pacify algorithms and protect their ratings, which damages their ability to capture value (Bucher et al., 2021).

Algorithmic management thus interlocks with performance management systems and dynamic pricing to lower workers' perceptions of their bargaining power in relation to the platform and value capture (Bowman and Ambrosini,

2000). Design features of platform firms make it hard for workers to evaluate tasks before taking them on (Dube et al., 2020) and to price tasks in ways that compensate adequately for what it costs them to produce value (Lepak et al., 2007).

Notwithstanding their heterogeneity, corporate platforms by and large seem to propagate a lower road in terms of value creation and value capture dynamics. By focusing explicitly on value capture as well as value creation, we can see that workers are not only creators of value with platform firms and custom- ers, but also competitors for exchange value with platform firms and their peers who they compete with as freelance workers. Research indicates that platform firms are so far largely winning the competition (Dube et al., 2020). Corporate platforms use their technology to leverage insights from workers on how to better create value for customers but often without compensating workers for these tacit insights or affording workers any real say in decisions on platform design or compensation (Waldkirch et al., 2021; Gegenhuber et al., 2021). Because all transactions can be captured by the platform, workers even may feel compelled to contribute and share their tacit knowledge without compensation because they anticipate how algorithms might interpret par- ticipation in voluntary and community activities when allocating gigs and channeling work towards, or away from, workers (Bucher et al., 2021). Birch and Cochrane (2021) cite the example of ride-hailing to argue that "Big Tech's novelty is the insertion of digital platforms as an intermediary between existing products/services and users (e.g., Uber), creating a new multi-sided ecosystem of exchange from which the digital intermediary can demand *both a toll and masses of data*" (emphasis added). Since a common strategy for online labour platform firms in sectors like food delivery and ride-hailing is to exit IPO after a platform has achieved a monopoly or dominant position in a segment and driven out competitors, this positions them to set more beneficial rules for platforms from which they can extract value at (ever) higher levels (Prassl, 2018) giving workers and customers fewer options to migrate to other plat- forms and get a better deal for their participation (Birch and Cochrane, 2021; Prassl, 2018). As such, we can expect that platforms' HRM practices over time transition from being more value creation-oriented towards becoming value capture-oriented activities.

Conclusion

Concerns have arisen about the rapid growth in platforms' ecosystems and "economy wide redesign of value creation, delivery and capture processes"

(Gawer, 2021: 2). These concerns, in our view, are warranted. Motivations for HRM practices rooted separately in value creation on the one hand, and value capture on the other, explain in more detail the reason platform firms adopt quite similar practices across different types of corporate platforms in app work, microtasking and creative crowdwork. Although value creation is a steadily growing topic in HRM scholarship in recent years, value capture has (with few exceptions) been largely overlooked to date. By incorporating a lens that explicitly considers how HRM can be used for both value creation *and* value capture, HRM in online labour platform ecosystems can be better understood in all its complex, and contradictory, nature. Insights from this context may also be helpful for researching how deploying algorithmic management in more traditional HRM settings impacts different stakeholders by focusing explicitly on both value capture and value creation, and outcomes for workers. Algorithmic workforce planning, work design, and performance management practices combine to make it both difficult for workers in corporate platform ecosystems to accurately anticipate whether it is worthwhile creating value for customers using the platform firm's technology, and difficult to bargain effectively for a fair share of the value that is captured. For this reason, it is important to examine HRM practices deployed by online labour platforms in terms of value creation and value capture, and to consider how HRM practices interlock to bolster efforts by platform firms to prevent value slippage to workers. This raises broader issues, beyond this chapter, including how societal value in protecting workers socially may be slipping to platform firms, whether this needs to be addressed, and how this can be addressed. With the diffusion of algorithmic management and insecure work contracts proceeding apace, traditional HRM scholarship can benefit from learning lessons from the platform ecosystems context. We argue for more research into different models of HRM used by corporate platforms, from a distinctly stakeholder perspective, where value capture is emphasized as well as value creation.

References

Adner, R. (2017), "Ecosystem as structure: an actionable construct for strategy", *Journal of Management*, 43 (1), 39-58.

Aloisi, A., 2016. Commoditized Workers. Case Study Research on Labour Law Issues Arising from a Set of "On-Demand/Gig Economy" Platforms. *Comparative Labor Law & Policy Journal*, 37(3), 653–690.

Amabile, T. M., 1996. *Creativity in context* (update to *The Social Psychology of Creativity*). Boulder, CO: Westview Press.

Amit, R. and Zott, C., 2001. Value creation in e-business. *Strategic Management Journal*, 22(6–7), 493–520.

Anwar, M. A. and Graham, M., 2020. Hidden transcripts of the gig economy: labour agency and the new art of resistance among African gig workers. *Environment and Planning A: Economy and Space*, 52(7), 1269–1291.

Birch, K. and Cochrane, D. T., 2021. Big Tech: Four Emerging Forms of Digital Rentiership. *Science as Culture*, 1–15.

Bondarouk, T. V. and Ruël, H. J. (2009). Electronic human resource management: Challenges in the digital era. *The International Journal of Human Resource Management*, 20(3), 505–514.

Boons, M., Stam, D. and Barkema, H.G., 2015. Feelings of pride and respect as drivers of ongoing member activity on crowdsourcing platforms. *Journal of Management Studies*, 52(6), 717–741.

Bowen, D. E. and Ostroff, C., 2004. Understanding HRM–firm performance linkages: The role of the "strength" of the HRM system. *Academy of Management Review*, 29(2), 203–221.

Bowman, C. and Ambrosini, V., 2000. Value creation versus value capture: towards a coherent definition of value in strategy. *British Journal of Management*, 11(1), 1–15.

Boxall, P. and Macky, K., 2009. Research and theory on high-performance work systems: progressing the high-involvement stream. *Human Resource Management Journal*, 19(1), 3–23.

Bucher, E. L., Schou, P. K. and Waldkirch, M., 2021. Pacifying the algorithm – Anticipatory compliance in the face of algorithmic management in the gig economy. *Organization*, 28(1), 44–67.

Chen, S. J., Lin, P. F., Lu, C. M. and Tsao, C. W., 2007. The moderation effect of HR strength on the relationship between employee commitment and job performance. *Social Behavior and Personality: An International Journal*, 35(8), 1121–1138.

Coff, R.W., 1997. Human assets and management dilemmas: Coping with hazards on the road to resource-based theory. *Academy of management review*, 22(2), 374–402.

Coff, R. W., 1999. When competitive advantage doesn't lead to performance: The resource-based view and stakeholder bargaining power. *Organization Science*, 10(2), 119–133.

Cushen, J. and Thompson, P., 2016. Financialization and value: why labour and the labour process still matter. *Work, Employment and Society*, 30(2), 352–365.

De Stefano, V., 2016. The rise of the just-in-time workforce: On-demand work, crowdwork, and labor protection in the gig-economy. *Comp. Lab. L. & Pol'y J.*, 37, 471.

Delmotte, J., De Winne, S. and Sels, L., 2012. Toward an assessment of perceived HRM system strength: scale development and validation. *The International Journal of Human Resource Management*, 23(7), 1481–1506.

Dube, A., Jacobs, J., Naidu, S. and Suri, S., 2020. Monopsony in online labor markets. *American Economic Review: Insights*, 2(1), 33–46.

Duggan, J., Sherman, U., Carbery, R. and McDonnell, A., 2020. Algorithmic management and app-work in the gig economy: A research agenda for employment relations and HRM. *Human Resource Management Journal*, 30(1), 114–132.

Frenken, K., Vaskelainen, T., Fünfschilling, L. and Piscicelli, L., 2020. An institutional logics perspective on the gig economy. In *Theorizing the Sharing Economy: Variety and Trajectories of New Forms of Organizing*. Emerald Publishing Ltd.

Gawer, A., 2021. Digital Platforms and Ecosystems: Remarks on the Dominant Organizational Forms of the Digital Age (1 August 2021). *Innovation: Organization & Management*, DOI: 10.1080/14479338.2021.1965888, Available at SSRN: https://ssrn.com/abstract=3900105.

Geary, J. and Trif, A., 2011. Workplace partnership and the balance of advantage: A critical case analysis. *British Journal of Industrial Relations*, 49, 44–69.

Gegenhuber, T., Ellmer, M. and Schüßler, E., 2021. Microphones, not megaphones: Functional crowdworker voice regimes on digital work platforms. *Human Relations*, 74(9), 1473–1503.

Gray, M. L. and Suri, S., 2019. *Ghost Work: How to Stop Silicon Valley from Building a New Global Underclass*. Eamon Dolan Books.

Howcroft, D. and Bergvall-Kåreborn, B., 2019. A typology of crowdwork platforms. *Work, Employment and Society*, 33(1), 21–38.

Irani, L. C. and Silberman, M. S., 2013 (April). Turkopticon: Interrupting worker invisibility in Amazon Mechanical Turk. In *Proceedings of the SIGCHI Conference on Human Factors in Computing Systems* (611–620).

Jacobides, M. G., Cennamo, C. and Gawer, A., 2018. Towards a theory of ecosystems. *Strategic Management Journal*, 39(8), 2255–2276.

Jarrahi, M. H., Newlands, G., Lee, M. K., Wolf, C. T., Kinder, E. and Sutherland, W., 2021. Algorithmic management in a work context. *Big Data & Society*, 8(2), 1–14.

Kang, S. C., Morris, S. S. and Snell, S. A., 2007. Relational archetypes, organizational learning, and value creation: Extending the human resource architecture. *Academy of Management Review*, 32(1), 236–256.

Kässi, O. and Lehdonvirta, V., 2018. Online labour index: Measuring the online gig economy for policy and research. *Technological Forecasting and Social Change*, 137, 241–248.

Keegan, A., & Meijerink, J. (2022). Dynamism and realignment in the HR architecture: Online labor platform ecosystems and the key role of contractors. Human Resource Management, 1–15. https://doi.org/10.1002/hrm.22120

Kellogg, K. C., Valentine, M. A., and Christin, A. (2020). Algorithms at work: The new contested terrain of control. *Academy of Management Annals*, 14(1), 366–410. https://doi.org/10.5465/annals.2018.0174.

Kittur, A., Nickerson, J. V., Bernstein, M., Gerber, E., Shaw, A., Zimmerman, J., Lease, M. and Horton, J., 2013 (February). The future of crowd work. In *Proceedings of the 2013 Conference on Computer Supported Cooperative Work* (1301–1318).

Kuhn, K. M. and Maleki, A., 2017. Micro-entrepreneurs, dependent contractors, and instaserfs: Understanding online labor platform workforces. *Academy of Management Perspectives*, 31(3), 183–200.

Kuhn, K. M., Meijerink, J. and Keegan, A., 2021. Human resource management and the gig economy: Challenges and opportunities at the intersection between organizational HR decision-makers and digital labor platforms. In *Research in Personnel and Human Resources Management*. Emerald Publishing Ltd.

Lee, M. K., Kusbit, D., Metsky, E. and Dabbish, L. (2015), *Working with machines: The impact of algorithmic and data-driven management on human workers*. Proceedings of the 33rd Annual ACM Conference on Human Factors in Computing Systems, New York, Association for Computing Machinery.

Lehdonvirta, V., Kässi, O., Hjorth, I., Barnard, H. and Graham, M. (2019). The global platform economy: A new offshoring institution enabling emerging-economy microproviders. *Journal of Management*, 45(2), 567–599.

Leicht-Deobald, U., Busch, T., Schank, C., Weibel, A., Schafheitle, S., Wildhaber, I. and Kasper, G., 2019. The challenges of algorithm-based HR decision-making for personal integrity. *Journal of Business Ethics*, 160(2), 377–392.

Leighton, P. and McKeown, T., 2015. The rise of independent professionals: Their challenge for management. *Small Enterprise Research*, 22(2-3), 119–130.

Lepak, D. P. and Snell, S. A., 1999. The human resource architecture: Toward a theory of human capital allocation and development. *Academy of Management Review*, 24(1), 31–48.

Lepak, D. P., Smith, K. G. and Taylor, M. S., 2007. Value creation and value capture: A multilevel perspective. *Academy of Management Review*, 32(1), 180–194.

Malik, A., Pereira, V. and Budhwar, P., 2017. Value creation and capture through human resource management practices: Gazing through the business model lens. *Organizational Dynamics*, 47, 180–188.

Meijerink, J. and Keegan, A. (2019) Conceptualizing human resource management in the gig economy: Toward a platform ecosystem perspective. *Journal of Managerial Psychology*, 34(4), 214–232.

Meijerink, J. and Schoenmakers, E., 2020. Why are online reviews in the sharing economy skewed toward positive ratings? Linking customer perceptions of service quality to leaving a review of an Airbnb stay. *Journal of Tourism Futures*. DOI: 10.1108/JTF-04-2019-0039.

Meijerink, J. G., Bondarouk, T. and Lepak, D. P., 2016. Employees as active consumers of HRM: Linking employees' HRM competences with their perceptions of HRM service value. *Human Resource Management*, 55(2), 219–240.

Meijerink, J., Keegan, A. and Bondarouk, T., 2021a. Having their cake and eating it too? Online labor platforms and human resource management as a case of institutional complexity. *The International Journal of Human Resource Management*, 1–37.

Meijerink, J., Boons, M., Keegan, A. and Marler, J., 2021b. Algorithmic human resource management: Synthesizing developments and cross-disciplinary insights on digital HRM. *The International Journal of Human Resource Management*, 1–18.

Newlands, G., 2021. Algorithmic surveillance in the gig economy: The organization of work through Lefebvrian conceived space. *Organization Studies*, 42(5), 719–737.

Porter, M. E. 1985. *Competitive Advantage*. Free Press.

Prassl, J., 2018. *Humans as a Service: The Promise and Perils of Work in the Gig Economy*. Oxford University Press.

Prassl, J. and Risak, M., 2015. Uber, taskrabbit, and co.: Platforms as employers-rethinking the legal analysis of crowdwork. *Comp. Lab. L. & Pol'y J.*, 37, 619.

Rosenblat, A., 2018. *Uberland*. University of California Press.

Rosenblat, A. and Stark, L., 2016. Algorithmic labor and information asymmetries: A case study of Uber's drivers. *International Journal of Communication*, 10, 3758–3784.

Ruël, H. and Van der Kaap, H., 2012. E-HRM usage and value creation. Does a facilitating context matter? *German Journal of Human Resource Management*, 26(3), 260–281.

Schor, J. B. and Vallas, S. P., 2021. The Sharing Economy: Rhetoric and Reality. *Annual Review of Sociology*, 47(1), 369–389.

Stanford, J. (2017), "The resurgence of gig work: Historical and theoretical perspectives", *The Economic and Labour Relations Review*, 28(3), 382–401.

Sundararajan, A., 2016. The Sharing Economy. *The End of Employment and the Rise of Crowd-Based Capitalism*. MIT Press.

Tassinari, A. and Maccarrone, V., 2020. Riders on the storm: Workplace solidarity among gig economy couriers in Italy and the UK. *Work, Employment and Society*, 34(1), 35–54.

Van Alstyne, M. W., Parker, G. G. and Choudary, S. P., 2016. Pipelines, platforms, and the new rules of strategy. *Harvard Business Review*, 94(4), 54–62.

van Doorn, N. and Badger, A., 2021. Dual value production as key to the gig economy puzzle. In *Platform Economy Puzzles*. Edward Elgar Publishing.

Van Doorn, N., Ferrari, F. and Graham, M., 2020. Migration and migrant labour in the gig economy: an intervention. Available at SSRN 3622589.

Veen, A., Barratt, T. and Goods, C., 2019. Platform-capital's "app-etite"for control: A labour process analysis of food-delivery work in Australia. *Work, Employment and Society*, 34(3), 388–406.

Wahyudi, E. and Park, S. M., 2014. Unveiling the value creation process of electronic human resource management: An Indonesian case. *Public Personnel Management*, 43(1), 83–117.

Waldkirch, M., Bucher, E., Schou, P.K. and Grünwald, E., 2021. Controlled by the algorithm, coached by the crowd–how HRM activities take shape on digital work platforms in the gig economy. *The International Journal of Human Resource Management*, *32*(12), 2643–2682.

Wareham, J., Fox, P. B. and Cano Giner, J. L. (2014), "Technology ecosystem governance", *Organization science*, 25(4), 1195–1215.

Wood, A. J., Graham, M., Lehdonvirta, V. and Hjorth, I., 2019. Good gig, bad gig: autonomy and algorithmic control in the global gig economy. *Work, Employment and Society*, 33(1), 56–75.

Wright, P. M. and McMahan, G. C., 1992. Theoretical perspectives for strategic human resource management. *Journal of Management*, 18(2), 295–320.

9   People management in entrepreneurial firms

Joonyoung Kim and M. Diane Burton

Introduction

Over the past 30 years, much has been written about vibrant startup organizations with charismatic leaders and ingenious management practices that attract and motivate top talent, encourage collaboration, support creativity and innovation, and provide generous rewards (Bosma & Kelley, 2018; Puranam & Håkonsson, 2015; Sheldon, 2012; Sorenson et al., 2021). Many believe that startups innovate and outcompete established firms because they avoid the traps of inertia and bureaucracy. In light of this emphasis on startups, entrepreneurship and entrepreneurial management, it is surprising that human resource (HR) management scholars have, for the most part, ignored the topic. Echoing prior calls (e.g., Galbraith, 1985; Heneman et al., 2000; Burton et al., 2019), we hope to make a compelling case for entrepreneurial HR research. In this chapter, we explain why it is needed, what we can hope to learn, and where researchers might most fruitfully focus their attention.

Just as the recognition that 'children are not merely small adults' was foundational to pediatrics becoming an independent medical specialty (Gillis & Loughlan, 2007), HR researchers have an opportunity to make a similar distinction. If HR researchers consider startups to be merely immature organizations, then startups are uninteresting because their size is smaller and their systems, processes, and practices are less well-developed. Lessons learned from established organizations could be applied to their younger counterparts, but their reverse is unlikely to be true. Alternatively, if HR researchers could consider startups to be a distinct category of organizations, then new possibilities open up. Recognizing entrepreneurial firms as a unique population with interesting genetic variability that is worthy of study, understanding how organizational variations emerge and evolve, and identifying when and why some variations thrive and others falter should improve the health and vitality of all kinds of firms - entrepreneurial and established.

The Stanford Project on Emerging Companies (SPEC) studies were among the earliest attempts in this vein to employ longitudinal data to understand how HR systems are first established and evolve over time in concert with organizational designs and business strategies (Burton, 1995; Baron et al., 1996). The motivation behind SPEC studies was rooted in the population ecology ideas, where population-level adaptation and evolution were the key focus of interest. In order to accurately understand the contexts and mechanisms by which HR systems vary and subsequently influence entrepreneurial firms, the design of the SPEC studies deliberately narrows some of the possible external sources of variation in HR systems. For example, focusing only on high-technology firms in Silicon Valley controls for the labor market and environmental conditions, as well as institutional influences that may shape organizational choices and outcomes (Burton, 2001). Also, gathering information on the earliest days of the organization enables studying how founding conditions and early decisions affect subsequent organizational evolution (Baron & Hannan, 2002). The SPEC research team documented that there are employment models or 'blueprints' that appear consistently in the sample of entrepreneurial firms (Baron et al., 1996) and that changes in these blueprints adversely affect employee turnover, bottom-line financial performance, and survival (Baron et al., 2001). The lessons from SPEC studies suggest the importance of focusing on the population of entrepreneurial firms - as opposed to relying on the sample of established firms or not making the distinction between entrepreneurial and established firms - and prudent research designs that take into account selection and sampling biases.

Why entrepreneurial firms are a useful context for HR studies

Entrepreneurial firms face fundamentally different structural challenges than established firms (Quinn & Cameron, 1983; Gilbert, 2005; Kimberly, 1979; Shane, 2003). They are plagued by a liability of newness (Stinchcombe, 1965) where they lack both resources and external legitimacy and have yet to create robust, repeatable processes. This allows for experimentation and adaptation that can yield new ways of organizing and managing. Additionally, entrepreneurs often operate in new and emerging industries or in new or emerging markets such that existing principles and theories cannot be applied without modification (Kotey & Slade, 2005; Taylor, 2006). Because of the structural challenges that distinguish entrepreneurial organizations from their established peers and the fact that they often operate in more uncertain environments, they offer a unique and potentially valuable business context for testing the existing principles and theories of HR and for elaborating new ones (Baron, 2003).

In addition, studying HR in entrepreneurial firms provides an opportunity to theorize and explore HR with a deeper understanding of the context in which a given HR structure was initiated. Immediately after an entrepreneurial firm is established, the founders (or founding team members) typically make a series of HR-related decisions (e.g., staffing) that constitute the organization"s HR model. Because the founders" choices are not limited by prior decisions or existing policies, researchers can examine causal relationships between HR and the environment (e.g., labor market conditions) or organizational characteristics (e.g., firm resources) without concern for causality (Burton, 2001). Also, because of the imprinting and path-dependent nature of early HR decisions (Baron et al., 1999), prior HR systems generally influence future HR systems within organizations. If a firm changes the ways in which it organizes and manages its employees, it is reasonable to assume that it has experienced events or shocks that prompted the changes. As in Penrose"s (1959) metaphor of the metamorphosis of a caterpillar into a butterfly, entrepreneurial firms may experience dramatic organizational transformation (DeSantola & Gulati, 2017) in which HR plays a role. Thakur (1998) has shown that the HR needs of entrepreneurial firms change as they mature. Studying HR in entrepreneurial firms may provide insights into the dynamics of how organizations manage their employees to adapt to changing environments. In doing so, researchers may gain a deeper understanding of the antecedents of HR systems and how they influence the performance of maturing entrepreneurial firms.

For example, we know that attracting and motivating talent is essential for all organizations. Because newly established firms lack both resources and legitimacy, they need to offer a compelling alternative work environment to prospective employees. Notably, many entrepreneurial firms have explored alternatives to traditional hierarchies and eschewed formal HR practices. Traditional HR practices are viewed as bureaucratic, rigid, and poorly suited to the rapid information flows and technological developments faced by entrepreneurial firms (Lee & Edmondson, 2017).

Consider how the online retailer Zappos adopted a novel organizational system called Holacracy and garnered considerable attention from both practitioners and academics (Bernstein et al., 2016). Holacracies are characterized by self-managing teams whereby designated managers are eliminated and individual employees have full autonomy in deciding how they will work (Robertson, 2015). Tony Hsieh, the founder and CEO of Zappos, adopted

Holacracy because he was concerned about decreasing productivity as the organization grew. He believed that self-organizing structures and systems would lead to increased innovation and productivity, improved employee satisfaction, and reduced turnover. Similarly, Valve, one of the most successful makers of computer games, has adopted non-hierarchical and informal HR practices where there are no job titles, no job descriptions, and no 'bosses' (Puranam & Håkonsson, 2015). Instead of being directed by managers, employees can choose how to use their time and talents. For instance, employees are free to initiate projects and choose which projects to work on (Lee & Edmonson, 2017). Valve"s intent with this approach to project staffing was to empower individual employees to steer their careers toward opportunities and away from risks.

Entrepreneurial firms" experiments with how they manage their employees are not only limited to organizational designs focusing on self-management and self-selection but also encompass other aspects of HR practices. For instance, Menlo Innovations, a software design and development company, hires its employees in mass job auditions instead of resumes and interviews where hiring managers make hiring decisions (Sheridan, 2015). These job auditions are designed to mimic the company"s operations, and candidates are set to work on a task, working in pairs with other candidates or current employees of the company. After each stage of the audition, the entire staff discuss what they have seen during the audition and make the decision. Gravity Payments, a credit card processing and financial services company, is an example of a novel experiment with compensation systems. The company raised its employees" minimum salary to $70,000, doubling from the previous $35,000 (Tayeb, 2021). Although this initiative drew significant skepticism at first, the company"s revenue has significantly increased every year since then. Because of the $70,000 initiative coupled with other employee-centric HR practices such as unlimited parental leave and paid time off, Gravity has not suffered from a labor shortage.

Experiments with novel HR practices are not always successful. In fact, some experiments are spectacular failures. For instance, Amazon built an artificial intelligence (AI) system to review job applicants" resumes with the aim of improving the search for top talent (Dastin, 2018). Despite good intentions, the AI system was trained to vet applicants by observing previous resumes submitted mostly from male applicants, and it ended up penalizing female applicants and garnered negative media attention. Realizing this problem, the company disbanded the project, but it continues to serve as a cautionary tale of the problems with algorithms and AI for hiring. Other well-known initiatives such as Holacracy (Bernstein et al., 2016) and Uber"s customer rating systems

(Dzieza, 2015) have also been harshly criticized for their unintended negative consequences.

The HR practices described above, whether or not they were successful, are attempts by entrepreneurial firms to distance themselves from traditional HR and bureaucracy and to experiment with new ways of organizing and managing employees. This type of experimentation with novel HR and organizational practices appears more prevalent in entrepreneurial firms operating in newer markets and sectors. In such places, new types of work and new ways of working emerge, forming the seeds for new experiments and shedding light on which might be employed in established firms. The failed experiments are instructive as they can reveal problematic practices when they are operating at a relatively small scale and are unlikely to do widespread damage to the labor market or the economy.

HR and entrepreneurial firms

Thus far, we have been quite general in our use of the terms 'entrepreneurial firm' and 'HR,' but catalyzing serious scholarly effort requires more precise definitions. Sadly, there is little consensus among entrepreneurship researchers in how they define entrepreneurship or entrepreneurial firms; and among HR researchers, there are many different foci. To make progress, we must narrow our focus and clearly specify the kinds of entrepreneurial firms that are of interest and the relevant aspects of HR.

What is an entrepreneurial firm?

For our purposes, we want to focus on the creation of new organizations and examine how HR may further the economic progress of new firms. To do this, we need to look at organizations in their early stages that are using novel and interesting HR practices. This approach is consistent with Carland et al. (1984) who defined an entrepreneurial firm as one whose principal goals are profitability and growth is based on innovative strategic practices; Klotz et al. (2014) who defined an entrepreneurial firm as a new venture that is in its early stages of development and growth; and others who are increasingly attending to these kinds of firms (Carlsson et al., 2013; Davidsson & Gruenhagen, 2021; Wiklund et al., 2011; Zott & Amit, 2007).

Because entrepreneurship involves the creation of an organization that did not previously exist, entrepreneurial firms are likely to be small initially, and entrepreneurship is often equated with small business ownership and management (Carland et al., 1984). However, the liabilities of newness (Stinchcombe, 1965) and smallness (Freeman et al., 1983) share some commonalities (e.g., resource constraints) but also are distinct in several aspects (Aldrich & Auster 1986). We are focusing on entrepreneurial firms rather than small firms, given the different material realities represented by their newness and smallness. We focus on new firms that are in their early stages of growth and are created by an individual or a group of individuals outside the context of previously established organizations. This definition of entrepreneurial firms is consistent with prior studies (Carlsson et al., 2013; Davidsson & Gruenhagen, 2021; Gartner, 1990; Low & MacMillan, 1988; Wiklund et al., 2011) but has a different focus than some definitions used in entrepreneurship research domains that are associated with entrepreneurial opportunities (e.g., Shane & Venkataraman, 2000) or self-employment (e.g., Van der Sluis et al., 2008). The reason that we are focusing on new and independently created organizations is that those are generally the places where novel and innovative HR practices are used.

What do we mean by HR?

There is also definitional confusion in what we mean by HR, which has numerous definitions and operationalizations (Ostroff & Bowen, 2000; Peccei & Van De Voorde, 2019). HR scholars tend to emphasize specific practices such as compensation, benefits, recruitment, selection, training and development either individually or in bundles or systems of practices (Boon et al., 2019; Combs et al., 2006; Guthrie, 2001; Huselid, 1995; Kehoe & Collins, 2017; Lepak et al., 2006). In contrast, in the entrepreneurship literature, researchers study a broad range of organizational aspects of building a new business as well as the people involved in business creation. These foci are distinct from how HR scholars recognize and use the term 'HR.' As a recent meta-analysis by Kim (2020) reveals, entrepreneurship scholars have studied (1) founding teams, (2) organizational design, (3) human capital, (4) social capital, (5) HR practices and systems, and (6) HR investments and functions. Among these, HR scholars have mostly focused on examining the antecedents and consequences of HR practices and systems and studying HR investments and functions. Ironically, these are the areas that have been the most understudied in the entrepreneurship literature. Thus, in this chapter, we focus on HR practices and systems and HR investments and functions to fill the gaps in the literature

and bridge entrepreneurship and HR research. However, we are not uncondi-
tionally excluding studies that cover founding teams, organizational design,
human capital, or social capital because, within those topics, some studies have
reported results that have critical implications for HR. For instance, Baron et
al. (1999) focused on founders and organizational structures of entrepreneurial firms and could be classified as a study of founding teams and/or organizational design. However, the key implications of the authors" findings are that
founders" employment and organizational models or blueprints have enduring effects on growth in managerial intensity. These effects may influence HR
practices and HR systems in the focal organizations, even after the founders
are no longer in charge. This has clear HR implications from the perspective of
HR scholars, although the topic may seem related only to founders or founding
teams. Note, however, that our focus is distinct from that of top management
team scholars, whose primary topics of interest are the human and social
capital of top management teams (e.g., Beckman & Burton, 2008; Kor, 2003;
Pitcher & Smith, 2001). Similarly, entrepreneurship research on ownership
and governance usually investigates how founders" statuses influence firm
performance, and there is no clear link to HR practices and systems. However,
some studies (e.g., Davila et al., 2010) examine founders who are reluctant to
adopt formal HR practices and systems because they fear losing control over
their employees and giving up their personalized management styles. Thus,
we attend to lines of research that may have a primary focus on founders or
ownership and governance but also have clear and direct HR implications.

What do we know about HR in entrepreneurial firms?

Although entrepreneurship and HR have seldom been jointly examined,
some studies have investigated HR in entrepreneurial firms. The SPEC studies
(Baron et al., 1996, 1999) were among the earliest to employ longitudinal data
on employment models from a wide sample of high-technology entrepreneurial firms. More specifically, the authors contended that founders form
employment models that vary across three dimensions: (1) attachment (i.e.,
work, love, or money), (2) basis of coordination and control (i.e., peer/cultural,
professional, formal, or direct), and (3) selection (i.e., skills, potential, or fit).
Among many possible combinations of these three dimensions, the authors
showed that entrepreneurial firms generally cluster into one of a few 'basic
model types' (Baron et al., 1999, p. 530) that exhibit a high degree of coherence
and internal consistency. For example, one extreme form is the bureaucratic
model, defined by attachment through challenging work, coordination and

control through formal systems, and skill-based selection. The commitment model is at the other end of the spectrum, which is defined by attachment through love, peer-group coordination, and control, and selection based on cultural fit. The authors showed how employment models chosen by founders are associated with different HR practices (Baron et al., 1999), different levels of managerial intensity (Baron et al., 1999), and different gender compositions (Baron et al., 2007). They also illustrate that these models exert an enduring influence on the organizations" future employment models even after the end of the founders" tenure (Baron et al., 2001).

Besides demonstrating the imprinting effects of founders" initial employment models, the SPEC authors also showed that altering these early employment models could have disruptive consequences on the organizations. Shifting from an early employment model to a different model increased employee turnover rates, particularly among senior employees (Baron et al., 2001). By demonstrating that early imprints have a powerful bearing on later administration and that changes in employment models may have negative impacts on entrepreneurial firms and their employees, the SPEC studies highlighted the importance of understanding the initial choices founders make concerning organizational administration and people management.

Another foundational stream of research on HR investments and functions was led by Welbourne and colleagues. For instance, Welbourne and Cyr (1999) examined the impact of having a senior HR executive in an entrepreneurial firm. They demonstrated that smaller, fast-growing IPOs experience the most gain from having senior HR executives. Chadwick et al. (2016) replicated and extended Welbourne and Cyr"s (1999) study and showed that the presence of an HR executive at the time of entrepreneurial firms" IPO is positively related to the ultimate success measure: post-IPO firm survival. The authors also found that firm size and leverage have a moderating effect on this relationship such that for entrepreneurial firms that have HR executives, the negative influence of firm size on firm mortality is greater and the positive effect of leverage on firm mortality is smaller. Welbourne et al. (2012) similarly found that firms allocating funding to HR are more likely to break through the growth ceiling quickly. The authors" theorization is rooted in the idea that allocating funding to HR allows an entrepreneurial firm to address multiple problems concerning management capacity, training and development, organizational structure, knowledge capacities, compensation, and motivation. Given the resource constraints that entrepreneurial firms encounter, their decisions about whether to invest in HR and/or have an HR executive reflect their strategic priorities (Sirmon et al., 2011).

A handful of studies have investigated how HR practices or systems influence entrepreneurial firms. Burton and O"Reilly (2004) found that high-commitment work systems in a young technology firm are associated with an increased likelihood of an IPO and a decreased likelihood of firm failure. They also demonstrated that high-commitment work systems and the espoused values of an entrepreneurial firm"s leadership interact with each other such that the benefit of one tends to amplify the other. The authors drew upon the social construction perspective and contended that leaders who espouse high-commitment values would provide informational and normative cues, conveying consistent and positive signals to employees with respect to HR practices (Meyer & Smith, 2000; Pfeffer, 1981). Similarly, Kerr et al. (2007) reported that having high-performance work systems in entrepreneurial firms is related to a higher level of entrepreneurial performance. They also found a positive association between the presence of an HR manager and having high-performance work systems. Similarly, Su and Wang (2018) found that an entrepreneurial firm"s output and behavior control systems enhance the positive influence of entrepreneurial orientation on firm performance. However, their findings suggest that an input control system - aligning employees" interests and values with the organizational goals - may negate the positive influence of entrepreneurial orientation on firm performance. The authors built on the dominant logic perspective to argue that an entrepreneurial firm"s input control system results in recruiting managers and employees who embrace experimenting with entrepreneurial initiatives and training them to be experimental. Consequently, input control may lead to excessive experiments and high uncertainty (Obloj et al., 2010) without carefully evaluating and commanding experimental decisions and actions (Hmieleski & Baron, 2009; Prahalad & Bettis, 1986).

Although only a few published empirical studies have focused on the impact of HR practices and systems and HR investments and functions on entrepreneurial performance, they have mostly found potentially positive influences on entrepreneurial firms and their employees. Still, in reality, entrepreneurial firms have not yet adopted HR practices and systems (Chadwick et al., 2013; Gilman & Raby, 2013; Harney & Dundon, 2006; Sels et al., 2006) and are reluctant to invest in HR to allocate limited resources in areas where the direct return is expected (e.g., infrastructure and technology; Deb et al., 2017). This research-practice gap warrants a need to more fully explore how and when HR influences entrepreneurial firms.

Opportunities for future research and mutual learning

In this section, we introduce opportunities for future research that are under-studied or may further our understanding of HR in entrepreneurial firms. In particular, we believe there are important research opportunities in the area of mutual learning, namely, what the HR and entrepreneurship literatures can learn from each other.

Mutual learning of dependent variables

In studying the impact of HR on individuals and organizations, the HR and entrepreneurship literatures have focused on distinct dependent variables. HR scholars have largely examined how HR influences individual-level and proximal outcomes (e.g., job satisfaction) and/or how these outcomes serve as the mechanisms through which HR affects organizational performance. In contrast, entrepreneurship scholars have paid more attention to firm-level and distal outcomes. Below, we explain these differences in dependent variables and suggest ways that researchers in the two fields can learn from one another.

Proximal outcomes and mechanisms

Research on HR in entrepreneurial firms has focused on the impact of HR on the firms" financial performance (e.g., IPOs, survival, profits). However, the mechanisms through which HR impacts entrepreneurial firms have been mostly neglected. The employee-related proximal outcomes that have been widely studied in the HR literature have not attracted scholarly attention in the entrepreneurship literature. Since HR scholars argued for the necessity of unpacking the 'black box' through which HR influences individual or organizational outcomes, a variety of mechanisms have been studied. Because HR practices impact employees, it seems intuitive to assume that they would influence employees in ways that will result in higher organizational performance (Wright & Ulrich, 2017). For instance, HR practices may impact the knowledge, skills, and abilities of employees (i.e., a firm"s human capital). Takeuchi et al. (2007) found that HR practices had a positive impact on the collective human capital of a firm. HR practices may also affect employee attitudes and behaviors, including motivation (e.g., Wright et al., 1998), affective commitment (e.g., Gong et al., 2009; Kehoe & Wright, 2013), organizational citizenship behaviors (e.g., Messersmith et al., 2011), and turnover (e.g., Jiang et al., 2012). Other lines of research have focused on how HR practices influence organizations" internal social structures to facilitate communication and collaboration among employees (Combs et al., 2006; Evans & Davis, 2005). For instance, Gittell et al. (2010) have suggested a relational model of high-performance work systems in which a set of HR practices strengthens relationships among employees who perform distinct functions, in turn positively impacting organizational performance.

Research on HR in the entrepreneurship domain has focused on distal outcomes such as financial performance. As a result, the mechanisms through which HR impacts entrepreneurial firms are only beginning to be explored. In the recent decade, there has been work on employee mobility (e.g., Campbell et al., 2012), lift-outs (e.g., Agarwal et al., 2016), acqui-hiring (e.g., Chatterji & Patro, 2014; Li & Wang, 2018), and non-compete agreements (e.g., Marx et al., 2009). For example, Agarwal et al. (2016) focused on a spin-out founder"s role as a team catalyst and found that spin-out founders more positively influence firm outcomes through recruiting larger and more experienced teams. Similarly, research on acqui-hiring - acquisition of a company to gain access to the firm"s employees (Chatterji & Patro, 2014) - suggests that it benefits acquiring firms" performance by the transfer of new and specialized knowledge, keeping up with technological progress, and exploiting synergies between the target and the acquiring firm (Li & Wang, 2018).

Despite these recent efforts to understand the mechanisms, sometimes, it has been assumed that the proximal outcomes and mechanisms unpacked in the HR and organizational behavior literatures would hold in entrepreneurial firms. However, that may not necessarily be the case. For instance, the strategic human resource management literature has shown that HR has a positive effect on employees" abilities, which in turn positively impacts organizational performance (Nyberg et al., 2014). In other words, ability or human capital usually serves as the mediator in the relationship between HR and organizational performance. Although this mechanism seems intuitive and therefore could be assumed to hold true for entrepreneurial firms as well, an alternative mechanism also makes sense, given the characteristics of entrepreneurial firms. De Winne and Sels (2010) found that founders" abilities/human capital were associated with a broad range of HR practices, which in turn positively affected the organizational performance of entrepreneurial firms. The authors posit that because the role and the influence of individuals, whether founders or employees, is broader in entrepreneurial firms than in their established peers, a talented individual may introduce a set of HR practices rather than being influenced by a pre-adopted set of HR practices. Alternatively, if an organization"s business success relies on a skilled, valuable, and unique workforce, it is likely that the focal organization will invest in HR practices and systems to attract and retain key talent (Bacon & Hoque, 2005). In both of these cases, HR serves as the mediator in the relationship between human capital and entrepreneurial performance. This discrepancy in mechanisms between entrepreneurial firms and established firms opens an interesting chicken-and-egg question. Does human capital affect the adoption of HR systems and practices, or do HR systems and practices have beneficial (or harmful) effects on human capital? If the former holds, entrepreneurial firms may benefit more from buying talent than making talent (Miles & Snow, 1984) because employees with superior abilities will introduce HR systems and practices that are required for success. For example, research on job crafting in entrepreneurial firms suggests that individual employees may shape their own jobs during and after hiring (Cohen & Mahabadi, in press) and thus, research in this vein describes a range of ways jobs are crafted around individuals" knowledge, skills, and abilities (Miner, 1987; Levesque, 2005). Conversely, if the latter holds, making talent would be a reasonable decision since HR systems and practices could increase employees" abilities, and the employees would then contribute more to entrepreneurial performance. There are research opportunities to extend and develop new theories on such potential effects of HR functions in entrepreneurial firms on proximal outcomes. Research on the role of HR outcomes in the relationship between HR and entrepreneurial performance may contribute to elucidating complex and diverse interactions. For instance, an HR system could influence an entrepreneurial firm"s survival by reducing employee turnover, or it could have a direct impact on the firm"s survival.

HR and creation of jobs

Entrepreneurship provides an important stimulus not only at the firm level but also at the societal level (Ireland & Webb, 2007) because of its impact on job creation (Birley, 1986). The creation of entrepreneurial firms is the source of most new employment in an economy (Audretsch & Thurik, 2001). Ouimet and Zarutskie (2014) reported that one in five employees works in a firm that has been in existence for fewer than five years. Despite the importance of entrepreneurial firms in job creation, 'entrepreneurship scholars have largely ignored employment-related topics, and employment scholars have largely ignored entrepreneurship-related topics' (Burton et al., 2019, p. 1051).

Although the above findings suggest that entrepreneurship increases the number of jobs, job creation and job quality have not been widely studied in the HR literature. Given HR"s role in the growth of organizations (Batt, 2002) and its influence on aspects of jobs that are closely associated with the employee-perceived job quality (Den Hartog et al., 2013), it is reasonable to assume that HR significantly affects both the quantity and quality of jobs. In contrast, in the entrepreneurship literature, diverse aspects of job creation have been studied as indicators of the performance of entrepreneurial firms (Baron & Tang, 2009; Rauch & Frese, 2005; Wiklund & Shepherd, 2005). For example, Baron and Tang (2009) found that entrepreneurs" social skills were significantly related to employment growth as they were mediated by the entrepreneurs" success in obtaining information and essential resources. It would be interesting to further examine the effects of HR practices, systems, investments, and functions on job creation. Entrepreneurship research often has policy implications because of the influence that entrepreneurship exerts on job creation and employment. Studying how HR affects job creation may expand the influence of HR research from the firm level to the society level.

Although diverse psychological and attitudinal or behavioral aspects of jobs have been the focus of HR research, job quality per se has not received scholarly attention in the HR literature. Scholars have examined how entrepreneurial firms treat their employees with respect to wages and benefits, finding that entrepreneurial firms are less generous (Burton et al., 2018; Litwin & Phan, 2013; Sorenson et al., 2021). Scholars have also studied how working at entrepreneurial firms influences careers (Burton et al., 2016). For example, several field experimental studies suggested the possibility that recruiters may attribute negative associations (e.g., fit and commitment concerns) to former founders when they attempt to enter wage employment (Botelho & Chang, 2020; Ding et al., 2020; Kacperczyk & Younkin, in press). Combining the results of these studies with findings from the HR literature may provide theoretical and practical insights on how HR influences both the quality of jobs in entrepreneurial firms and the characteristics of people who inhabit them.

Mutual learning of topics

HR and entrepreneurship scholars have studied different topics when investigating the organizational and people aspects of organizations. By studying HR in entrepreneurial firms, particularly by investigating the novel HR practices being employed in such organizations, HR scholars may be able to gain insights that have not been tapped before in the literature. Likewise, entrepreneurship scholars studying HR can learn from the ways that HR scholars have assessed the value of HR in organizations. Although HR practices and systems have tended to be portrayed as bureaucratic and formal from the perspective of entrepreneurs and those who study them (e.g., Sheldon, 2012), it is too early to draw firm conclusions because the value of such practices and systems in entrepreneurial firms has not been widely studied. Scholars of HR and general management, including entrepreneurship, have taken different perspectives on what HR represents and entails. These issues are explained in greater detail below.

Where to find novel HR practices

As Gartner (1985) asserts, 'entrepreneurs do not operate in vacuums - they respond to their environments' (p. 700). Entrepreneurs and employees of entrepreneurial firms are embedded in their firms, which are embedded in the business context. It is critical to investigate the contexts of the organizations in which HR is studied. In studying HR in entrepreneurial firms, one must consider the organizational setting. Given that the promise of studying HR in entrepreneurial firms lies in the expectation that they will be useful places to study novel HR practices, it is essential to choose a context where such practices are likely to be used.

Industry could be used as the criterion for selecting the context for a study. Industry is a source of variance in the adoption of HR practices among entrepreneurial firms (Lancker et al., in press). Industry conditions are an important consideration because different industries face varying levels of environmental uncertainty. For these reasons, the limited research on HR in entrepreneurial firms has a clear high-tech bias (Harney & Alkhalaf, 2021). High-tech industries are defined as those 'in which rapid technological change and high inputs of scientific research and development expenditure are producing new, innovative and technologically advanced products' (Keeble, 1990, p. 361). In general, high-tech industries face much higher uncertainty than low-tech industries. Organizations in high-tech industries face more dynamic environments and use sophisticated and complex technologies that typically require extensive knowledge and research (Utterback, 1996). Given that environmental uncertainty leads to greater job demands and more task complexity (Jin et al., 2017), high-tech firms may be more likely than other firms to experiment with novel HR practices to better cope with uncertainty. Consequently, it may appear that organizations in high-tech industries should be the top contextual choice for researchers considering the study of HR.

However, focusing disproportionately on high-tech firms raises two issues. First, high-tech firms do not represent the entire population of entrepreneurial firms (Harney & Alkhalaf, 2021). Aldrich and Ruef (2018) pointed out that entrepreneurship researchers have focused on the 'black swans' of the entrepreneurial world, such as large Silicon Valley high-tech firms, when in reality, entrepreneurial firms that issue IPOs and attract venture capital financing are extremely rare. They note that mundane and ordinary startups, in lifestyle or other traditional sectors, account for the vast majority of entrepreneurial firms; thus, entrepreneurship scholars have focused on one extreme and neglected the more typical and mundane. The disproportionate focus on high-growth, well-financed high-tech firms may result in unrealistic biases about entrepreneurial firms and entrepreneurs.

We agree with Aldrich and Ruef"s (2018) analysis and advocate the study of more mundane entrepreneurial firms, but that is not the only reason that we believe it problematic to use industry as the criterion in choosing a context for the study of HR. A single industry may not be representative of the population of entrepreneurial firms that have the novel HR practices that we are interested in and excited about. For instance, when Uber was founded, the industry that it said it would revolutionize was the taxi industry (Kim, 2015). Similarly, Amazon was characterized as a mail-order bookselling business when it was founded (Gartenberg, 2021). If a researcher used industry as the criterion to select entrepreneurial firms that are likely to create revolutionary change, neither Uber nor Amazon would have been chosen. However, they have both grown into large and successful firms in which many types of novel HR practices are being employed. If researchers had had the opportunity to study HR in those firms from the beginning, they could have gained insights into HR"s contributions to firm evolution. Consequently, we argue that industry criteria should not be used to choose entrepreneurial firms for study. Researchers need to look further to identify novel HR experiments. More importantly, researchers need to be preemptive in identifying potentially fruitful contexts in which to study HR; otherwise, it will be impossible to observe how HR systems unfold and interact with the internal and external environments of entrepreneurial firms. Being preemptive requires predictors to pinpoint entrepreneurial firms that are likely to be revolutionary and conduct novel HR experiments.

In the search for predictors, it might be useful to focus on stakeholders who can influence entrepreneurial firms - in particular, stakeholders who care about employment relations and the quality of employment. To the extent to which their stakeholders are focused on employee relations and the quality of employment, entrepreneurial firms are likely to focus on building well-managed people management systems, despite limited resources and multiple investment priorities. In such contexts, entrepreneurial firms may bow to external pressures to create better organizations for employees, and therefore are more likely to experiment with novel HR practices to satisfy stakeholders" mandates. Environments in which these stakeholders and their mandates may be found include impact investing; environmental, social, and corporate governance (ESG); and government-sponsored incubators.

For instance, impact investing - defined as 'actively placing capital in enterprises that generate social or environmental goods, services, or ancillary benefits such as creating good jobs, with expected financial returns ranging from the highly concessionary to above market' (Brest & Born, 2013) - might be a place to look because impact investors can have an outsized impact on the quantity and quality of jobs in entrepreneurial firms. To meet the demands of impact investors and gain access to financial resources, entrepreneurial firms may attempt to design and implement management practices that positively affect employees" health and economic security and the well-being of the community in which they operate. For instance, in the early days of Tesla, DBL Investors - a group of venture capitalists and impact investors - encouraged the company to explore locations in the San Francisco Bay Area because the people at DBL were committed to creating high-quality jobs there (Brest & Born, 2013). Today, Tesla is one of the most innovative companies in the world (Babal, 2020) and has experimented with unconventional HR policies such as a minimalist employee handbook and insisting that employees initiate conversations about feedback (Babal, 2020; Kelly, 2020). Rethink Impact is another example of a group of impact investors who are focused on employment relations and the quality of employment. They encourage gender diversity and gender equity in the companies that they back. Similarly, many ESG and government-sponsored incubation programs seek to find companies that attend to the well-being of employees by evaluating them via HR-related metrics such as the number of employees receiving a healthcare benefit and the female ownership percentage. Similarly, entrepreneurial intermediaries such as incubators and accelerators vary a great deal in terms of who they serve and how they approach their mission (Cohen, 2013), but some, particularly those affiliated with governmental economic development mandates, are explicitly tasked with job creation (Clayton et al., 2018). The extent to which entrepreneurial firms are attending to pressure from such critical stakeholders regarding employment relations will probably affect their likelihood of possessing novel HR practices that could provide HR scholars with exciting research opportunities.

Broader perspective on HR and HR responsibilities

Empirical studies in the entrepreneurial HR literature find that the presence of an HR department or an HR executive is associated with stronger firm performance (e.g., Welbourne & Cyr, 1999; Chadwick et al., 2016). However, practitioners continue to question the usefulness of HR functions (Hammonds, 2005) and many practitioners" articles treat HR as of limited value and report on high-tech firms" attempts to automate and outsource HR operations (e.g., Tobenkin, 2019). Note that both advocates and critics are focusing narrowly on the HR department when they discuss HR responsibilities. But note also that when scholars and practitioners in the field of general management talk about HR, their focus is quite different from that of HR scholars and practitioners. Instead of using the term 'HR,' they use other phrases such as 'people management' (e.g., Cappelli, 2020) and focus on how general managers and the leadership may (or should) manage their employees. Consider the World Management Survey and the subsequent studies of the antecedents and consequences of management practices in organizations (e.g., Bender et al., 2018; Bloom & Van Reenen, 2007). These management practices include employee monitoring, goal setting, and incentives, all of which are core to the HR literature but are here described more generally as management. The HR department seems to be narrowly circumscribed to encompass only minor administrative roles (e.g., payroll preparation). This disconnect between understandings of HR as a formal department or specific formalized practices versus HR as everything related to people management in organizations may explain why there has been relatively little interest in entrepreneurial HR. Another challenge to studying HR in entrepreneurial firms is that the formal HR practices and systems of interest in the HR literature are often not present, and in fact may not be suitable, in entrepreneurial firms. HR is usually characterized by formal policies and procedures, and decision-makers in entrepreneurial firms tend to believe that such protocols do not work well in fast-moving environments (Katz et al., 2000). The business environments in which entrepreneurial firms operate are generally highly uncertain (Navis & Glynn, 2010). Therefore, regardless of any preset plans, founders of entrepreneurial firms may not have the luxury of rigorously selecting employees (Leung et al., 2006). If they have to work with whatever employees are available to them, traditional HR practices (e.g., rigorous selection) may not be applicable. Additionally, carefully crafted job and work designs are often considered foundational in HR systems and closely linked with other HR practices (Parker et al., 2017), but employees in entrepreneurial firms often have broader roles than their counterparts in established firms (Campbell, 2013; Sørensen, 2007). Often their roles are not defined, and they may be asked to do any task that is in front of them. For these reasons, entrepreneurial firms typically rely on informal HR practices (Hornsby & Kuratko, 2003) rather than formal and systematically developed practices (Leung, 2003). But much in the way that linguistic innovations appear in spoken colloquial language before they are formalized into dictionaries for written language, it is possible that the interesting HR innovations first appear informally as entrepreneurial experiments in ways of managing, and we are missing them because we are not looking in the right places.

The entrepreneurial tendency to resist formal HR practices and systems may also be attributed to entrepreneurs" assumptions that they would be culturally unsuitable. Entrepreneurial firms tend to resist formality to maintain a high-energy and 'garagelike' atmosphere (Galbraith, 1985); entrepreneurs may believe that formal HR practices are not a good fit with such an atmosphere or that managing their employees through formal HR practices rather than personally may represent a loss of control (Wasserman, 2017). The prevalence of informal HR practices in entrepreneurial firms is also driven by the fact that these firms are run by small founding teams (or even one founder) who engage in a wide variety of activities, including HR (Åstebro & Thompson, 2011; Mathias & Williams, 2018). Entrepreneurs, as well as employees who choose to work for entrepreneurial firms, are distinct from those who work for established firms (Ouimet & Zarutskie, 2014). Also, employees in new and established firms are likely to have different motives for joining and staying with their organizations. For instance, employees in new firms may have a relatively lower preference for job security and salary and a higher preference for independence and responsibility than their peers in established firms (Roach & Sauermann, 2015). Therefore, HR practices that are known to work well in established firms may not be effective in the management of employees of entrepreneurial firms.

Another reason for this possible misfit between formal HR practices and entrepreneurial firms is that entrepreneurial firms are typically small and face severe constraints in mobilizing the financial resources required to sustain them through the periods of growth (Baker & Nelson, 2005; Katila et al., 2008). In entrepreneurial firms, investment in HR may not be their priority because they have resource constraints and many competing strategic priorities. Given the resource-intensive nature of systematic HR practices, entrepreneurial firms may not invest their limited resources in HR programs even when they might be beneficial (Deb et al., 2017; Miner, 1973).

Clearly, there is a large disconnect between HR, general management, and entrepreneurship in how they perceive HR; however, it seems that a broader perspective on HR responsibilities and activities that includes people management more generally would be beneficial in studying the influence of HR in entrepreneurial firms. Entrepreneurial HR scholars should not only focus on the role of the HR function but also include people management generally and all of the formal and informal systems relating to people management. HR critics should recognize that it is both inaccurate and unfair to dismiss an HR function as a department that handles only administrative duties. To elaborate on these ideas, we introduce Netflix"s people management practices.

People think of Netflix as a highly innovative organization, not only because of its products and services but also because of its people management and culture. As described by McCord (2014) and elaborated in a recent book, its cultural foundation is a 'freedom & responsibility' framework (Hastings & Meyer, 2020). Employees are given the discretion to make their own decisions with almost every aspect of their jobs, even the timing and number of their vacation days, as long as they take responsibility for their actions. Netflix has ended formal performance reviews and switched to informal 360-degree reviews in which people are asked to candidly tell their colleagues what they should stop, start, or continue. These people management practices are considered cutting-edge and have been adopted by many other high-tech entrepreneurial firms. Interestingly, although people generally consider Netflix as an innovative company with a pioneering culture and style of people management, almost no one thinks that it has a leading HR department. Yet culture is one of HR"s primary responsibilities; if Netflix has a superior culture, it is almost equivalent to having a good HR function. If we define HR from a broader perspective, good or bad people management systems and workplace cultures indicate whether HR is doing a good job. In this conceptualization, HR is not equivalent to what an organization"s HR function does. Such a narrowly defined concept of HR fails to depict the wholistic function of HR in entrepreneurial firms. In our view, what an HR department does is associated with the description of its functional duties, not the overall quality of HR in the organization. In fact, there has been a trend for more and more companies to outsource the functional and administrative roles of HR departments (Tobenkin, 2019), shrinking the size and functional scope of the departments. This trend does not indicate that the importance of people is shrinking. Rather, it indicates that the people matter more than ever, and the managing of people cannot be (and should not be) confined to a single department. From an HR standpoint, the key takeaway from the study of Netflix is that its managers and leadership lead HR through high-quality people management systems, and the HR function is just one of the HR actors that enable such systems (e.g., by designing HR practices). It is no longer the entity that is solely responsible for people management overall. This is another reason that studying HR in entrepreneurial firms is interesting. In new and small firms, it is clear that managers and the leadership are responsible for HR. In fact, in many of these firms, an HR department does not exist, and the fact that managers and leaders handle HR is unambiguous. Studying HR in such contexts enables us to take a broader view of HR and understand it from a more holistic perspective.

Mutual learning of methods

The HR and entrepreneurship literatures have adopted different research methods to investigate their research questions. Below, we explain how the literatures can learn from each other to gain a more fine-grained understanding of HR in entrepreneurial firms.

Qualitative and mixed methods research

Although the entrepreneurship literature has progressed from empirical surveys to more contextual-oriented research (Amit et al., 1993), most studies of HR in entrepreneurial firms have used quantitative data to investigate the effectiveness of HR. Although quantitative researchers provide insights by building theories and testing hypotheses driven by them, they often ignore the contexts of their quantitative and statistical findings. To address these concerns, we recommend that HR researchers move from quantitative to qualitative or mixed methods research to contextualize the findings of the quantitative studies. Research on organizations has always benefited from grounded, inductive, and qualitative methods (Eisenhardt, 1989; Strauss & Corbin, 1998; Yin, 1994).

Combining qualitative and quantitative information could provide even deeper insights. The two approaches are complementary (Jones, 1988) in that quantitative methods allow researchers to test their hypotheses, and qualitative methods permit them to triangulate and elaborate their quantitative findings (Jick, 1979). We recommend that HR researchers be more open to such qualitative and/or mixed studies while continuing to conduct quantitative studies.

Comparative studies

Most existing HR studies have been conducted in established firms or by using a sampling frame that was not focused on distinguishing entrepreneurial firms from established firms. Therefore, it is still unclear whether the effects of HR practices and systems and investments and functions that have been widely studied in the HR literature apply to both entrepreneurial firms and established firms. Comparative studies that contrast the antecedents and consequences of HR in entrepreneurial and established firms would be valuable.

Longitudinal research designs and temporal dynamics in HR

Although time is an 'important dimension of the discovery, creation, and exploitation process' (Busenitz et al., 2003, p. 302), longitudinal research designs are used infrequently to study HR in entrepreneurial firms. Although this is a criticism that could be applied to organizational research in general (Daily et al., 2002; Schwenk & Dalton, 1991), studying HR in entrepreneurial firms through longitudinal studies is particularly important because of the unique characteristics of entrepreneurial firms. Such research could provide insights into how HR and its impact on entrepreneurial firms emerge and change over time. The context of entrepreneurial firms is particularly valuable in studies focusing on temporal dynamics via multiperiod research. Researchers may trace the development of a firm from its founding and see how HR contributes to its growth and maturation. By treating time as a variable of interest, researchers may be able to investigate many unanswered questions. For example, we know that HR develops over time, but little is known about the factors and processes that enable or inhibit its development or the associated performance implications.

Conclusion

Of course, we recognize that delivering on the promise of studying HR in entrepreneurial settings will require overcoming a number of perils and pitfalls. First, it can be challenging to obtain data. Researchers have to identify recently founded firms that fit their research purposes. Moreover, HR researchers have traditionally obtained much of their data from HR departments, and many entrepreneurial firms do not have HR departments (Katz et al., 2000). Also, given that entrepreneurial firms generally rely on informal rather than formal HR practices, it is difficult for researchers to gather data on their HR practices via surveys and archival data.

Additionally, we recognize that the business context facing entrepreneurial firms is quite distinct from that of established firms, which makes it both interesting and challenging to study HR in this setting. There is little HR literature in this area. Therefore, it is unclear whether HR practices and systems that have been widely studied and proven effective in established firms are effective in entrepreneurial firms as well. By addressing this gap in the literature, researchers may offer practical insights on the extent to which entrepreneurial firms would benefit by adopting such HR practices and systems. We are confident that many of the challenges and risks associated with HR research in entrepreneurial firms can be overcome with rigorous and creative research designs and by recognizing that HR in this setting often occurs outside of HR departments. But by being open to this new context - one which is likely to be revolutionized by novel HR practices - we believe that HR scholars will be able to explore uncharted research areas. In doing so, it is important to take a broad perspective on HR rather than being focused on the functional roles of HR departments. Relatedly, entrepreneurship scholars and entrepreneurs may be able to benefit by taking stock of what HR scholars have discovered as there is benefit in understanding the mechanisms that connect people-related practices to firm-level outcomes.

We conclude with a note of caution. We fear that anti-employee, anti-employment, and anti-HR sentiments are increasing in entrepreneurial settings. For instance, despite Uber"s financial success, its employment models and reliance on gig workers have been criticized by the public and scrutinized by law enforcement authorities (Chung, 2021). Although relying on temporary workers and independent contractors may seem an optimal choice that delivers financial benefits to an organization, there is no guarantee that doing so will be sustainable in the long run. Indeed, numerous negative effects have been suggested by HR scholars (e.g., Broschak & Davis-Blake, 2006). Of course, we are not arguing that relying on gig workers or other optimization-focused people management practices should be avoided at all costs. Rather, we urge entrepreneurs to think about people management more seriously from the outset, to recognize the path-dependent nature of choices that they are making, and to consider the societal costs and benefits in addition to the financial. We ultimately hope that by seeing the relevance of people management to the creation of healthy and robust organizations, entrepreneurs may be able to reap greater social and financial benefits.

References

Agarwal, R., Campbell, B. A., Franco, A. M., & Ganco, M. (2016). What do I take with me? The mediating effect of spin-out team size and tenure on the founder-firm performance relationship. *Academy of Management Journal*, 59(3), 1060–1087.

Aldrich, H. E. & Auster, E. R. (1986). Even dwarfs started small: Liabilities of age and size and their strategic implications. *Research in Organizational Behavior*, 8, 165–198.

Aldrich, H. E. & Ruef, M. (2018). Unicorns, gazelles, and other distractions on the way to understanding real entrepreneurship in the United States. *Academy of Management Perspectives*, 32(4), 458–472.

Amit, R., Glosten, L., & Muller, E. (1993). Challenges to theory development in entrepreneurship research. *Journal of Management Studies*, 30(4), 815–834.

Åstebro, T. & Thompson, P. (2011). Entrepreneurs, jacks of all trades or hobos? *Research Policy*, 40(5), 637–649.

Audretsch, D. B. & Thurik, A. R. (2001). What"s new about the new economy? From the managed to the entrepreneurial economy. *Industrial and Corporate Change*, 10, 267–315.

Babal, S. (2020). *How Tesla step-up its HR game?* https://hrnxt.com/hr/how-tesla-step -up-its-hr-game/14488/2020/02/14/.

Bacon, N. & Hoque, K. (2005). HRM in the SME sector: Valuable employees and coercive networks. *International Journal of Human Resource Management*, 16(11), 1976–1999.

Baker, T. & Nelson, R. E. (2005). Creating something from nothing: Resource construction through entrepreneurial bricolage. *Administrative Science Quarterly*, 50(3), 329–366.

Baron, J. N. & Hannan, M. T. (2002). Organizational blueprints for success in high-tech start-ups: Lessons from the Stanford Project on Emerging Companies. *California Management Review*, 44, 8–36.

Baron, J. N., Burton, M. D., & Hannan, M. T. (1996). The road taken: Origins and evolution of employment systems in emerging companies. *Industrial and Corporate Change*, 5, 239–275.

Baron, J. N., Hannan, M. T., & Burton, M. D. (1999). Building the iron cage: Determinants of managerial intensity in the early years of organizations. *American Sociological Review*, 64(4), 527–547.

Baron, J. N., Hannan, M. T., & Burton, M. D. (2001). Labor pains: Change in organizational models and employee turnover in young, high-tech firms. *American Journal of Sociology*, 106, 960–1012.

Baron, J. N., Hannan, M. T., Hsu, G., & Kocak, O. (2007). In the company of women: Gender inequality and the logic of bureaucracy in start-up firms. *Work and Occupations*, 34(1), 35–66.

Baron, R. A. (2003). Editorial: human resource management and entrepreneurship: Some reciprocal benefits of closer links. *Human Resource Management Review*, 13(2), 253–256.

Baron, R. A. & Tang, J. (2009). Entrepreneurs" social competence and new venture performance: Evidence on potential mediators and cross-industry generality. *Journal of Management*, 35, 282–306.

Batt, R. (2002). Managing customer services: Human resource practices, quit rates, and sales growth. *Academy of Management Journal*, 45, 587–597.

Beckman, C. & Burton, M. D. (2008). Founding the future: The evolution of top management teams from founding to IPO. *Organization Science*, 19(1), 3–24.

Bender, S., Bloom, N., Card, D., Van Reenen, J., & Wolter, S. (2018). Management practices, workforce selection, and productivity. *Journal of Labor Economics*, 36(S1), S371–S409.

Bernstein, E., Bunch, J., Canner, N., & Lee, M. (2016). Beyond the Holacracy hype: The overwrought claims - and actual promise - of the next generation of self-managed teams. *Harvard Business Review*, 94(7/8), 38–49.

Birley, S. (1986). The role of new firms: Births, deaths and job generation. *Strategic Management Journal*, 7, 361–376.

Bloom, N. & Van Reenen, J. (2007). Measuring and explaining management practices across firms and countries. *Quarterly Journal of Economics*, 122(4), 1351–1408.

Boon, C., Den Hartog, D. N., & Lepak, D. (2019). A systematic review of human resource management systems and their measurement. *Journal of Management*, 45(6), 2498–2537.

Bosma, N. & Kelley, D. (2018). *Global entrepreneurship monitor 2018/2019 global report*. Global Entrepreneurship Research Association, London.

Botelho, T. L. & Chang, M. (2020). The perception and evaluation of founder experience by hiring firms: A field experiment. *Academy of Management Best Paper Proceedings*.

Brest, B. P. & Born, K. (2013). When can impact investing create real impact? *Stanford Social Innovation Review*, 22–31.

Broschak, J. P. & Davis-Blake, A. (2006). Mixing standard work and nonstandard deals: The consequences of heterogeneity in employment arrangements. *Academy of Management Journal*, 49(2), 371–393.

Burton, M. D. (1995). The evolution of employment systems in high technology firms. Unpublished PhD Dissertation, Department of Sociology, Stanford University.

Burton, M. D. (2001). The company they keep: Founders" models for organizing new firms. In C.B. Schoonhoven and E. Romanelli (eds.), *The Entrepreneurship Dynamic: Origins of Entrepreneurship and the Evolution of Industries*, Stanford, CA: Stanford University Press.

Burton, M. D. & O"Reilly, C. (2004). Walking the talk: The impact of high commitment values and practices on technology startups. *Working Paper Series*. Cornell Digital Commons.

Burton, M. D., Dahl, M. S., & Sorenson, O. (2018). Do startups pay less? *ILR Review*, 71(5), 1179–1200.

Burton, M. D., Fairlie, R. W., & Siegel, D. (2019). Introduction to a special issue on entrepreneurship and employment: Connecting labor market institutions, corporate demography, and human resource management practices. *ILR Review*, 72, 1050–1064.

Burton, M. D., Sørensen, J. B., & Dobrev, S. (2016). A careers perspective on entrepreneurship. *Entrepreneurship Theory and Practice*, 40(2), 237–247.

Busenitz, L. W., PageWest, G., Shepherd, D. A., Nelson, T., Chandler, G. N., & Zacharakis, A. (2003). Entrepreneurship research in emergence: Past trends and future directions. *Journal of Management*, 29(3), 285–308.

Campbell, B. A. (2013). Earnings effect of entrepreneurial experience: Evidence from the semiconductor industry. *Management Science*, 59(2), 286–304.

Campbell, B. A., Ganco, M., Franco, A. M., & Agarwal, R. (2012). Who leaves, where to, and why worry? Employee mobility, entrepreneurship and effects on source firm performance. *Strategic Management Journal*, 33, 65–87.

Cappelli, P. (2020). Stop overengineering people management. *Harvard Business Review*, September/October.

Carland, J. W., Hoy, F., Boulton, W. R., & Carland, J. C. (1984). Differentiating entrepreneurs from small business owners: A conceptualization. *Academy of Management Review*, 9, 354–359.

Carlsson, B., Braunerhjelm, P., McKelvey, M., Olofsson, C., Persson, L., & Ylinenpää, H. (2013). The evolving domain of entrepreneurship research. *Small Business Economics*, 41, 913–930.

Chadwick, C., Guthrie, J. P., & Xing, X. (2016). The HR executive effect on firm performance and survival. *Strategic Management Journal*, 37(11), 2346–2361.

Chadwick, C., Way, S. A., Kerr, G., & Thacker, J. W. (2013). Boundary Conditions of the High-Investment Human Resource Systems-Small-Firm Productivity Relationship. *Personnel Psychology*, 66, 311–343.

Chatterji, A. & Patro, A. (2014). Dynamic capabilities and managing human capital. *Academy of Management Perspectives*, 28(4), 395–408.

Chung, A. (2021). *Supreme Court rejects Uber bid to avoid driver pay lawsuit*. https://www.reuters.com/article/usa-court-uber-idCNL2N2N4156.

Clayton, P., Feldman, M., & Lowe, N. (2018). Behind the scenes: Intermediary organizations that facilitate science commercialization through entrepreneurship. *Academy of Management Perspectives*, 32(1), 104–124.

Cohen, L. E. & Mahabadi, S. (in press). In the midst of hiring: Pathways of anticipated and accidental job evolution during hiring. *Organization Science*.

Cohen, S. (2013). What do accelerators do? Insights from incubators and angels. *Innovations: Technology, Governance, Globalization*, 8(2), 19–25.

Combs, J., Liu, Y., Hall, A., & Ketchen, D. (2006). How much do high-performance work practices matter? A meta-analysis of their effects on organizational performance. *Personnel Psychology*, 59, 501–528.

Daily, C., McDougall, P., Covin, J. G., & Dalton, D. (2002). Governance and strategic leadership in entrepreneurial firms. *Journal of Management*, 28(3), 387–412.

Dastin, J. (2018). *Amazon scraps secret AI recruiting tool that showed bias against women*. https:// www .reuters .com/ article/ us -amazon -com -jobs -automation -insight/amazon-scraps-secret-ai-recruiting-tool-that-showed-bias-against-women -idUSKCN1MK08G.

Davidsson, P. & Gruenhagen, J. H. (2021). Fulfilling the process promise: A review and agenda for new venture creation process research. *Entrepreneurship Theory and Practice*, 45(5), 1083–1118.

Davila, A., Foster, G., & Jia, N. (2010). Building sustainable high-growth startup companies: Management systems as an accelerator. *California Management Review*, 52(3), 79–105.

Deb, P., David, P., & O"Brien, J. (2017). When is cash good or bad for firm performance? *Strategic Management Journal*, 38, 436–454.

Den Hartog, D. N., Boon, C., Verburg, R M., & Croon, M A. (2013). HRM, communication, satisfaction, and perceived performance: A cross-level test. *Journal of Management*, 39(6), 1637–1665.

DeSantola, A. & Gulati, R. (2017). Scaling: Organizing and growth in entrepreneurial ventures. *Academy of Management Annals*, 11(2), 640–668.

De Winne, S. & Sels, L. (2010). Interrelationships between human capital, HRM and innovation in Belgian startups aiming at an innovation strategy. *International Journal of Human Resource Management*, 21(11), 1863–1883.

Ding, W. W., Lee, H. J., & Shapiro, D. L. (2020). Are ex-entrepreneurs penalized during job-searches? It depends on who is hiring. *SSRN Electronic Journal*.

Dzieza, J. (2015). *The rating game*. https://www.theverge.com/2015/10/28/9625968/ rating-system-on-demand-economy-uber-olive-garden.

Eisenhardt, K. M. (1989). Building theories from case study research. *Academy of Management Review*, 14, 532–550.

Evans, W. R. & Davis, W. D. (2005). High-performance work systems and organizational performance: The mediating role of internal social structure. *Journal of Management*, 31, 758–775.

Freeman, J. H., Carroll, G. R., & Hannan, M. T. (1983). The liability of newness: Age dependence in organizational death rates. *American Sociological Review*, 48, 692–710.

Galbraith, J. R. (1985). Evolution without revolution: Sequent computer systems. *Human Resource Management*, 24(1), 9–24.

Gartenberg, C. (2021). *Bezos" Amazon: From bookstore to backbone of the internet.* https://www.theverge.com/2021/2/3/22264551/jeff-bezos-amazon-history-timeline -look-back-company.

Gartner, W. B. (1985). A conceptual framework for describing the phenomenon of new venture creation. *Academy of Management Review*, 10, 696–706.

Gartner. W. B. (1990). What are we talking about when we talk about entrepreneur-ship? *Journal of Business Venturing*, 5, 15–28.

Gilbert, C. (2005). Unbundling the structure of inertia: Resource versus routine rigidity. *Academy of Management Journal*, 48, 741–763.

Gillis, J. & Loughlan, P. (2007). Not just small adults: The metaphors of paediatrics. *Archives of Disease in Childhood*, 92(11), 946–947.

Gilman, M. & Raby, S. (2013). National context as a predictor of high-performance work system effectiveness in small-to-medium-sized enterprise (SMEs): A UK–French comparative analysis. *International Journal of Human Resource Management*, 24, 372–390.

Gittell, J. H., Seidner, R., & Wimbush, J. (2010). A relational model of how high-performance work systems work. *Organization Science*, 21(2), 490–506.

Gong, Y., Law, K. S., Chang, S., & Xin, K. R. (2009). Human resources management and firm performance: The differential role of managerial affective and continuance commitment. *Journal of Applied Psychology*, 94(1), 263–275.

Guthrie, J. (2001). High-involvement work practices, turnover, and productivity: Evidence from New Zealand. *Academy of Management Journal*, 44(1), 180–190.

Hammonds, K. H. (2005). Why we hate HR. *Fast Company*, 97(8), 40–47.

Harney, B. & Alkhalaf, H. (2021). A quarter-century review of HRM in small and medium-sized enterprises: Capturing what we know, exploring where we need to go. *Human Resource Management*, 60, 5–29.

Harney, B. & Dundon, T. (2006). Capturing complexity: Developing an integrated approach to analysing HRM in SMEs. *Human Resource Management Journal*, 16(1), 48–73.

Hastings, R. & Meyer, E. (2020) *No Rules Rules: Netflix and the Culture of Reinvention.* New York: Penguin Random House.

Heneman, R. L., Tansky, J. W., & Camp, S. M. (2000). Human resource management practices in small and medium-sized enterprises: unanswered questions and future research perspectives. *Entrepreneurship Theory and Practice*, 25(1), 11–26.

Hmieleski, K. M. & Baron, R. A. (2009). Entrepreneurs" optimism and new venture performance: A social cognitive perspective. *Academy of Management Journal*, 52(3), 473–488.

Hornsby, J. S. & Kuratko, D. F. (2003). Human resource management in US small businesses: A replication and extension. *Journal of Developmental Entrepreneurship*, 8(1), 73–92.

Huselid, M. A. (1995). The impact of human resource management practices on turn-over, productivity, and corporate financial performance. *Academy of Management Journal*, 38(3), 635–672.

Ireland, R. D. & Webb, J. W. (2007). A cross-disciplinary exploration of entrepreneur-ship research. *Journal of Management*, 33(6), 891–927.

Jiang, K., Lepak, D. P., Hu, J., & Baer, J. C. (2012). How does human resource manage-ment influence organizational outcomes? A meta-analytic investigation of mediating mechanisms. *Academy of Management Journal*, 55, 1264–1294.

Jick, T. D. (1979). Mixing qualitative and quantitative methods: Triangulation in action. *Administrative Science Quarterly*, 24, 602–611.

Jin, L., Madison, K., Kraiczy, N. D., Kellermanns, F. W., Crook, T. R., & Xi, J. (2017). Entrepreneurial team composition characteristics and new venture performance: A meta-analysis. *Entrepreneurship Theory and Practice*, 41(5), 743–771.

Jones, M. O. (1988). In search of meaning: Using qualitative methods in research and applications. In Jones, M.O., Moore, M.D. and Synder, R.C. (Eds), *Inside Organizations: Understanding the Human Dimension*, Sage, London.

Kacperczyk, O. & Younkin, P. (in press). A founding penalty: Evidence from an audit study on gender, entrepreneurship, and future employment. *Organization Science*.

Katila, R., Rosenberger, J. D., & Eisenhardt, K. M. (2008). Swimming with sharks: Technology ventures, defense mechanisms and corporate relationships. *Administrative Science Quarterly*, 53, 295–332.

Katz, J. A., Aldrich, H. E., Welbourne, T. M., & Williams, P. M. (2000). Guest editor"s comments: Special issue on human resource management and the SME: Toward a new synthesis. *Entrepreneurship Theory and Practice*, 25(1), 7–10.

Keeble, D. (1990). High-technology industry. *Geography*, 75(4), 361–364.

Kehoe, R. R. & Collins, C. J. (2017). Human resource management and unit performance in knowledge-intensive work. *Journal of Applied Psychology*, 102(8), 1222–1236.

Kehoe, R. R. & Wright, P. M. (2013). The impact of high-performance human resource practices on employees" attitudes and behaviors. *Journal of Management*, 39(2), 366–391.

Kelly, J. (2020). Tesla"s leaked employee handbook is as unconventional as founder Elon Musk. https://www.forbes.com/sites/jackkelly/2020/02/14/teslas-leaked-employee-handbook-is-as-unconventional-as-its-founder-elon-musk/?sh=5a2a251c7ec2.

Kerr, G., Way, S. A., & Thacker, J. (2007). Performance, HR practices and the HR manager in small entrepreneurial firms. *Journal of Small Business & Entrepreneurship*, 20(1), 55–68.

Kim, J. (2020). The intersection between HR and entrepreneurial performance: Review and roadmap for future research. *Academy of Management Proceedings*, 2020(1), 14565.

Kim, T. (2015). The taxi wars: Uber is 'destroying the taxi industry'. http://america.aljazeera.com/articles/2015/9/16/taxi-wars-uber-destroying-the-taxi-industry.html.

Kimberly, J. R. (1979). Issues in the creation of organizations: Initiation, innovation, and institutionalization. *Academy of Management Journal*, 22, 437–457.

Klotz, A. C., Hmieleski, K. M., Bradley, B. H., & Busenitz, L. W. (2014). New venture teams: A review of the literature and roadmap for future research. *Journal of Management*, 40, 226–255.

Kor, Y. Y. (2003). Experience-based top management team competence and sustained growth. *Organization Science*, 14, 707–719.

Kotey, B. & Slade, P. (2005). Formal human resource management practices in small growing firms. *Journal of Small Business Management*, 43, 16–40.

Lancker, E. V., Knockaert, M., Audenaert, M., & Cardon, M. (in press). HRM in entrepreneurial firms: A systematic review and research agenda. *Human Resource Management Review*.

Lee, M. Y. & Edmondson, A. C. (2017). Self-managing organizations: Exploring the limits of less-hierarchical organizing. *Research in Organizational Behavior*, 37, 35–58.

Lepak, D. P., Liao, H., Chung, Y., & Harden, E. E. (2006). A conceptual review of human resource management systems in strategic human resource management research.

In J. J. Martocchio (Ed.), *Research in Personnel and Human Resource Management* (pp. 217–271). Greenwich, CT: JAI Press.

Leung, A. (2003). Different ties for different needs: Recruitment practices of entrepreneurial firms at different developmental phases. *Human Resource Management*, 42, 303–320.

Leung, A., Zhang, J., Wong, P., & Foo, M. (2006). The use of networks in human resource acquisition for entrepreneurial firms: Multiple 'fit' considerations. *Journal of Business Venturing*, 21, 664–686.

Levesque, L. L. (2005). Opportunistic hiring and employee fit. *Human Resource Management*, 44(3), 301–317.

Li, K. & Wang, J. (2018). Human capital and knowledge spillover in mergers and acquisitions. *SSRN Electronic Journal*.

Litwin, A. S. & Phan, P. H. (2013). Quality over quantity: Reexamining the link between entrepreneurship and job creation. *ILR Review*, 66(4), 833–873.

Low, M. B. & MacMillan, I. C. (1988). Entrepreneurship: Past research and future challenges. *Journal of Management*, 14(2), 139–161.

Marx, M., Strumsky, D., & Fleming, L. (2009). Mobility, skills, and the Michigan non-compete experiment. *Management Science*, 55(6), 875–889.

Mathias, B. D. & Williams, D. W. (2018). Giving up the hats? Entrepreneurs" role transitions and venture growth. *Journal of Business Venturing*, 33, 261–277.

McCord, P. (2014). How Netflix reinvented HR. *Harvard Business Review*, 92, 70–76.

Messersmith, J. G., Patel, P. C., Lepak, D. P., & Gould-Williams, J. S. (2011). Unlocking the black box: Exploring the link between high-performance work systems and performance. *Journal of Applied Psychology*, 96(6), 1105–1118.

Meyer, J. P. & Smith, C. A. (2000). HRM practices and organizational commitment: Test of a mediation model. *Canadian Journal of Administrative Sciences*, 17, 319–331.

Miles, R. E. & Snow, C. C. (1984). Designing strategic human resources systems. *Organizational Dynamics*, 13, 36–52.

Miner, A. S. (1987). Idiosyncratic jobs in formalized organizations. *Administrative Science Quarterly*, 32(3), 327–351.

Miner, J. B. (1973). Personnel strategies in the small business organization. *Journal of Small Business Management*, 11, 13–16.

Navis, C. & Glynn, M. A. (2010). How new market categories emerge: Temporal dynamics of legitimacy, identity, and entrepreneurship in satellite radio, 1990–2005. *Administrative Science Quarterly*, 55, 439–471.

Nyberg, A. J., Moliterno, T. P., Hale, D., & Lepak, D. P. (2014). Resource-based perspectives on unit-level human capital: A review and integration. *Journal of Management*, 40, 316–346.

Obloj, T., Obloj, K., & Pratt, M. G. (2010). Dominant logic and entrepreneurial firms" performance in a transition economy. *Entrepreneurship Theory and Practice*, 34, 150–170.

Ostroff, C. & Bowen, D. E. (2000). Moving HR to a higher level: HR practices and organizational effectiveness. In K. J. Klein & S. W. J. Kozlowski (Eds.), *Multilevel Theory, Research, and Methods in Organizations: Foundations, Extensions, and New Directions* (211–266). Hoboken NJ: Wiley.

Ouimet, P. & Zarutskie, R. (2014). Who works for startups? The relation between firm age, employee age, and growth. *Journal of Financial Economics*, 112, 386–407.

Parker, S. K., Morgeson, F. P., & Johns, G. (2017). One hundred years of work design research: Looking back and looking forward. *Journal of Applied Psychology*, 102(3), 403–420.

Peccei, R. & Van De Voorde, K. (2019). The application of the multilevel paradigm in human resource management–outcomes research: Taking stock and going forward. *Journal of Management*, 45, 786–818.

Penrose, E. T. (1959). *The Theory of the Growth of the Firm*. Oxford: Blackwell.

Pfeffer, J. (1981). Management as symbolic action: The creation and maintenance of organizational paradigms. In L. L. Cummings & B. M. Staw (Eds.), *Research in Organizational Behavior* (1–52). Greenwich, CT: JAI Press.

Pitcher, P. & Smith, A. D. (2001). Top management team heterogeneity: Personality, power, and proxies. *Organization Science*, 12, 1–18.

Prahalad, C. K. & Bettis, R. A. (1986). The dominant logic: A new linkage between diversity and performance. *Strategic Management Journal*, 7, 485–501.

Puranam, P. & Håkonsson, D. D. (2015). Valve"s way. *Journal of Organization Design*, 4(2), 2–4.

Quinn, R. E. & Cameron, K. (1983). Organizational life-cycles and shifting criteria of effectiveness: Some preliminary evidence. *Management Science*, 29, 33–51.

Rauch, A. J. & Frese, M. (2005). Effects of human capital and long-term human resources development on employment growth of small-scale businesses: A causal analysis. *Entrepreneurship Theory and Practice*, 29(6), 681–698.

Roach, M. & Sauermann, H. (2015). Founder or joiner: The role of preferences and context in shaping different entrepreneurial interests. *Management Science*, 61(9), 2160–2184.

Robertson, B. J. (2015). *Holacracy: The New Management System for a Rapidly Changing World*. New York: Henry Holt and Company.

Schwenk, C. & Dalton, D. R. (1991). The changing shape of strategic management research. In P. Shrivastava, A. Huff, & J. Dutton (Eds.), *Advances in Strategic Management* (277–300). Greenwich, CT: JAI Press.

Sels, L., De Winne, S., Maes, J., Delmotte, J., Faems, D., & Forrier, A. (2006). Unravelling the HRM–performance link: Value-creating and cost-increasing effects of small business HRM. *Journal of Management Studies*, 43(2), 319–342.

Shane, S. (2003). *A General Theory of Entrepreneurship: The Individual Opportunity Nexus*. Northampton, MA: Edward Elgar.

Shane, S. & Venkataraman. S. (2000). The promise of entrepreneurship as a field of research. *Academy of Management Review*, 25, 217–226.

Sheldon, K. (2012). 8 reasons to choose a startup over a corporate job. *Fast Company* (March 13).

Sheridan, R. (2015). The most unusual and effective hiring process you"ll ever see. https://www.inc.com/richard-sheridan/the-most-unusual-and-effective-hiring-process-you-ll-ever-see.html.

Sirmon, D. G., Hitt, M. A., Ireland, R. D., & Gilbert, B. A. (2011). Resource orchestration to create competitive advantage: Breadth, depth, and life cycle effects. *Journal of Management*, 37, 1390–1412.

Sørensen, J. B. (2007). Bureaucracy and entrepreneurship: Workplace effects on entrepreneurial entry. *Administrative Science Quarterly*, 52(3), 387–412.

Sorenson, O., Dahl, M. S., Canales, R., & Burton, M. D. (2021). Do startup employees earn more in the long run? *Organization Science*, 32(3), 587–604.

Stinchcombe, A. (1965). Social structure and organizations. In J. March (Ed.), *Handbook of Organizations*. Chicago: Rand McNally.

Strauss, A. L. & Corbin, J. M. (1998). *Basics of Qualitative Research* (2nd ed.). Thousand Oaks, CA: SAGE Publications.

Su, Z. & Wang, D. (2018). Entrepreneurial orientation, control systems, and new venture performance: A dominant logic perspective. *Entrepreneurship Research Journal*, 8, 1–17.

Takeuchi, R., Lepak, D. P., Wang, H., & Takeuchi, K. (2007). An empirical examination of the mechanisms mediating between high-performance work systems and the performance of Japanese organizations. *Journal of Applied Psychology*, 92(4), 1069–1083.

Tayeb, Z. (2021). After this CEO raised his company"s minimum wage to $70,000, he said the number of babies born to staff each year grew 10-fold and revenue soared. https://www.businessinsider.com/gravity-payments-dan-price-ceo-raise-minimum -wage-revenue-2021-8.

Taylor, S. (2006). Acquaintance, meritocracy and critical realism: Researching recruitment and selection processes in smaller and growth organizations. *Human Resource Management*, 16(4), 478–489.

Thakur, S. P. (1998). Size of investment, opportunity choice and human resources in new venture growth: Some typologies. *Journal of Business Venturing*, 14, 283–309.

Tobenkin, D. (2019). HR needs to stay ahead of automation. https:// www .shrm .org/ hr -today/ news/ hr -magazine/ spring2019/ pages/ hr -needs -to -stay -ahead -of -automation.aspx.

Utterback, J. M. (1996). *Mastering the Dynamics of Innovation*. Boston: Harvard Business Press.

Van der Sluis, J., van Praag, M., & Vijverberg, W. (2008). Education and entrepreneurship selection and performance: A review of the empirical literature. *Journal of Economic Surveys*, 22, 795–841.

Wasserman, N. (2017). The throne vs. the kingdom: Founder control and value creation in startups. *Strategic Management Journal*, 38(2), 255–277.

Welbourne, T. M. & Cyr, L. A. (1999). The human resource executive effect in initial public offering firms. *Academy of Management Journal*, 42(6), 616–629.

Welbourne, T. M., Neck, H., & Meyer, G. D. (2012). The entrepreneurial growth ceiling. *Management Decision*, 50(5), 778–796.

Wiklund, J. & Shepherd, D. (2005). Entrepreneurial orientation and small business performance: A configurational approach. *Journal of Business Venturing*, 20(1), 71–91.

Wiklund, J., Davidsson, P., Audretsch, D. B., & Karlsson, C. (2011). The future of entrepreneurship research. *Entrepreneurship Theory and Practice*, 35(1), 1–9.

Wright, P. M. & Ulrich, M. D. (2017). A road well traveled: The past, present, and future journey of strategic human resource management. *Annual Review of Organizational Psychology and Organizational Behavior*, 4, 45–65.

Wright, P. M., McMahan, G. C., McCormick, B., & Sherman, W. S. (1998). Strategy, core competence, and HR involvement as determinants of HR effectiveness and refinery performance. *Human Resource Management*, 37(1), 1–9.

Yin, R. K. (1994). *Case Study Research* (2nd ed.). Thousand Oaks, CA: SAGE Publications.

Zott, C. & Amit, R. (2007). Business model design and the performance of entrepreneurial firms. *Organization Science*, 18(2), 181–199.

10 Future directions

Peter D. Sherer

The chapters in this book speak to the important variety in theory and forms of HRM arrangements. Table 10.1 provides an integration of key themes that run through the chapters, with the idea of encouraging future theory and research. Several of the themes are shared across a number of chapters and clearly need to be the subject of theory and research. Other themes appear in just a few chapters, but they are equally important for researchers to address. What the themes highlight too is that our theoretical understanding of processes goes hand-in-hand with research that addresses the variety in forms of HRM arrangements, and that we need both types of research to move the field of Strategic HRM ahead.

Micro foundations are critical issues that authors address in different ways. Sanders addresses micro dynamics through the attributions that employees make about HRM practices and systems. Chadwick et al.'s discussion of human capital also provides a building block of micro foundations. Collins speaks to the mediating processes by which HPWS lead organizations to be effective. Tolbert's cautions to be clear on our conceptualization of HPWS have the implication that different logics are likely to involve different micro dynamics. Addressing these theoretical arguments are critical if we are to understand the processes by which HRM systems and practices have effects on employees and organizations.

The chapters on variety in HRM practice and systems do not directly address micro foundations but they are important in enriching our theoretical arguments on micro dynamics. As Cappelli and Baek's and Swart et al.'s chapters suggest, novel micro dynamics are likely to arise when leased employees and standard employees work together. And there is something of a debate between the authors of these chapters that needs to be addressed. Cappelli and Baek argue that there are many negative aspects to these interactions, including reduced morale and higher turnover; Swart et al. argue that commitment, along with social capital, is a critical element to bringing together networks of employees of different companies. Keegan and Meijerink point to the novel ways in which online labor platforms motivate workers to supply their labor,

Table 10.1   Key themes and future directions

	Micro-Foundations	Social Capital	Human Capital	Resource Orchestration	Institutional and Social Processes	Work Force Flexibility	HR beyond the HR Function/ Leadership	Value Creation/Value Capture	Societal and Economic Issues
Tolbert	X	-	-	-	X	-	-	-	X
Sanders	X	-	X	-	-	-	-	-	-
Chadwick et al.	X	-	X	X	X	X	-	X	-
Collins	X	X	X	X	-	-	X	-	-
Cappelli & Baek	X	-	X	-	X	X	X	-	X
Swart et al.	X	X	X	X	-	-	X	-	-
Keegan & Meijerink	X	-	X	-	-	-	X	X	X
Kim & Burton	X	-	X	-	X	-	X	-	X

and how firms have used algorithms to monitor and incentivize workers. It will be important as time goes by to observe how platform workers learn to circumvent and "game" these platforms, as workers have done in the past (Matthewson, Dennison, & Morgan 1931; Montgomery, 1979), and how firms counteract. Kim and Burton speak to the different abilities, motivations, and opportunities in entrepreneurial firms as compared to mature firms. As they cogently point out, we need to understand these firms as distinct in their own right, which suggests they may have very different dynamics that need to be understood.

A great deal of attention in the chapters is placed on leadership and on thinking of HR beyond the HR function, returning to a theme for which Beer et al. (1984) argued. Collins makes a plea to study leadership and managerial capability. Kim and Burton argue that entrepreneurial firms need to be examined in terms of people management because so much of how they manage their workforce is outside of the HR function, if there even is an HR function. The same argument is made for professional service firms, where much of the critical people management is done outside of the HR function (Sherer, 1995, 1996). Chadwick et al.'s focus on value creation and capture points to the role of firm leadership's calculations of how to maximize rents. Sanders's discussion of the attributions that employees and managers make about HRM practices and systems ultimately goes back to leaders and the organizational designs they set. Cappelli and Baek's liquid workforce is a creation of leadership, and not necessarily the HR function. Swart et al.'s networked organizations are outside of the HR function although there are HRM-like practices that need to be established. Keegan and Meijerink's online labour platforms are the creation of leaders outside of the HR role and, given the central role of independent contractors and IT, the HR function often has no obvious role with these workers.

Given all that was said, it is clear that strategic HRM needs to move beyond the HR function and study the management of people or what some would call "human assets." A great deal of the strategic management of people in organizations involves leadership outside or in addition to the HR function. This suggests returning to the themes of organizational design, with its focus on the contingencies that lead organizational leaders to architect and shape configurations of organizational structures, reward systems, information systems, people, culture, processes, and the like (e.g., Galbraith, 1995; Miller & Friesen, 1984; Nadler & Tushman, 1997). How these fields got separated and compartmentalized is something of a mystery. Nonetheless, while organizational design theory and research by scholars has waned over the years (Greenwood & Miller, 2010), it was once an important area of study. A compelling case can be made that Strategic HRM and organizational design need to be brought together in a renewal of both.

Not surprisingly, human capital is addressed in several chapters, with its specific focus in Chadwick et al. Resource orchestration, how to coordinate and deploy human capital, is explicitly addressed in Collins and Chadwick et al., but it is important in Cappelli and Baek's liquid workers operating side by side with traditional employees, and in Swart et al.'s networks. We clearly need research that looks not just at the different skills and resources that individuals bring to an organization, but also at how they coordinate, and how social capital plays a role in this. An important question for theory and research is to determine whether individuals identify with the project as a larger super-ordinate goal (Sherif et al., 1954), as Swart et al. suggest, or if they ultimately socially identify with just their organizations, which then potentially acts as a source of division.

Collins makes an explicit case for social capital as a critical mediator in the HRM Practices-Firm Performance relationship, and Swart et al. point to its importance to make networks work. These authors make strong cases for social capital. Certainly, more work is needed on the role of social capital, given the important role it holds in contemporary theory and research on organizations.

Several of the chapters speak to institutional processes. Notably, Tolbert directly addresses the possibility that competitive processes alone may not explain the limited incidence of HPWS. Cappelli and Baek do not directly address institutional processes but their point that use of liquid workforce is ubiquitous yet does not appear to have direct value to firms, or their employees may suggest that institutional processes are at work. Kim and Burton's entrepreneurial firms whose founders imprint their HRM models on their firms, an argument dating back to Stinchombe's (1965) foundational work on imprinting effects, also bear more attention. We know a great deal more about institutional processes since the time of the early institutional labor economists that needs to be incorporated into strategic HRM research. Institutional processes can provide further insights into how their interaction with competitive processes influence firm behavior.

Discussion about the role of HRM practices in societal and economic well-being in this book take us beyond the singular focus on firm performance. Cappelli and Baek and Keegan and Meijerink ask questions that speak to the economic and social well-being of workers under work arrangements that are increasingly popular, but for which regulation has not kept pace with developments in the field. Cappelli and Baek paint a less than optimistic picture of whether leased employment is good for workers. Keegan and Meijerink point to how firms have created value and captured it through online labour platform, and that value creation has generated work for workers, but workers share of the wealth generation has been limited. Kim and Burton suggest that we need to look deeper into the role of HRM practices on job creation. Swart et al. paint a far more optimistic picture, suggesting that networks of workers and organizations require high levels of commitment and, correspondingly, engagement, which presumably is good for workers. These works are important steps to expanding the outcomes that we look at regarding HRM systems and practices and reflect a growing interest in what it means to have socially responsible HRM (e.g., Aust, Matthews, & Muller-Camen, 2020). Future work will allow us to see more fully what the benefits and costs of HRM systems and practices are on the multiplicity of stakeholders, not just firms.

Finally, implicit in Table 10.1 is the question of how we conduct research on Strategic HRM. The almost total reliance on cross-sectional data through surveys and regression analyses meant variance-based approaches were given almost exclusive attention at the expense of process-based methodologies that address questions of how (Brady, Collier, & Seawright, 2006, 2010; Van de Ven, 2007). Qualitative methods were almost nonexistent in Strategic HRM, despite the ethnographic tradition and other more qualitative approaches that existed in studies that preceded the field (Cole, 1979; Dore, 1973; Kerr, 1958). We see limited use of mixed method research approaches involving a qualitative and quantitative methodology combined in a single study (Greene, 2007, 2012; Teddlie & Tashakkori, 2003). Nonetheless, such mixed method approaches allow researchers not only to explain variation but also to examine the mechanisms by which it occurs, a point of concern for Strategic HRM since the ground-breaking studies of the 1990s. Clearly, if we are to move forward, we will need to see greater variety in the methods that are used.

As this book demonstrates, the possibilities for Strategic HRM are numerous if not endless. The greater variety and complexity in the strategic management of human resources highlights the importance of the field, building from the past, and the need for renewed theory and research. The authors of this book have provided not a unitary direction but several paths to the future. My hope is that these many different paths flourish.

References

Aust, I., Matthews, B., & Muller-Camen, M. 2020. Common Good HRM: A paradigm shift in Sustainable HRM? *Human Resource Management Review*, 30(3), 100705.

Beer, M., Spector, B., Lawrence, P. R., Mills, D. Q., & Walton, R. E. 1984. *Managing Human Assets*. New York: The Free Press.

Brady, H. E., Collier, D., & Seawright, J. 2010. Refocusing the discussion of methodology. In H. Brady. and D. Collier (Eds.), *Rethinking Social Inquiry: Diverse Tools, Shared Standards*, 15–32. UK: Rowman & Littlefield.

Brady, H. E., Collier, D., & Seawright, J. 2006. Toward a pluralistic vision of methodology. *Political Analysis*, 14, 353–368.

Cole, R. E. 1979. *Japanese Blue Collar: The Changing Tradition* (Vol. 86). Berkeley, CA: University of California Press.

Dore, R. 1973. *British Factory-Japanese Factory: The Origins of Diversity in Industrial Relations*. London: Allen & Unwin.

Galbraith, J. R. 1995. *Designing Organizations*. San Francisco: Jossey-Bass Publishers.

Greene, J. C. 2012. Engaging critical issues in social inquiry by mixing methods. *American Behavioral Scientist*, 56, 755–773.

Greene, J. C. 2007. *Mixed Methods in Social Inquiry*. Hoboken, NJ: John Wiley & Sons.

Greenwood, R. & Miller, D. 2010. Tackling Design Anew: Getting Back to the Heart of Organizational Theory. *Academy of Management Perspectives*, 24, 78–88.

Kerr, C. 1958. The balkanization of labor markets. In E.W. Bakke et al. (Eds), *Labor Mobility and Economic Opportunity*, 92–110. Cambridge, MA: Technology Press of MIT.

Matthewson, S., Dennison, H. S., & Morgan, A. E. 1931. *Restriction of Output Among Organized Workers*. New York: Viking Press.

Miller, D. & Friesen, P. 1984. *Organizations: A Quantum View*. Englewood Cliffs, NJ: Prentice Hall.

Montgomery, D. 1979. *Workers' Control in America: Studies in the History of Work, Technology, and Labor Struggles*. New York: Cambridge University Press.

Nadler, D. A. & Tushman, M. L. 1997. *Competing by Design*. New York: Oxford University Press.

Sherer, P. D. 1996. Toward an understanding of the variety in work arrangements: The organization and labor relationships framework. In C. L. Cooper & D. M. Rousseau (Eds.), *Trends in Organizational Behavior*, 99–122. New York: John Wiley. Also appears *in Journal of Organizational Behavior*, 3: 99–122.

Sherer, P. D. 1995. Leveraging human assets in law firms: Human capital structures and organizational capabilities. *Industrial and Labor Relations Review*, 48, 671–691.

Sherif, M. H., Harvey, O. J., White, B. J., Hood, W. R., & Sherif, C. 1954 (Reprinted in 1988). *Experimental Study of Positive and Negative Intergroup Attitudes between Experimentally Produced Groups: Robbers Cave Experiment*. Norman: University Oklahoma.

Stinchombe, A. L. 1965. Social structure and organizations. In J. G. March (Ed.), *Handbook of Organizations*, 142–193, Chicago: Rand McNally.

Teddlie, C. & Tashakkori, A. 2003. Major issues and controversies in the use of mixed methods in the social and behavioral sciences'. In A. Tashakkori and E. Teddlie, E. (Eds.), *Handbook of Mixed Methods in Social & Behavioral Research*, 3–50, Thousand Oaks, California: Sage.

Van de Ven, A. H. 2007. *Engaged Scholarship: A Guide for Organizational and Social Research*. Oxford University Press on Demand.

Index